Entwined
~♦ By ♦~
Adoption

OUR STORY OF INFERTILITY, TEEN PREGNANCY, AND FAITH

Nancy Faltermeier & Kelly Sumner

"SCRIPTURE QUOTATIONS TAKEN FROM THE NEW AMERICAN STANDARD BIBLE®, COPYRIGHT© 1960, 1962, 1963, 1968, 1971, 1972, 1973, 1975, 1977, 1995 BY THE LOCKMAN FOUNDATION USED BY PERMISSION." (WWW.LOCKMAN.ORG)

Copyright © 2017 by Nancy Faltermeier & Kelly Sumner

All rights reserved. No part of this publication may be reproduced, distributed or transmitted in any form or by any means, without prior written permission.

SwordSower Publishing
P. O. Box 98
Eastlake, CO 80614
www.swordsowerpublishing.com
SwordSower Logo – Jan Marie Wirth

Cover Design - Nancy Faltermeier

Editor – Marjorie Vawter

Publisher's Note: This is a work of non-fiction, while stories are true, names and locales have been changed to protect identity. Any resemblance to actual people, living or dead, or to businesses, companies, events, or institutions is completely coincidental. Although every precaution has been taken to verify the accuracy of the information contained herein, the author and publisher assume no responsibility for any errors or omissions. No liability is assumed for damages that may result from the use of information contained within.

Book Layout © 2016 BookDesignTemplates.com

LCCN - 2016914214

Entwined by Adoption/ Nancy Faltermeier & Kelly Sumner. -- 1st ed.
Print Edition ISBN 978-1-945391-06-4
Kindle Edition ISBN 978-1-945391-07-1

Publisher's Cataloging-In-Publication Data
(Prepared by The Donohue Group, Inc.)

Names: Faltermeier, Nancy. | Sumner, Kelly.
Title: Entwined by adoption : our story of infertility, teen pregnancy and faith / Nancy Faltermeier & Kelly Sumner.
Description: 1st ed. | Eastlake, CO : SwordSower Publishing, [2016] | Includes bibliographical references.
Identifiers: ISBN 978-1-945391-06-4 (print) | ISBN 978-1-945391-07-1 (Kindle)
Subjects: LCSH: Faltermeier, Nancy. | Sumner, Kelly. | Adoption--Religious aspects--Christianity. | Infertility, Female--Religious aspects--Christianity. | Teenage pregnancy--Religious aspects--Christianity.
Classification: LCC HV875.26 .F35 2016 (print) | LCC HV875.26 (ebook) | DDC 248.8/6196692--dc23

This Book is Dedicated to...

... the Lord who takes the dust of our lives and transforms it into something of radiance and splendor. Without His orchestration in our lives this book would not exist.

Our husbands, Scott and John for their support and understanding these past years as we muddled through this huge endeavor.

Our children for their sacrifices as we scraped together time to accomplish this project.

Acknowledgments

We send all our thanks to our editor, Marjorie Vawter, who polished our words to shine like diamonds and to the members of our critique groups who gave us encouragement and wise suggestions. You know who you are.

Also a special thanks to Vickie Andre for her biblical assessment of our work.

Introduction

During the opening general session of a writer's conference, I noticed a young woman leaving the meeting early. Across the hall she appeared strikingly similar to my son's birthmother. I dismissed the thought that it might be her.

Later, as I returned to my room, my roommate spoke of a woman she felt I needed to meet. The next morning the woman she spoke of was none other than my son's birth-mom. Another miracle God had performed in our relationship. That day this book was born. It is our prayer this work will be a blessing to you, the reader.

Contents

PART ONE *The Entwining*...1
Chapter 1 The Quest...1
Chapter 2 Hope and Worry..9
Chapter 3 The Early Years...15
Chapter 4 All Things New..23
Chapter 5 Many Fearful Things...33
Chapter 6 The Big Mystery..49
Chapter 7 Breakthroughs...65
Chapter 8 Losing What I Love...71
Chapter 9 Second Time Around...79
Chapter 10 Attraction and Betrayal..................................83
Chapter 11 Changes...99
Chapter 12 Burned by Fire...115
Chapter 13 New Challenges...131
Chapter 14 Divine Appointments.....................................137
Chapter 15 Practice Run..147
Chapter 16 The Valley of Death.......................................153
Chapter 17 The Decision..161
Chapter 18 Doubt...173
Chapter 19 Entwined..177
PART TWO *White Diamonds*..183
Lesson One Graphite: The Stuff of Diamonds..................185
Lesson Two The Hope Diamond.......................................193

Lesson Three **The Rob Red Diamond** 203
Lesson Four **The Dresden Green Diamond** 213
Lesson Five **The Steinmetz Pink Diamond** 219
Lesson Six **The Royal Purple Heart Diamond** 229
PART THREE Black Diamonds 243
Lesson 1 Graphite 245
Lesson 2 Yellow Diamonds 251
Lesson 3 Green Diamonds 255
Lesson 4 Purple Diamonds 261
Lesson 5 Brown Diamonds 267
Lesson 6 Red Diamonds 271
Endnotes 275

PART ONE
The Entwining

Our Story

The Entwining

KELLY'S STORY

May 28, 1993

I wanted to die. My swollen abdomen ached in emptiness. My soul shattered like a thousand shards of glass, cutting deep as they pierced my inner core. The child I sheltered in my womb for the past nine months was gone. Life held little meaning. The hollowness within engulfed me into a dark void. I wept for a dream that couldn't be. The roar of blood pulsed through my ears beating a mantra I didn't want to hear.

My breasts, heavy and laden with milk, protested against the ace bandage that bound them. There would no longer be a baby to relieve them of their burden. I stood before the window of my bedroom and the images outside blurred. So this was loss. How did anyone survive this?

My hand trembled as I reached for the phone on my desk. The number I knew by heart. I tried to dial, only to fumble and dial the wrong number. Over and over again I attempted the call that must be made. Against my will the familiar voice on the other end of the line crackled forth.

"This is Jeanie."

I swallowed past the mountain lodged in my throat. "It's me."

"Kelly? I've been so worried about you, how are you?"

"Not good."

"Is there anything I can do?"

"Yes." The words fell out in a constricted voice. "Call Nancy and John. Tell them they have a son."

Chapter 1
The Quest

NANCY'S STORY

January 1985

A female voice entered my consciousness as a hand shook my shoulder. "Time to wake up, Nancy. Come on, wake up."

I forced an eye open as the nurse padded away. Rolling my head to the left, I found John sitting beside my gurney with a devilish grin.

He squeezed my hand. "What's my mother's name?"

I searched my foggy brain. I knew it started with a G. "It's Guinevere."

John broke out into a hearty laugh. "Are you sure?"

All I wanted was to close my eyes and go back to sleep. "It starts with a G. Right?"

A smirk creased his face as he stifled a snicker. "Yes."

"Is the surgery over? Did they find anything?"

"Yes, it's over, but I don't know anything yet."

"Geneva. Your mother's name is Geneva."

"Are you sure?"

"Yes, you're devious."

The nurse returned with a cup of lime soda and a package of saltines. She set them on the table beside me and adjusted the gurney, raising me into a sitting position. "How do you feel?"

"Tired."

She slid the table across the bed in front of me. "You might want to eat those crackers and sip the pop to keep from getting nauseated."

"Thanks." I tore open the package of crackers and began to nibble.

Doctor Hill appeared in his scrubs as he shoved the curtain aside. "I have good news. The laparoscopy went well, and we didn't find anything amiss. When we did the hysterosalpingogram, the dye flowed nicely through your Fallopian tubes. They're open with no obstructions. So everything looked good. There shouldn't be anything preventing you from getting pregnant."

John looked up at the doctor. "So, now what do we do?"

The doctor smiled. "Just relax and keep trying."

I reached for John's hand. "That's good. We'll just keep trying."

The doctor laid a hand on my arm. "I suggest you take a nice vacation and relax. It should happen in due time."

***

January 1986

I stirred my coffee and stared out the high-rise, break room window, not comprehending the view of downtown Denver. My husband John and I still pursued the elusive child with no success.

Carrie, my friend and coworker, sat across the table. "What's wrong?"

She knew me well and always seemed to sense when I was down. I tried to will away the army of tears gathering to march down my face. "I started. It's so frustrating. No baby again this month. Relaxing and trying isn't working. All we accomplish is more failure."

"I'm sorry." She sipped her coffee and surveyed the break room. "There's something wrong. Maybe you should try my doctor. He mentioned an infertility doc he knows."

"Infertility specialist? I didn't even know there was such a thing."

"It's a new, cutting-edge medical specialty."

"The insurance probably won't pay for treatment."

"I'm sure they'll give you the 'it's experimental' routine, but I'd sure give it a try."

"Maybe I will. We can't quit until we've tried everything. It may lead to more letdown, but another year has passed and still no baby. I'm ready for a new doctor."

***

End of January 1986

The nurse led John and me down the hall and into the doctor's personal office. "Take a seat. He will be with you shortly."

We took seats as she left us alone in the office.

John pursed his lips but said nothing. I sat across from Dr. McWilliam's nameplate on his desk. I'd taken Carrie's advice to try her doctor. He sent me to this man, an infertility specialist. This physician was dedicated to helping couples achieve their dream of having children.

My stomach flip-flopped as I shifted in my chair. We were there to get the results of our infertility workup, which included blood tests, an endometrial biopsy, laparoscopy, hysterosalpinogram, and a sperm count.

Pictures of the doctor's wife and children hung on the wall. It didn't look like his wife had trouble getting pregnant. Tacked to a corkboard on the opposite wall, faces of a couple dozen babies smiled down at us. It gave me hope. Perhaps he could help us.

John's jaw seemed tense, and I couldn't help wondering if he regretted marrying a woman who couldn't get pregnant. A wave of nausea washed over me, and I sucked a deep breath to calm the butterflies' dive-bombing in my stomach.

The door opened and Dr. McWilliams entered holding our chart. He smiled. "John. Nancy."

He sat behind his mahogany desk and opened our file. "The laparoscopy and hysterosalpinogram confirm there are no structural issues. The endometrial biopsy showed the lining of your uterus, Nancy, could support a pregnancy. So that's all good news."

I stiffened. Was the problem with John? *Help me, Lord, to deal with this the way I should.*

Dr. McWilliams continued. "John's sperm count is clearly

in the normal range. So we have nothing major preventing pregnancy."

John spoke up. "So why isn't she getting pregnant?"

The doctor smiled. "I think I have an answer for that."

I swallowed hard. "So something is wrong."

"Your blood work showed a low progesterone level. It may be that you are conceiving but with a low progesterone level you can't sustain a pregnancy. You are probably miscarrying before you know you're pregnant."

John's jaw seemed to relax. "Can something be done?"

"Yes, we use a drug called Clomid. It's a hormone that raises the progesterone level in most women."

"Great. When can I start taking it?"

"On your next cycle. You have good insurance that will cover the treatment, so I see no reason not to give it a try."

John and I left the doctor's office with optimism. Our struggle with infertility might almost be over.

***

May 1986

I slammed the car door and peered across the top of my lime-colored sedan. The long and abandoned city street, still shrouded in darkness, held rare patches of dim light, mirroring the black void I carried within myself, a hollow sorrow.

I trudged down the street toward the high-rise office building where I worked. If I wanted to see the infertility doctor later that day, I needed to come to work before dawn. As I strode down the street at an unwilling pace, I glanced at my watch as I passed under a street lamp. The dial said 5:20 a.m.

Why was I doing this? I couldn't answer the question. The vacuum in my heart grew deeper with the constant march of time. As irrational as it was, I couldn't shake the longing to fill my empty arms, no matter the cost. I begged daily. "Lord, please, free me from the ironclad bondage of desire for a child."

But it was all to no avail.

I came to a storefront window. In the waning light of the street lamp my reflection stared back at me from the glass. That's me all right, the one always standing on the outside looking in. Always on the fringe of the "parent club," excluded from conversations about late-night feedings and diaper rash. Isolated and alone, I was the proverbial square peg.

For at least five days each menstrual cycle, I faced the perils of the transient world. Lying before me in the center of the sidewalk, I came upon a third man sleeping on a grate venting heat from underground. Clutching the straps to my purse and tote bag tighter, I sloshed into the gutter to pass him by. Back onto the sidewalk, I glanced behind me, scanning for danger. I'm reminded of the foes lurking to devour my soul. Wolves of bitterness, envy, and doubt howled loud within me as I tried to keep my ire toward God at bay.

I lagged as the traffic light glowed WAIT but crossed the empty street anyway and arrived at my office building. Shoving an unlocked glass door open, I stepped inside. Sad moans of empty escalators greeted me, rising and descending in spite of no one using them. Padding onto a moving step, I ascended as I pulled my company ID badge from my purse.

At the top, I discovered the security desk unmanned. "Great. I might be the only one in the building." Passing the empty security station, I entered a bank of elevators and punched the UP button. As the elevator door slid shut, I closed my eyes and begged. "Keep me safe, Lord. And please, let me get pregnant this month. I don't want to do this anymore."

An ill-lit hallway greeted me as I arrived on floor thirteen. I tramped down the corridor to the office, opened the door, and searched the wall for the light switch with fumbling fingers. All the while hoping no vagrant hid sleeping under a desk somewhere. At last I snagged the elusive button, and lights flickered across the expansive room illuminating the entire southwest corner of the floor.

Like a mouse in a maze, I wove my way through the hallways constructed of movable four-and-a-half-foot walls. I plopped all my belongings onto the desk in my cubicle and removed my jacket. Navigating the maze again toward the opposite dark corner of the floor, I turned on more lights. After starting a pot of coffee, I returned to my desk, sat, changed my tennis shoes to high heels, and pitched everything except my pepper spray into the bottom drawer.

Snatching my mug, I returned to the coffeepot and filled my cup. Once back at my workstation, I peered at my overloaded inbox sitting on my desk and sighed. I sipped coffee and pushed the ON button to the computer. As it booted up, I leafed through the incoming work.

The clock on the wall read 5:35 am. It would be an hour-and-a-half before coworkers would start to filter in. So I focused on the mountain of work before me and hoped to conquer the stack.

The door creaked. A quick glance at the clock told me it was 6:00 a.m. My heart galloped and my fingers froze on the keyboard. I strained to listen, latched onto my pepper spray, and with great stealth stood and leaned over the desk. My short five-foot frame just allowed me to peek over the cubicle wall. Justina, one of my coworkers, walked the maze.

I stood tall. "Oh, it's you."

She jumped. "You scared me." She waddled toward her desk. "What are you doing here so early?"

"Have a doctor's appointment."

"Didn't you go to the doctor yesterday?"

"Yeah, they have to draw blood every day this week until they find it's the optimum time to make a baby."

"Really?"

"I'm beginning to feel like a pin cushion. The doc is planning to send me home today with a vial and a syringe. That's so my friend can stick me with it on Sunday. Even on the weekends, I'm fair game."

I sat and resumed typing. "I'm glad for your company. It's spooky here all alone."

Justina shuffled to me and dangled an arm over the short wall. "I bet. It's harrowing to come in early. Seems like a whole different world out there before six forty-five. No one manned the guard's station. What's up with that?"

"Still?" I scrutinized Justina's form with envious eyes. Her eight-month pregnant belly protruded from her open coat. "Somebody's falling down on the job. It's unsettling. Who knows what kind of unsavory character could be roaming these dark halls?"

She removed her coat. "I don't know why you want a baby so bad. You know what I keep telling you. You'll lose your freedom and sleep the minute its head pops out."

I set my jaw and stared at the computer screen. "That may be, but you'd go crazy if someone took away your kids."

"True."

"I rest my case."

Justina leaned against my cubicle wall, holding her empty coffee mug. "I've got a doctor's appointment, too. He's just a few blocks away. I'm glad I don't have to come in as early as you do. It's hairy enough as it is. Did you start a pot of coffee?"

"Yeah, it's waiting for you."

My fingers pounded harder on the keyboard than necessary, as Justina lumbered off. "Why, God, do you bless a woman like that with children?" I whispered under my breath. "It's not fair. She's never been married. Yet, You've given her four. I feel cursed, like You're punishing me. What have I done so wrong?"

My attention caught John's handsome face staring back at me from his picture on my desk. I hated the toll infertility treatments had on our love life. Drained of all spontaneity, doctors, basal thermometers, and blood tests now ruled our lives. Our passion—now reduced to a duty to perform, or abstain from, overtook our freedom of intimacy.

I battled tears threatening to spill over and swallowed hard. "Please, Jesus, if You don't want us to have kids, then please take this desire away. Help me not to want a baby. I don't understand why I want one so bad."

***

Two Days Later

Sunday afternoon, I rang my friend Debbie's doorbell, holding a plastic bag with a vial of hCG and a syringe. Three years had passed, since we started this quest. I hoped Clomid would be our ticket, but now the doctor added hCG shots.

Debbie answered the door. "Come in, come in. Can I take your jacket?"

I removed my coat and handed the garment to her.

"I have water heating in the teakettle." She hung up my jacket and reached for the plastic bag in my hand. "Thought we could get the deed done first and then settle in for some girl talk."

"Sounds good to me. I'm glad one of my best infertility buddies is a nurse. Otherwise, I would have been forced to skip this cycle."

She led me down the hall to her room. "I hear you. They've started me on these shots, too."

"It's rude of the doctor to take a vacation." I joked. "The audacity. It shouldn't be allowed."

Debbie smirked at me as she poked the syringe into the vial. "Drop your pants."

I tugged the clothing off one hip. "You know, I'll get even someday."

She jabbed my rear with the hormone-laden syringe. "There, you might want to rub it."

I rubbed the spot and replaced my pants. "You're good. I barely felt that. Some nurses drill for oil."

"Yep, once we pass the syringe and orange course, they send us to oil drilling."

"Great."

"What kind of oil would you . . . I mean, tea would you like?"

"Very funny."

Chapter 2
Hope and Worry

NANCY'S STORY

July 1987

Blacks, grays, and whites contorted across the monitor of the ultrasound machine. Mary, the technician, maneuvered the vaginal ultrasound head for a better vantage point to view my ovary. Spots of black appeared, and I recognized them as eggs ready for my body to release. Hope rose in me, but I stuffed it down. I'd been through this routine numerous times and possessed a layman's understanding of what we looked for. Certain we had found what we sought, I studied Mary to read her expression.

She smiled, while taking measurements and pictures. "I see several good-sized eggs in there. The doctor will be pleased."

I resisted her optimism. "Well, we need more than an egg. Conception. Now that I could get excited about."

She pressed a button and glanced at the printer as it started to hum. "Yes. But there won't be a conception without good eggs."

"True."

She flipped on the light. "You can get dressed and then open the door." She picked up pages from the printer and waved them in her hand. "After the doc takes a look at these, he'll be in to talk to you."

Once dressed, I opened the door. What would make this cycle any different than all the failed ones? How long should we keep trying this fruitless endeavor? The doctor told us everything looked fine, but we still had no success.

Dr. McWilliams entered the room carrying the ultrasound pictures. "I count seven good eggs, in these pictures. That's seven chances to get pregnant."

"Yeah," I broke in, "but I produced about that many eggs the last few months, and I'm still not pregnant."

"You're right."

I resisted the urge to lash out. "So now what's wrong?"

"Some women have a side effect to Clomid, which makes their body hostile to sperm. I suspect you're one of them."

"Great. That's just great."

"It's a problem easily overcome in most cases."

"Really? How's that?"

"We inseminate you with your husband's sperm. The procedure bypasses the hostile area." He laid a hand on my shoulder. "This evening would be the optimum time to do it."

I pursed my lips. "I'll have to talk to John."

"I understand." He gave my shoulder a squeeze. "Give him a call, and if you decide to do the procedure, call my receptionist. She'll make arrangements with the hospital and set a time for you to meet me here this evening. I encourage you to try this. I've seen a lot of success with women like you."

***

Later that evening, Dr. McWilliams stood, peeled off his latex gloves, and tossed them into the trash. "You need to lie there for thirty minutes."

I glanced at the clock on the wall. It was 9:35 p.m. He opened the door, turned, and faced John and me, smiled, and raised crossed fingers. "I'll keep them crossed. We're going to make this happen."

Then he left us.

With a pillow tucked under my rear and my feet in the stirrups, I would lie there. I would stay put until the cows came to visit, if that's what it would take for the elements to get together and make a baby.

***

August 1987

I joined my parents at their home in Dolan Springs, Arizona. Earlier that day, we attended my ninety-four-year-old grandfather's funeral. I helped my mother set the table for dinner and returned to the kitchen for more dishes.

Momma held out a plate full of dill pickles. "Here, set these on the table."

I took the plate and returned to the dining room, eyeing the pickles. They looked luscious. Craving overtook me and I almost took one, but refrained. I could wait until dinner. It was odd, however, since I usually didn't care for pickles.

Out-of-town relatives filled the house, and we all squeezed around my mother's large dining room table. I sat next to Momma and near the pickles. After my father blessed the meal, Momma passed the pickles to the person sitting on her opposite side.

I could wait. The pickles would come soon enough.

As I filled my plate with other items, I kept an eye on the pickles that dillydallied their way toward me. A bowl of potato salad came just ahead of my obsession, and I scooped a spoonful onto my plate. As I turned to receive the pickle plate, the person next to me snatched up the last one. I stifled a gasp. Heat ascended into my face. I had to have a pickle. I eyed the long green spears donning everyone's plate but mine. In a pickle, I took a quick scan of Momma's plate. I'd not be begging one from her. She hadn't taken one.

"Hey, Dad, how bad do you want that pickle?"

Momma hopped up, snatching the empty plate. "We have more, I'll get them."

She returned to the table and handed me a full plate. "I didn't think you ate pickles."

"I don't usually, but for some reason I'm really craving one."

My cousin snickered. "You know what they say about women craving pickles. You might have something baking in the oven."

I smiled, but said nothing. *I wonder . . .*

***

I sat in the waiting room of Dr. McWilliams's office bouncing my knee. Minutes earlier I'd given a urine sample for pregnancy testing. Now I waited with hope and dread. If only I would receive the news I so desired, but I braced for the words I'd heard before, dashing my hopes.

By the time I flew back to Denver from my grandfather's funeral, my monthly cycle was late. Coupled with the pickle incident, my expectations were higher than ever. I told myself it was dangerous to anticipate a positive result. Anxious to know the truth, I waited with the clock on the wall that rested between each tick and tock.

At last, the nurse called me back into an examining room. Her face broke into a smile. "Congratulations! You're pregnant!"

"Are you sure?" Could I believe her? She wouldn't joke about something like this, would she?"

She showed me the tester with a bold plus sign in the center of a circle. "As sure, as we can be." Handing the test to me, she said. "Here, you might want to keep this as a memento. We need to schedule an ultrasound to make sure everything looks good."

My heart dropped. "Does he think something's wrong?"

"Oh, no, it's standard procedure. Here's a business card for the OB/GYN the doc recommends you go to."

I took the information. "Thanks."

John would be thrilled. All our troubles were over. We'd finally figured out the combination to getting me pregnant. Life should be smooth sailing from here on out.

***

September 3, 1987

Mary, the ultrasound tech, squirted gel over my abdomen. Eager, I scanned the ultrasound monitor for the first glimpse of our baby. We were at the sixth week of gestation.

I spotted a pulsating dot. "Is that the baby?"

She smiled. "Yup, it's your baby's heartbeat."

"I'm awestruck at how fast it beats. I can't believe I'm

finally pregnant."

Dr. McWilliams stepped in and examined the monitor. "Congratulations, Nancy. Everything looks good." He patted my shoulder. "I like to see success."

Mary handed me an ultrasound picture. "You'll probably want to have this. You can put it in your baby book"

"Thank you. I will."

***

December 1987 – Twenty Weeks Gestation

As the months passed, I did everything in my power to give our baby the best chance at a healthy life. I downed prenatal vitamins and exercised daily. My dreams of motherhood would finally come true.

One cold and blustery day, John and I went to the mall to do some Christmas shopping. We planned to spend the holidays in Estes Park with John's family for a reunion, and I wanted to get the shopping done early.

As we walked the mall, a sharp pain stabbed under my right rib. I sat on the edge of a brick planter and tugged at the elastic in my clothing. It seemed to help, so I stood and walked on.

John frowned. "What's wrong?"

"A sharp pain stabbed under my right rib. It might be caused by the maternity girdle, but now, I'm not so sure. It's way too early to be having pain like this."

We decided to cut our shopping trip short and return home. I called my OB/GYN, Dr. Swensen, as soon as we arrived at the house.

"Many women have gallbladder problems during pregnancy." The doctor said. "That's what I think it is. I'll have my nurse set up an appointment for an ultrasound. She'll give you a call with the details."

The next day, I stayed home from work. They had scheduled the ultrasound for that afternoon. I couldn't help but worry.

"Please, Lord, keep our baby safe. Please don't let us lose

this baby."

I picked up my Bible, hoping to receive comfort from the Lord. It fell open to Psalm thirty-one. Verses fourteen and fifteen leapt out at me: "But as for me, I trust in thee, O LORD, I say, 'Thou art my God.' My times are in Thy hand."

"My times are in Thy hand? What are you telling me, Lord?"

The words comforted me, yet it came with uneasiness. Something would not go my way

~♦♦♦~

Chapter 3
The Early Years

KELLY'S STORY

The summer of 1980

With the eruption of Mount St. Helen came the end of my parent's marriage. After thirteen years, my mother called it quits and filed for divorce. At the tender age of four, I didn't comprehend its implication. Though the memories of a child are often blurry and unclear, the events leading to the final straw are burned into the recess of my mind, creating an outcome that forever changed my life.

Tossing and turning, I pulled my pillow over my head trying to block out the yelling coming from the other room, but it only muffled their voices. The bunk bed creaked as I rolled my four-year-old body over onto my stomach.

My sister whispered. "Kelly, are you awake?"

"Yeah"

"I'm scared"

I peered down over the side of the bunk.

Ann's three-year-old, tear-streaked face looked up at me. "I don't like it when Mommy and Daddy fight."

Scooting to the ladder, it squeaked under my weight as I climbed down. Pulling back Ann's covers, I climbed in next to her. "I'll sing to you."

"Twinkle, twinkle little star . . ."

Ann's curls bobbed back and forth in protest. "No, 'Jesus Loves Me.'"

Closing my eyes, I started to sing. My voice cracked under the strain of keeping up the pretense of normality.

Ann scooted closer to me, her heavy sigh fluttered across my cheek as I continued on, as much for my sake as for hers. Our parents could still be heard but were almost drowned out by the sweet lullaby. When Ann finally drifted off to sleep, I slipped out of her bed, pulled the blankets around her, and returned to my own.

The next time I opened my eyes, sunlight filtered in through the window blinds. Feeling the damp sheets underneath me, I shivered with dread. My nightgown clung to my body as I scurried down the ladder to the floor. Changing into clean clothes, I tucked my wet nightgown under some garments in the full hamper and walked to the family room.

Ann watched cartoons on the couch and turned as I walked in. "I'm hungry. Where's Mommy?"

I put my finger to my lips. Noises came from Ben's room down the hall. "Shhh, Ann. Try to be quiet and let Mommy and Daddy sleep. I'll get us some cereal."

Walking to the cabinet, I grabbed the cereal and two bowls. Pouring it into the bowls, I tried not to spill but dumped most of it onto the table. Grasping the milk, I opened the carton like Mommy did and attempted to pour some into the bowl.

Mommy walked in with Ben on her hip and snatched the carton from my hand. "Whoa Kelly, let me do that."

"Look, Mommy, I'm making breakfast. Did I do good?"

"Yes, honey, I see that. Good job." She poured the milk into the bowls.

Climbing into my chair, I looked up at her. Her eyes were puffy and red, and her hair was in disarray. "Are you sad, Mommy?"

Ann snickered. "You look funny, Mommy."

I kicked her under the table. "No, you don't."

Ann glared at me. "Ouch. Mommy, Kelly kicked me."

Mommy sighed. "Don't kick your sister."

Ann smirked at me, and I glared back as she turned to Mommy. "Where's Daddy? He promised to take us to the park today."

Mommy sat at the table and rested her head in her hands. "Your father isn't here."

Ann fidgeted. "Where is he?"

Mommy wiped an errant tear away. "I don't know, honey. Daddy isn't going to live here anymore."

Ann and I looked at each other. "Why not?" We said in unison.

With tears in her eyes, she looked back at us. "Daddy has a problem, but you're too young to understand. Eat your cereal before it gets mushy."

Once I finished my cereal, I went into the bathroom. What did Mommy mean by Daddy had a problem? Was it me? I brushed my teeth and went back to the kitchen. "I finished brushing my teeth, Mommy. Can I go out and play?"

She stood at the sink washing dishes. "That's good. Come here for a minute."

She picked me up and set me on the counter with my legs dangling off the side. "I want to tell you something."

"What?"

She smiled. "You're adopted."

What did that mean? I sensed it was bad. My tricycle sat near the door begging me to go for a ride. "Okay. Can I go out and play now?"

She rolled her eyes. "What that means is, you didn't come out of my tummy. You had a different mommy at first, and you came out of her tummy."

I scrunched up my face. "Oh . . . can I go outside and play now?"

"All right, I just wanted to tell you."

***

What my mother didn't tell me that day was that she'd been desperate for a child. After trying for five years to conceive with no success, they adopted me. But, within two months of bringing me home, she received the joyful news, she was pregnant. Just four short minutes before my first birthday, my sister Ann was born.

At four, I didn't grasp the concept of being adopted. I knew long before, though, that I was different. My four-year-old mind might not have understood the terminology or why my mother felt the need to tell me at such a terrible moment is unclear. Given the turmoil between my parents and the volatile atmosphere we lived in, perhaps the irrational need to give me such information at that time made sense to her, but I wondered for years if my adopted state played into their breakup.

Dad didn't come home that night or the next. When he did come to see us, he took us to his new place—a mobile home located a few miles away. We begged him to come home, but after a month went by, then six, we realized he wasn't coming back.

***

Spring 1982

Now in kindergarten, the strain of my parent's separation affected me. I struggled in reading, and my teacher showed concern about my progress. My parents each handled the divorce in different ways. My mother struggled to maintain a full-time job. Trying to be helpful, Dad would find clothes at garage sales but paired polka dots and stripes in colors that didn't match.

During this stage in my life, I began to notice the relationship I had with my parents was different than what they had with my siblings. My school performance deteriorated, causing my first grade teacher to suggest I be held back a year. I don't know what worried me most, disappointing my parents or being put into the same grade as my sister.

***

May 1983

Dad didn't do well single and dated several women he met in his adult Bible study at a new church he attended. The relationships never lasted long enough for us to get to know any of them, until Molly. She had kind blue eyes, the type that could look right through you. With her red hair, she stood out unlike anyone I had ever met. She had a son David, my age, and a daughter Bethany, two years younger. I hit it off with them right from the start.

By August, three months later, the whirlwind romance resulted in wedding bells, shocking everyone when Dad moved into Molly's house, thirty minutes away. All this came as a major surprise to my mother.

As the impending school year approached, my academic future still hung in the balance. I began to withdraw. On our weekends with Dad, I competed with four other kids and often felt left out. Ben and David played sports, while Ann and Bethany engaged in make-believe Barbie dramas. Molly spent hours talking with me, trying to pull me out of my shell. Once she got wind of my school situation, she inquired at the schools near her, for programs that might suit me.

***

One Friday afternoon she took me to an elementary school near her house. As we waited in the office for the receptionist to get off the phone, a woman came in.

Her dark hair, long and curly, hung past her shoulders, reminding me of Esmeralda from the *Hunchback of Notre Dame*.

The receptionist hung up the phone and looked at Molly. "Can I help you?"

She cleared her throat. "I called about seeing if you might have a place for my stepdaughter, Kelly."

The receptionist paused then smiled. "Oh yes, that's right, I did check into that. I'm really sorry. our special education program is full."

Molly tried again. "They don't need to open a full space for her, she only struggles in reading."

The phone rang. As the receptionist lifted the receiver, she whispered, "Sorry, the class is full."

With sagging shoulders Molly looked down at me. "Well, we tried. I really thought God told me to bring you here today."

We stepped toward the door, but the woman with the long curly hair blocked our path. "I couldn't help but overhear your conversation about the special education program."

Molly paused. "Yes, well, it doesn't matter now, they're full."

"Is this your daughter?" the woman asked as she turned and knelt down so that she and I were at eye level.

"Yes, this is my stepdaughter. Kelly, say hello."

Is she going to think I'm stupid too? I kept my eyes on the floor. "Hi."

The woman lifted my chin. "Hi, Kelly, my name is Jennifer Simmons, but you'll call me Ms. Simmons."

"Nice to meet you."

She stood and shuffled her feet, eyeing the floor. "I normally don't do this, but . . . there's something about Kelly. I'm going to open a space for her."

Molly's mouth dropped to the floor. "What?"

The woman chuckled. "I'm going to take her on myself. I thought I wouldn't be taking any students this year, but I've just changed my mind."

Molly stammered. "Wait . . . Who are you?"

The woman held out her hand. "I'm sorry. I'm Jennifer Simmons, the director of the special education program here. I'd really like a chance to work with Kelly, if you would let me."

Molly clasped her hand. "Yes, we would be so grateful. Thank you. I'm Molly, by the way."

Molly turned to the receptionist. "What do we need to do now?"

Jennifer patted her shoulder. "I'll take care of it. We have your information, right?"

Molly nodded. "Thank you, thank you so much."

Jennifer winked at her and knelt to me. "I will see you in a couple of weeks."

I nodded, not sure what had just happened.

***

God had done several miracles in my life, and I didn't even know it. Miracle number two soon followed. My mother allowed me to live with Dad and Molly. Hoping to at least give me a chance to catch up to my class, she reluctantly let me go.

The third happened when my best friend, who had lived two doors down from my mother's house, moved during the summer. I missed her and thought of her often. I was shocked when, on my first day of second grade, in a new school, she was not only in my class but sat right next to me. God opened up a place for me at a new school, and He arranged for a friend to be with me.

My transition to my dad's house seemed pretty easy, thanks to Molly. I liked her, and she went out of her way to make me feel welcomed. The uncomfortable part of this arrangement came when I returned to my mother's house every other weekend.

One such weekend, as my mother cooked dinner, I told her about school. She rushed around the kitchen as I talked.

While I set the table, I said, "Molly showed me this really cool way to set the table."

Mother grabbed a platter for the meat. "That's nice, honey. Tell me about school."

"Oh, well, Ms. Simmons says I'm catching up real quick to my class. She doesn't think I'll need to stay in her special class next year. Molly says . . ."

Mother slammed the platter down on the table causing the glasses to clamor. "Kelly, can we not talk about Molly anymore? I am your mother! I don't want to hear about her."

I looked down at the table, holding back tears. *Why did I do that? I know I need to be careful and not bring up Molly, it makes her mad.* "Sorry, Mom."

I couldn't do anything right.

Ben and Ann walked in and we sat to eat. I didn't bring up Molly again or what went on at Dad's house. As the months went by, the constant upheaval of going back and forth led to a diminished relationship with my mother. With my father in and out of treatment centers for alcohol and drug addiction, Molly became my rock.

Chapter 4
All Things New

KELLY'S STORY

1984

We all sat in the family room waiting for Dad's big announcement. Ben and Ann were with us for the weekend, and all of us kids were stumped.

Dad put his arms around Molly's shoulders and faced us. "We wanted it to be a surprise, so we waited until everyone was here to announce that we're moving."

Groans followed, as my siblings grumbled about missing their friends. I sat up straighter. "Where are we moving to?"

He smiled. "Not too far from here. You guys won't even have to change schools, if you don't want to."

Molly took a hold of his hand. "It's a much bigger house, and it's out in the country."

My heart beat faster. Country, new home. Maybe a horse? "Can we have horses?"

She nodded. "It is a horse property, but it would take a lot of work before we can even consider getting a horse."

Both Molly and Dad knew about my love of horses, and I almost allowed myself to hope, until Dad shook his head emphatically. "Don't be putting ideas in her head, Molly. We're not getting a horse. They're smelly, attract flies, not to mention the cost of food and vet bills."

One look at him had all my hopes and dreams of having a horse one day come crashing down. He would never cave on the issue. I stared down at the ground. Molly came over and sat next to me, laying her arm across my shoulders. "Hey, it'll be all right, Kelly."

I shrugged. "I hope so."

Dad's face turned red as he watched us. "Molly, don't go filling her head with dreams of having horses. The only way I would ever get a horse is if it were free."

He and the others left the room, leaving Molly and I staring after them. I turned to her. "If it were a piano or something interesting to Ben, I'm sure he would do it."

She squeezed my shoulders. "Don't think like that. Your Dad loves you."

I shrugged again. "Not as much as them."

"Did I tell you I read in the paper the other day about a horse program for kids?"

I sat up straighter. "Really?"

"Yep, it's called Westernaires. They teach all about horses, from learning about their anatomy, to caring for them, and riding them. I think I can convince your dad to let you join."

Like a tulip bulb opening up in spring, the sun shone down on me. I clapped my hands. "Oh my gosh! Really?"

She smiled. "I'll talk it over with your dad tonight. It's every Saturday in the beginning, and it can branch out from there. I'd be willing to take you, and maybe Dave and Bethany might want to join, too."

A dark cloud formed when I thought about dad. When his mind was set on something, nothing could change it. Would he say yes? Probably not. "Dad will say no. If it were piano lessons or tennis lessons maybe, but not that."

She pushed my chin up with her finger and looked straight at me. "Hey now, what's impossible with God?"

Changing Dad's mind was impossible. But could God? "Nothing, Molly?"

"That's right. Nothing. We'll keep praying that God will soften your dad's heart."

Moving into the new house hadn't been so bad. I'm not sure how it worked out, but I got my own room. Dave and Bethany agreed to share their rooms with Ann and Ben on the weekends when they came. Friendly neighbors surrounded us; many of them owned horses. I longed for a horse and counted down the days to my ninth birthday. Dad agreed to let us join Westernaires, but I had to be nine to do it.

One day after Molly had met a friend for lunch, she came home all excited.

My school project lay scattered on the table. "Hey, how'd your lunch go?"

She tossed her purse on the counter and raced over to me. "You're not going to believe this. At lunch today, Mindy told me the Girl Scouts are giving away free horses."

Free horses? That got my attention.

Her smile lit up her face. "Well, they're asking girls to write a letter stating why their home would make a good place for a horse. It's a long shot, but I think you should write them."

For a chance at a horse, I'd write a hundred letters if need be. Could I actually win one? Excited, I got up to look for paper and a pen. "Who do I write it to?"

Molly reached for her purse and pulled out a sheet of paper. "It's all here."

She brought it over and handed the information to me. "I can't help you write it, Kelly. The rules say the letter has to be written by a girl."

I stared at the blank paper. Why would they pick me? *Lord, if ever I asked for something, this is the deepest desire of my heart.* I wrote hoping the words would come to me.

Dear Girl Scout Board,
My name is Kelly and I am writting you cause I heard you were givin away horses. I have loved horses all my life. I am eight now, but almost nine. I am going to be in Westernners when I turn nine, so I can learn more about horses.
My home is a good place for a horse. We have lots of room. I would feed it, brush it, ride it, and put bows in its hair. I would take good care of a horse, I promise, scouts onor. Have a good day.
Love,
Kelly

Once I signed my name, I looked over the letter. Satisfied, I'd done my best, I took it to Molly. "I'm finished, Molly. Do you want to see?"

She reached for the letter. "Sure, I would love to."

I held my breath as she read it. Scared she might not like it, I searched her face for a signal. Was it good enough for someone to pick?

She raised her eyes to mine and smiled. "I love it. You did a wonderful job."

I exhaled. "Oh good, I was afraid it might be awful."

"Nope, I think it's perfect. We can put it in the mail tomorrow."

I scrunched my face. "How long do you think it will take to find out?"

"I don't know, but God does. We'll pray and we'll see what happens."

During the next two weeks, I prayed every chance I had. I didn't want to get my hopes up, trusting God would answer my prayers. Molly and I didn't tell anyone about the letter, and as the weeks continued on with no word, I figured they didn't pick me.

One night as I lay in bed, Molly came in and sat next to me. "Hey, you're up pretty late tonight. Are you all right?"

Not really. What if we never hear about a horse? I bunched the blanket in my fist. "I'm fine. I guess God doesn't want me to have a horse."

She reached over and brushed the hair from my face. "Oh Kelly, we don't know that. I've been praying, too, and I'm wondering if maybe it's not the right time yet. We need to get a fence up, and I don't know how open your father is to doing that right now."

A tear slid down my cheek. "I know, I just thought maybe. Doesn't God love me?"

She wiped away a tear rolling down her check too. "Hey now, of course He loves you. Why would you ask that?"

Because why would he love me? I looked down at my covers as more tears spilled out. "He doesn't answer my prayers."

"What do you mean?"

"I've been praying for a long time that God would make

Dad stop drinking, but it doesn't work."

She tucked the blankets around me. "I love you, and that isn't ever going to change. Don't give up on your dreams, honey. God loves you, and I know He has something big in store for you."

Headlights flashed in the window, Molly looked over at my alarm clock and frowned. "I guess your dad's home, late again."

When the door slammed, she stood up. "I better go see how he is. I'll see you in the morning."

Dad and Molly talked downstairs. His slurred words weren't lost on me.

Great. He's drunk again, the third time this week.

***

January 1985

Days went by in a blur. I went to school and did my chores at home. Dad's drinking soon became the elephant in the room we didn't talk about. As it became more frequent, we saw less and less of him. On weekends Ben and Ann visited, he wouldn't drink. It seemed like we had our dad back. After a while, though, I noticed a pattern, he would force himself to be sober for Ben and Ann. Why wouldn't he do it for Molly, Bethany, Dave, and me?

I continued to visit my mother, now married to Joe, every other weekend. I was lost, like I didn't belong in either household and wondered if God had forgotten me too.

***

March 1985

The phone rang as I opened the door. Throwing my backpack down I ran to grab it. "Hello."

An unfamiliar male voice spoke. "Hello, may I please speak to Kelly?"

Who was this? I paused. "This is Kelly."

"Hi, my name is Sam. I got your name and number from the Girl Scout Board."

My heart pounded faster. *Oh my gosh, did I get picked?*

"Your name was selected along with a few others for a free

horse."

Did I hear him correctly? "Really? Okay."

"We have a few to choose from. They're all retired trail horses and would make great riding horses. Do you have any particular color you might like?"

I took a deep breath. "I really like palominos and buckskin horses."

He chuckled. "Well then, I have a perfect match for you. Her name is Cloud, and she's a buckskin quarter horse. She's gentle around everyone, has a bit of an issue with being caught though, but once you have a halter on her, she's sweet as pie."

"I . . . have a horse named Cloud? Really? She's mine?"

"Well, I need to talk to your parents, but if everything works out all right, yes."

I scanned the room for Molly, finding Bethany. "Beth, go find Mom. Quick."

Beth shot me a curious look before she turned and left the room. A few seconds later Molly came in with a puzzled look. I held out the phone for her.

"This is Molly."

I hung on her every word. After a few minutes she put the phone back on the receiver and turned to me with a look of shock on her face. "You were picked."

"I have a horse?"

Bethany ran over. "What? What were you picked for?"

Molly stared at us. "I have to call your dad. I want you both to go outside for a little while."

I realized at that moment my dream still hung in the balance. It all would come down to whether Dad would agree.

Once outside, Beth turned to me. "Do you think Dad will agree?"

"I don't know, Beth. I sure hope so."

We sat there for what felt like hours before Molly came to get us. She smiled as she sat down. "I talked to your dad and then with Mrs. Peterson down the street, and it's all settled."

My heart drummed faster. *Oh no, he said no.*

"What's settled?" asked Beth

Molly grinned from ear to ear. "You have a horse, Kelly."

I expected I'm so sorry but . . . "Wait. What?"

Bethany moved closer to us.

Molly smiled. "We need to build a fence, barn, and warming shed. Until then, Mrs. Peterson is going to board the horse for us."

Oh Lord, You do love me. I brushed away tears of joy.

"I have a horse!"

***

A few months later, with the fence built and everything in order, we brought home not one horse, but two. Mrs. Peterson gave us a pony named Apache. An older pony, he was as stubborn as a mule, but we loved him. He died a short time after the move, but for the time we had him, we loved him.

By the end of that summer we not only had Cloud and Apache but also a new two-year-old horse named Teddy Bear. Every chance I had, I spent with the horses. They somehow made the mess I lived in more tolerable.

I found out years later that Molly had gone toe to toe with my dad. At first he said no, but Molly fought back until he caved, using his own words, "The only way I'll get a horse is if it's free." Owning not one but three horses is one of the best memories I have of my childhood. Looking back now, I realize the sacrifices that were made in order for me to have one.

God had made it possible.

The horses were an incredible gift during a desperate time. Even now, remembering those moments bring tears to my eyes.

***

Fall 1985

The weekend at my mother's house was over, and I couldn't wait to get home. Even though I was only nine, I sensed my visits were an intrusion into their lives now. Ann and Ben each had friends, and they spent most of their time with them. Gone were the relationships I had with them when we were younger. I reached for my backpack and noticed we passed by the point where we usually met Dad to make the transfer.

Wait, why isn't she stopping? "Aren't we meeting Dad?"

Her grip tightened on the steering wheel. "No. Molly called this morning and said he couldn't make it. I'm taking you to the house."

If her stiff upper lip and deep sigh weren't enough to clue me in to her anger, with this new hiccup in her plan, the glare she sent me said it all. "I'm sorry you have to take me all the way home."

Her face softened. "It's not your fault. I just get frustrated when your dad changes plans at the last minute. He isn't the only one with a full-time job."

I looked out the window. "I know."

We drove the rest of the way in silence. When we pulled into the driveway, I gripped the door handle before we came to a complete stop. Slipping my backpack over one shoulder got out and waved. "Bye, Mom, thanks for the ride."

"Bye, honey, I'll see you in a couple weeks." She eyed the front porch. "Do you want me to wait till you're inside?"

I adjusted my backpack. "No, it's okay, the porch lights are on. I know you need to get home."

"Well . . . okay then. I love you."

Her taillights disappeared as I reached the porch. The lights burned brightly as I tried to open the door and found it locked. I rang the doorbell, to no avail. I dug in my backpack for my key and couldn't find it. I dumped the contents onto the porch, but still no key. My hands shook as I stuffed everything back into my bag. I was alone.

I left my backpack on the steps and went around back to see if the sliding glass doors were unlocked. My lip trembled and tears gathered when I found them locked as well. Where is Molly? Is she coming back?

As I rounded the corner of the house, Cloud greeted me with a loud neigh. My spirits lifted. She and Teddy pranced along the fence line. Changing direction, I headed toward them, watching in puzzlement as they pawed the ground. They wanted to be fed. I glanced at my watch, it said six thirty p.m., way past their feeding time.

As I approached Teddy, he rubbed his soft muzzle against my arm. "I know, boy. I'm back. I'll get you some food right now."

Cloud tended to be a little skittish around people but followed behind, as I opened the door to the barn. I grabbed four sections of hay, and took them over to the fence making two piles. Teddy barely gave me time to move before he barreled over to the hay. Both horses dove right in.

Walking toward them as they ate, I passed the water trough. At half full it needed filling. What happened? Why haven't the horses been fed? Molly always feeds them when I'm gone. Something bad must have happened.

I picked up a brush to groom Teddy while he ate. "What happened, boy, where is everyone?"

He snorted.

I brushed him in silence. When he stopped eating, I approached Cloud. As long as she ate, and I didn't have a halter in my hand, she would let me come near her.

"Hi, pretty lady."

She turned her head and eyed my hands and then went back to eating.

"No, I'm not going to catch you tonight." I ran my hand over her back.

Brushing her seemed a healing balm to my emotional weekend. I could tell my horses anything and trust them to still love me. "I hate going to my mother's every other weekend. I don't think they care if I'm there or not."

Tears welled, but I paid them no attention as they spilled over and cascaded down my cheeks. "It's always the same. I'm an intrusion into their perfect lives."

Teddy came over and nudged my shoulder with his nose. "I love you too, boy." I turned to pat his neck so he wouldn't feel left out.

An hour later, Molly found me still grooming them. "I thought you might be here."

I dropped the brush and ran into her arms. "I was so worried when no one was home."

She sighed and held me close. "I'm sorry, honey. Bethany and I just got home. I hoped you had your key, but when I saw your backpack by the front door, I felt horrible."

I pulled back to look at her in the dim light, her eyes were puffy and tired. "Are you all right?"

"It's been a long day."

Her face told me it had to do with Dad. "Dad? Right?"

"Yeah." She walked over to pat Teddy. "I see you fed these guys. Thank you."

She bent over to retrieve the brush and began running it along Teddy's shoulders. "How did your weekend go?"

Not looking at her I walked back over to Cloud. "All right."

I could feel her eyes boring into my back as I began to play with Cloud's mane.

"That bad?"

"Same as always."

"I'm sorry."

I wiped a lone tear away and shrugged. "Not your fault."

We stood in silence for a while, each to our own thoughts. When she returned the brush to the barn, her defeated frame walked back toward me. "Come on, we need to go inside. You have school tomorrow."

I followed her to the gate. "Is Dad home?"

"No, he's in the hospital on a seventy-two-hour watch."

Of course, why did I ask? I looked back at the horses. "Alcohol and prescription drugs again?"

She nodded.

We walked up the path toward the house. He would be back in three days, promising it would never happen again and then tell us how sorry he was.

"Didn't your mother wait to see if you could get into the house when she dropped you off?"

"No, we thought someone was home since the porch lights were on."

She remained silent until we reached the door. "I'll make sure you have your key next time."

I looked at the floor. "It was my fault, Molly. I forgot to put the key in my bag."

She lifted my chin. "Kelly, you're nine. You're tall for your age, but you're still a child. It's not your fault. I should have been here."

~ ♦♦♦ ~

Chapter 5
Many Fearful Things

NANCY'S STORY

December 1987

Later that afternoon, the tech slathered my swollen belly with gel. She proceeded to place the ultrasound head on my tummy and slid it around. Although I could see the monitor, I had no clue what I looked at, since she viewed a different area of the abdomen.

I fished for information. "What are you looking at?"

"Your gallbladder."

"Do you see the baby?"

"Yes."

"Does the baby look okay?"

"As far as I can tell, but I'm not a doctor."

The tech fell silent. I'd not be getting any information out of her. There was a clock on the wall, but the darkened room made it impossible to read. The tech took measurements and pictures. She moved the head a smidgen and took more. It seemed as if she hunted for something, measuring and snapping pictures of every inch of my abdomen. Her silence spoke volumes.

Something was wrong.

Although the test felt similar to a massage, it did little to calm my trepidation. Aware the ultrasound took much longer than expected, ominous fingers of dread crept into my being.

I tried again. "Is the baby all right?"

The ultrasound tech wiped gel off my tummy. "I have to leave that call to the doctor." She turned off the monitor and ultrasound machine. "I'll be back."

She stepped out, closed the door, and left me lying in a lightless room. Sinister darkness closed in on me, wrapping me in a nightmare I wanted to wake up from.

"Please, Jesus," I whispered. "Keep my baby safe."

I wished John were there.

My times are in Thy hand. The words of my morning Bible reading crossed my mind.

"Yes, Lord. I know my times are in Your hand, but what about my baby? Please, don't take this child from me." Tears welled. "I can't bear it."

Trust Me.

"I'm trying. I'm not sure I know how." I dried my tears and breathed a deep sigh.

Time crawled in the blackness. With every passing moment, the sense of foreboding became more palpable. The darkened walls breathed gloom and dread, and I wondered if I'd been forgotten by the tech.

Forgotten by God.

At least an hour passed before the door opened, and the tech returned. A well-built man followed her in.

The tech motioned toward the man. "This is the radiologist."

The doctor shook my hand and gave me his name. "I'm going to take a look."

Once again the tech squeezed gel onto my growing tummy. The doctor took the ultrasound head and probed my abdomen. No one spoke, their eyes riveted on the monitor. My heart thumped in my ears like a war drum announcing doom. Couldn't they tell me what was wrong? I needed to ask, but fear of grim news held my tongue.

After fifteen minutes of pure silence, the radiologist spoke. "Does anyone in your family have cysts on their kidneys?"

"No, not that I know of."

"Anyone with kidney disease?"

"No."

"Were you adopted?"

"No. Why?"

"That's odd." The doctor fell quiet for a time as he continued to search my abdomen. "I suppose you could be the mutation."

"The what?"

"Do you think you could have been switched at birth?"

"Are you kidding me?"

The doctor shrugged. "It does happen."

"I don't think so. I look too much like my dad. Is the baby okay?"

"The baby looks fine."

I breathed a big sigh of relief. "That's good to hear."

"You, on the other hand, have a genetic kidney disease called Polycystic Kidney Disease or PKD. Cysts grow on the kidneys and liver. Most people who have the disease don't start having problems until they hit their forties or fifties. Until ultrasound systems were developed, people didn't know they had the disease until their kidneys started to shut down. Others are diagnosed at autopsy, after dying from another cause."

In most cases this news would have been devastating, but at the time, my entire focus was on the baby. And the baby looked fine.

***

Mid-January 1988 – Twenty-five Weeks Gestation

One evening I stood at the stove cooking, a sudden gush of warm fluid ran down my inner thigh. Alarm bells pealed off in my mind.

I called to John who sat in the living room watching TV. "I think my water broke."

He rushed into the kitchen. "Do you think you need to go to the hospital?"

"Yes. It's way too early." To still the mental turmoil roiling in my mind, I had to do something. "Let me change my pants before we go."

At the hospital, Dr. Swensen happened to be on call and met us in the emergency room with a wheelchair. I detected what seemed to be concern in his eyes. "Let's wheel you up to the fifth floor where I can do an ultrasound."

On the fifth floor, a nurse helped me lie on an empty bed. The doctor rolled in an ultrasound, turned on the machine, squirted lotion on my abdomen, and began to search my tummy as the nurse flipped off the light.

Tears loomed in the wings to escape my control. John stood to the side in silence, and I could only imagine what he thought.

Tension-filled minutes passed.

Finally, a smile broke across Dr. Swensen's face. "Everything's fine."

I struggled to wrap my mind around what he'd just said, since I expected bad news. "Really?"

"Yes, I just saw your baby bounce its head on your bladder. There's plenty of embryotic fluid and all is still intact. You've just got a little stinker."

Tears escaped. "Are you kidding me?"

The doctor laid a hand on my shoulder. "Everything's fine, but if it happens again, you'll still need to come in. We can never be sure, in cases like this, until we take a look."

***

Beginning of February 1988 – Twenty-Eight Weeks Gestation

Carrie and I viewed the clock with disdain. Our coffee break, now over, signaled we needed to go back to work.

She stood with a moan. "Breaks are never long enough."

"I agree."

I began to waddle my way toward the door as a sharp pain grabbed my upper inner thigh. "Ouch!" It jabbed me at every step. "What's wrong with my thigh? It packs a punch when I put weight on my right leg."

Carrie gave a knowing smile. "It's probably round ligament pain. I got it with every one of my pregnancies. It's normal."

"That's good, but is there anything I can do for the pain?"

"I'd try heat or ice. Sometimes it just goes away on its own."

"If it still hurts like this at lunchtime, I'll go down to medical and see if they can help me out."

At lunchtime I found myself limping into the company's medical department.

A woman sat behind the counter. "Can I help you?"

"I think I'm struggling with round ligament pain. Wondered if someone could do something to help me."

"Take a seat. I'll tell the nurse."

Not long after, the nurse came for me. In the examining room, I told her about the pain in my leg.

She picked up a blood pressure cuff. "I have to take your blood pressure before I can do anything. It's policy."

Placing the cuff around my arm, she pumped it up, and watched the gauge. Her eyes widened. "I'm taking it again."

Repeating the procedure, she stared at the gauge with interest. She allowed the pressure to release, snatched up a sticky notepad, and wrote something down. "I don't care about your round ligament pain but these numbers are another matter. What's your doctor's name and phone number? You're not returning to work today. Your blood pressure is about to burst through the roof."

I dug through my purse and handed my doctor's card to her. This was mystifying to me. I felt fine, except for the pain in my upper thigh.

"Lie down on the examining table and rest while I'm gone. I'll be back."

It was nice to receive the news I couldn't go back to work when I felt fine. On the other hand, was the baby okay?

A few minutes later the nurse returned and gave me a sticky note. "This is the time your OB/GYN wants to see you today in his office. How did you get to work?"

"I drove."

"Do you have someone who can pick you up? It's not wise for you to be behind the wheel."

"I feel fine."

"That may be, but with that high blood pressure anything can happen. I can't let you leave here alone. You need to get someone to drive you to the doctor."

"I suppose I could call my husband."

She moved the telephone across the desk toward me. "Here, call him."

I called John. He would pick me up in time for the doctor's appointment.

"My husband's coming for me." I said, as I hung up.

"When?"

"Around three o'clock."

"You can lie down in sick bay until he arrives."

"I'm hungry. Can I get some lunch?"

She pursed her lips and sighed. "I suppose, but only if you stay in the building."

"I was planning to go to the cafeteria."

She glanced at her watch. "I'll let you go, but you must be back in forty-five minutes. I don't like this, but you need to eat."

I ate my lunch while my mind pinged from one thought to another. Was I risking my baby's life, or my own, for food? I didn't eat much.

When I returned, the nurse wasted little time putting me to bed in a dark room. Another dark room. Darkness vexed me like a pesky flea intent on sucking away the light of hope and life.

***

Later that afternoon, Dr. Swensen released the blood pressure cuff. "I feared this would happen with your kidneys. You have toxemia, which means bed rest until you deliver."

"I have to stay in bed for the next three months?"

"Yes, if you want to keep the baby cooking. Can I trust you to lie in bed or on the couch if I send you home?"

"I'll do whatever is good for the baby."

He turned toward John. "This means no cooking, cleaning, or anything else she can't do lying down." He turned to me. "You can get up to go to the bathroom. That's it. This could be life threatening for both baby and mom, if it's not taken seriously. Now, call me immediately if anything unusual takes place."

***

Four days later I lay on the couch watching an old sitcom rerun. John returned home from work and gave me a kiss as I rose to use the restroom.

I returned to the couch and called to him in the kitchen. The words stuck in my throat. "I'm spotting."

That evening they admitted me to the hospital and a private room on the maternity ward. A nurse brought a long triangular cushion to use as a wedge behind my back. "The doctor ordered this. You need to lie on your left side only because your blood pressure is less if you do. This will keep you from rolling over on your back or to your right side."

"Are you serious? Sounds like Chinese torture."

"I'm afraid so."

For the next two weeks, I dutifully lay on my left side resisting the desperate desire to change position. Each day became touch and go. On Valentine's Day morning, the doctor warned me he might need to deliver the baby later in the day. I prayed for healing mercies and bolstered my resolve to lie on my left side for the full three months.

A nurse came in a half hour later with a wheelchair. "I'm going to give you a tour of the neonatal care unit. Doctor's orders."

Glad for a reason to get off my left side, I donned my robe and slipped into the wheelchair. As she wheeled me toward the intensive care nursery, I took deep breaths trying to untie the knot forming in my stomach. The realization had dawned. The doctor didn't expect me to make it full term.

Please, Lord, protect my baby.

Inside the intensive care nursery, my nurse introduced me to the neonatologist and the attending nurses there. The doctor handed me booklets on premature infants and their possible complications. The nurse rolled me past the tiniest babies I'd ever seen. Tubes protruded from their belly buttons with ventilator hoses coming from their mouths.

I squared my shoulders. My baby wasn't going to be one of those. No, I'd lie on my left side until the sun burned out, if need be.

Back in my room, I read the booklets. Denial became my

insulator. None of those things would happen to my child. No, I would stay on my left side until I gave birth to a full-term baby. I would *will* it into being. Sheer determination would give my child a normal birth.

The doctor bolstered my thinking when he returned to my room. "Looks like we won't have to deliver today, after all. We've bought more time. However, I would like to perform an amniocentesis."

I frowned with a shake of my head. "I don't think that's necessary. I'm giving birth to this baby no matter what defects it might have."

"That isn't the reason for performing it. The procedure will determine how developed your baby's lungs are. We want to give the baby the best chance at survival and to keep the child in the womb as long as possible. I'm not expecting you to make your due date."

I bit my lower lip. "I've heard there are risks to the baby during an amniocentesis."

"Yes, there are, but in this case, the baby risks more by not having one. We need to be prepared for the baby's condition."

A half hour later, he returned with the longest needle I'd ever seen. I wished for John's presence, held my breath, and prayed the wicked instrument would not harm my baby. The doctor pierced my belly with the lengthy needle, retrieved amniotic fluid, and left.

Later that day, I received steroid shots to speed up the development of my baby's underdeveloped lungs. My baby and I stood on the precipice of disaster. I clutched my abdomen to protect my unborn child from hurling into the black abyss. How could I back away from this danger?

But the only thing I could do was pray.

***

February 21, 1988

Food delivery carts rolled down the hall wafting the smells of eggs, bacon, and coffee. Mealtimes broke up the monotony of lying in a hospital room, day after day on my left side. I waited with expectation, but my breakfast never came. Thinking they'd forgotten me, I pushed the call button for the nurse.

"What can I do for you?" The nurse said as she entered.

"The breakfast crew seemed to have skipped me."

"No. We're holding your breakfast until the doctor is sure he won't need to deliver your baby today. As soon as we get word, I'll bring it to you, if I can."

"Okay, thanks." I wasn't giving birth to my child today, or any other day for that matter, not until my baby was full term. I would *will* it to be, and that was final.

At 11:00 a.m., the nurse returned with my breakfast. I ate with contentment. My determination strategy was working. As I devoured my morning meal, I tried to remember what I had ordered for lunch. The feast would be arriving soon, and I probably wouldn't have the appetite for more food. Happy the baby would stay snug in my womb that day, I surfed the TV for something interesting to watch.

Thirty minutes later, my phone rang. A coworker needed guidance on how to handle part of my job. After after we finished business, we continued to chat.

The doctor bolted into my room. "I thought I told them to block your calls. You should be resting, not working from your hospital bed."

"What? I . . ."

"Sorry. Your kidneys are failing. We need to induce now, if you and the baby are to survive."

I spoke into the phone. "I have to go."

My coworker wished me luck, and we hung up.

The doctor stood at the end of my bed. "We'll try to induce, but if the baby doesn't do well, we'll need to do a C-section. Toxemia will kill you both if we don't deliver today. You might want to call your husband."

The doctor left, and I dialed the business where John worked several times but only received busy signals.

Nurses poured in pushing IV racks and carts of supplies.

I dialed again. Still busy.

Then I called the operator.

"This is Sue, may I help you?"

"I need an emergency break-in on a line for John Faltermeier."

"This is a true emergency?"

My voice wavered as tears escaped. "Yes."

No amount of determination would prevent what was happening. My baby's life hung in the balance—and mine as well.

Lord, help us.

A nurse grabbed my free arm and sterilized it for an IV.

"Ma'am, that line is a business line. I can't clear the line for you."

I stifled a sob. "I know it's a business." The nurse inserted the IV line into my arm. "Operator, please, this is an emergency."

"I'm not supposed to do this, but I'll give it a try. If they're not willing to relinquish the line, there's nothing I can do."

"Thank you."

Another nurse wrapped a monitor around my belly to monitor the baby's heartbeat.

The operator broke in on the line. "This is the operator. I have an emergency break through call for a John Faltermeier."

A male voice responded. "For John, you say?"

"Yes, that's right."

"Just a minute."

A sigh of relief escaped my lips as I heard the man calling for John in the distance. Moments later John's voice came on. "Hello?"

"John, my kidneys are failing. They're delivering the baby today. You need to get here as soon as possible."

"I'm leaving now. Love you. Bye."

I handed the receiver to the nurse. She smiled as she hung the phone up. "I'm sorry. I needed to give you IV meds that will cause you to give up the breakfast you just ate."

As soon as the words left her mouth, I felt like heaving. For the next half hour, I vomited.

The doctor returned to break my water. Everything within me screamed "no". Yet he would force my baby into the world with the hope of saving both our lives. Two nurses pushed down on my tummy as the doctor pushed upward internally. Finally it broke, and we were beyond the point of no return.

I had to accept things were out of my control. My precious unborn child hurtled along with me, over the edge and into the dark crevasse below. Thrust upon the river of unknowns, my baby would enter into this harsh world ten weeks early.

The doctor left the room as early labor pains set in. Details from the booklets on premature infants occupied my mind. The devastation of reality and anxiety for the future overcame the denial that had insulated me, thus far, from my circumstance. A tsunami swept us away—my infant and me—to a place we did not wish to go. Could anyone help us? There was nothing to do but to ride the massive wave and pray we didn't drown.

When John arrived, they gave him scrubs to put on. The nurse checked the baby's monitor. Concern seemed to etch her face as she left the room. Five minutes later she returned with the doctor.

Without a word, the doctor studied the monitor. Then he turned toward John and me. "The baby is in distress, and this is still early labor. The baby won't make it if we don't do a C-section." He turned toward the nurse. "Prep her for surgery."

From that point on, things became a blur. They rolled me to my side, gave me an epidural, moved me to a gurney, and wheeled me to the operating table as John padded at my side. Once on the operating table they set up a drape so that I couldn't see what they were doing. John sat at my head with his hand on my shoulder.

For a time, I felt sensations of tugging and pulling. Then a small bellow came as the baby cried.

"Congratulations!" The doctor said. "It's a girl."

John squeezed my shoulder and smiled.

The doctor spoke. "Your appendix looks inflamed. I think we should remove it while we have you opened up. We'd hate to have to do surgery again in a week or two."

I looked over at John. He shrugged.

"Okay, I guess. I don't want to face surgery again."

John eyed the doctor. "You're the doc. Do what you think's best."

The neonatologist brought the baby to me, and held her in front of the drape so I could see her. "She's a sweet baby girl."

Wrapped tight in a blanket, my precious girl peered out at me with one eye open and her tiny hand balled up against her face. For one snapshot of time, I saw her. Then they whisked her away.

"I'm sorry." The neonatologist said as she walked away. "We need to get her to the intensive care nursery pronto."

I didn't see my baby again for two whole days.

A sharp pain stabbed under my rib. "Ouch! I felt that."

The doctor ordered more medication, and all went black.

***

I awoke in an unfamiliar hospital room. Recovery. I couldn't move from the neck down due to the extra drugs numbing my body. Too drugged to be alarmed, I found John watching an ice skating competition on TV. The skaters gliding across the screen made my eyes cross, and I fell back asleep.

That evening, I woke to the sound of John's voice. "Hi Dad, hi Mom. I'm calling to tell you, you have a new granddaughter."

He gave more details and chatted as I dozed. I pried my eyes open as he said his good-byes. His brave face vanished as soon as the receiver hit the cradle. His brow furrowed as he stood and turned his back to me and peered out the high-rise window. I doubted he really saw the Denver city lights.

It didn't take much for me to imagine what nettled his mind. Would he lose his wife, his child or both? What did the future really look like? Would he share it with his complete family, or alone? Would he live on with a heartbroken wife, or raise a motherless child? How would he face what lay ahead? Life would be different from this day forward. I tried to pray for him but only drifted off again.

I spent two more days in recovery, sleeping, and regaining the use of my limbs. Finally, two nurses wheeled me on a gurney to postpartum. On the way, we came to a window in the hallway and one of the nurses tapped on the glass.

"Would you like to see your baby?" the other asked.

I rose up on one elbow. "You better believe it."

The mini blinds opened, and a nurse on the other side of

the window smiled. She pointed at a tiny baby sprawled out on an open infant-sized bed. Attached to my infant, tubes, wires, and a ventilator obstructed my view. Above her bed a colorful, handmade sign read *Baby Faltermeier.*

I tried to rise a bit higher to get a better look but pain from the sutures prevented me. "She's so tiny." I said. "I didn't realize how small she is. When can I see her?"

"As soon as you can get to a wheelchair without collapsing on us." A nurse said. "Perhaps tomorrow."

***

That evening John sat with me in my hospital room. A knock sounded on the door and the neonatologist, Dr. Zarlento, entered. "Hello, I'm wondering if you've named your baby."

I hung my head. "No. We never settled on a girl's name, and I've been so drugged since her birth. I can't think."

"Well, the poor child needs a name. We're tired of calling her Baby Faltermeier. Did you have a boy's name picked out?"

"Yes."

"Why don't you see if there's a girl's version of the name and call her that. Many couples do that in your situation. Let us know her name as soon as you decide. However, this is not the reason for my visit."

My heart stampeded as I reached for John's hand.

She continued. "Oftentimes we see patent ductus arteriosus problems in premature infants."

I squeezed John's hand harder. "What does that mean?"

"There's a valve on the heart that usually closes at birth. Your daughter's valve hasn't closed. Preemies do much better once it closes. We've tried to shut your baby's valve chemically, but she hasn't responded to the treatment. I plan to try the medication once more, but if the valve refuses to close, we will need to surgically do it. If the operation is necessary, we will need to transfer her to Children's Hospital."

My heart hit bottom. She wasn't even two-and-a-half pounds yet. "She's so tiny. The procedure sounds risky."

The doctor shook her head. "Actually, most preemies do

better after the surgery but with all operations there are risks. As I said, we'll try the medication first. Hopefully the third time will be the charm, and she won't need the operation. I'll keep you updated."

What else could go wrong?

She left us sitting in stunned silence. Our baby was too small and young to face such a dangerous surgery. My heart palpitated against my chest. I had to do something to protect my little girl. Truth was, we were still helplessly falling, plunging deeper and deeper into the black abyss. John and I clung to one another and prayed. We prayed the medication would do its job, and did the only thing we could do for our child. We named our precious little girl, Brianna Lyn.

I didn't get much sleep that night. The cries of healthy babies made their ways to my ears as I pleaded for the life and health of my child. The idea of my tiny little girl facing major surgery on her third day of life was unbearable.

***

The next day, they allowed me to get up and John wheeled me to the ICN so we could spend time with our little Brianna. He rolled me up to the radiant table where our baby lay. The table, heated by lights above, was controlled by a sensor taped to her body.

"Hi Brianna," I said, petting the back of her hand with my index finger. "I'm your mommy."

She gave no response, except for the rapid breathing helped by the ventilator down her throat. IV's inserted in her belly button, the medical staff used for feeding and blood transfusions. Monitors attached to her small body tracked her breathing, heart rate, and oxygenation.

"Please, Jesus," I whispered, "heal her heart valve without surgery. She needs You. I need You. Please save my daughter's life. I believe You're not a God who defrauds. After all my begging for this child, please don't take her from us now."

The neonatologist stepped up behind me. "I had to make her go to sleep. She kept trying to pull the ventilator out."

"Why isn't she in an incubator?"

"We put the sickest kids on the radiant tables. They are as warm as the incubators, but we can get to them faster. How's Mom?"

"Well enough to visit."

"That's good. She's going to need a healthy mother."

"We named her Brianna Lyn, last night after you left us."

Dr. Zarlento pulled out a pen and pad from her lab coat pocket. "How are you spelling it?"

"B-R-I-A-N-N-A."

"Good, I'll have a nurse make a new sign for her. I arranged for a breast pump to be sent to your room. Did you get it?"

"Yes. The nurse said she brought down the milk I pumped."

"Good. That's the best for the baby." She patted me on the back and left the unit.

I stared at Brianna and wished her to be the size of a normal infant. Her little arms were only as thick as my index finger, her head was the size of an orange, and her tiny fingernails were like dots. Would she ever grow to average size?

***

Later that day Dr. Zarlento entered my room. I couldn't help but stiffen. Bad news was coming. I was sure of it. John's jaw seemed tense as I reached for his hand.

Dr. Zarlento smiled. "Brianna's heart valve appears to have closed. I don't think she will need surgery after all. The third time seems to have been the charm."

I wanted to jump out of bed and hug the doctor. "That's great news. I'm so glad and relieved. You have no idea."

The doc stepped toward the door. "I have an idea. I was thrilled to see her turn around and came at the first opportunity to tell you both. She should do much better from now on."

As the doctor left us, John and I thanked the Lord for His intervention. He had miraculously saved Brianna from catastrophe. Now, if she could dodge all the other hazards of preemies, we would host a grand celebration.

***

February 23, 1988

The nurse entered with a wheelchair. Dressed to go home, I stood and settled into the rolling chair. She handed me the balloons and flowers well-wishers brought me during my stay and smiled. "Congratulations, you get to go home."

"Yeah, but I'm leaving my baby behind."

"I'm sorry. That's got to be hard, but when you do get to bring her home, all this will be forgotten."

"I sure hope so."

When I arrived home, my mother and father stepped out of the house to greet me. They had traveled from Arizona to help us. As I entered my home, I found presents for Brianna piled high in the living room. My coworkers gave up the idea of holding a baby shower for me and delivered gifts instead.

Although grateful for all their kindnesses, circumstances cheated me. Why didn't my giving birth play out the way it does for most people? Something nagged me. Would Brianna live to use the gifts lavished upon her?

Chapter 6
The Big Mystery

NANCY'S STORY

Early March 1988

While I recovered from the C-section, we fell into the routine of visiting Brianna morning and evening. My parents drove me to the hospital in the mornings, and John and I returned at night. Dr. Zarlento instructed me to pump breast milk at the times of Brianna's feedings and freeze the milk for her. So even though my baby did not come home with me, I still rose in the middle of the night to pump.

The long walks into the hospital to see Brianna were slow and painful due to the sutures, but I wouldn't allow a little pain to keep me from seeing my child. I talked to her, hoping she remembered my voice, and the sound of it would comfort her. She'd lost a few ounces but now was gaining weight. It's a great feat for a preemie to gain an ounce and we rejoiced over each one.

March 1, as we did every day, Momma and I scrubbed, put on sterile gowns over our street clothes, and entered the ICN. As I strolled to the radiant table where Brianna slept, I smiled. "Look, Mom. They removed the ventilator."

Momma scooted beside me. "Finally, I get to see my grandbaby without that tube in her mouth."

"The tubes for feeding and blood transfusions are gone from her belly button, too. That's a good sign."

An oxygen hood encompassed Brianna's head. It looked similar to an inverted clear plastic bowl with a tube protruding from its side.

Becky, the nurse, stepped up to us. "If all goes well, we'll be putting her into an isolette this evening."

Momma shoved up the glasses on her nose. "A what?"

"We hope to put her into an incubator later today." Becky said and turned to me. "Well, Mom, would you like to hold your baby?"

"You bet! She's ten days old, and I've yet to hold her."

Sharon, another nurse, came over to us. "I'll get you a chair."

Becky removed the oxygen hood but left the tube near Brianna's nose. She then put a tiny pink and blue striped knit cap over her head and wrapped her tight in a blanket.

Sharon placed a chair near Brianna's radiant table and motioned for me to sit.

Becky picked up Brianna with great care. "Now, when I give her to you, you will need to hold the oxygen tube to her nose."

With gentleness, Becky laid Brianna into my arm. Sharon stood behind her with the oxygen hose and placed it in my free hand. I held the tube to Brianna's tiny nose and looked into her little face for the first time. The sun shone brightly in that moment. God had rescued us from the depths.

Both nurses huddled over us like nervous mothers. Sharon asked Becky, "What time is it?"

Becky shoved up her sleeve and peered at her watch. "It's 10:20." She then turned to me. "You can only hold Brianna for five minutes. Sorry. She's not that strong yet."

Momma never came to the hospital without her camera. She snapped pictures as soon as Brianna lay in my arms.

As I held my baby girl, I noticed how little she weighed. It seemed as if I held only the weight of the blanket.

Momma snapped another picture. "She's a doll."

Before long, Becky stood over us. "I'm sorry. I must take her now. She needs to be fed and put her back on the radiant table."

Becky took my baby and sat. She laid Brianna on her lap facing her and threaded a tube down her throat.

Momma's outward cringe mirrored my own. "Oh, my!"

Becky raised a bag of my breast milk and squeezed it down the tube. "These babies must be gavage fed until their sucking reflex develops. Once they learn to suck, we can bottle feed them."

I shook my head. "I'm glad she won't remember all this."

After Brianna's feeding, Becky placed her back on the radiant table and under the oxygen hood. Brianna cried, but no sound came from her.

My heart wrenched. "Brianna's crying, but she's not making any noise."

"Yes, that happens." Becky said. "Her throat and vocal chords have been irritated by the ventilator. She'll get her voice back."

Later that night, John and I returned and were pleased to find Brianna in an isolette. We rejoiced at her improvement. Yes, things were looking up.

***

One morning, I found Brianna with blood transfusing through an IV inserted at the left side of her head. This set me on edge every time I encountered this. But because of her tiny size, when they tested Brianna's blood, they needed to replace the blood. It disturbed me to see her in such a way, but I'd console myself with the thought that we were both alive. The sun was shining, and we no longer descended toward destruction.

Later that evening, when John and I returned, we found bruises on both of Brianna's tiny hands and both of her ankles. Now lodged in the right side of her head, sat the blood transfusion IV. Tears surfaced. When would this end? What else must she endure?

***

March 11, 1988

My incision seemed to be healing, but I wondered when my energy would return. As the days wore on, I felt worse. One evening, I ran a high fever. John drove me to the emergency room. When the intake nurse took my temperature, the fever had risen to 103 degrees. She promptly wheeled me to a room in the emergency department, bypassing the full-waiting area.

Another nurse met me with a number of questions, gave me a gown to change into, and left. A few minutes later, a young doctor entered the room with the nurse trailing behind. The nurse mumbled something, turned around, and disappeared. The doctor rolled his eyes with a labored sigh. I got the sense I was an intrusion, and I wanted to dress and slink out.

The doctor pulled on latex gloves and sighed again. "You probably have an infection from giving birth. I'll check your uterus as soon as the nurse returns."

The nurse rushed in with instruments on a tray. The doctor rolled his eyes again, and the silent friction between the two of them rose as unease settled over me. The nurse asked me to lay back and put my feet in the stirrups. Not sparing a second after I responded to her request, the disgruntled physician began the examination. Pain bolted through me, and I slapped the wall with my hand. "Ouch!"

The doctor stood, jammed his foot on the lever to the trashcan, peeled off the gloves, threw them in, and let the lid bang shut. "Call OB/GYN. She's their patient."

As he opened the door to leave, he turned and said, "You have an infection in your uterus. OB/GYN will be down to see you."

He left and the door slammed behind him. The nurse threw me an apologetic glance. "I'll call OB/GYN." She forced a smile. "Someone should be down shortly."

The nurse opened the door to leave as John met her at the threshold.

I waved. "Hi, hon."

The nurse shrugged and allowed John to enter then closed the door.

I smiled. "Did they get all my info?"

"Yeah. What did you do to upset the doctor? He shot out of here spitting nails."

"Don't blame me. He and the nurse were at odds. I just hunkered down in the crossfire."

The nurse returned with a large plastic bag with handles. "We're admitting you, so here's a bag for your clothes."

"Are you kidding me? I've already spent three weeks here."

She handed me the bag. "Sorry. It shouldn't be long. They'll most likely put you on IV antibiotics, and you'll be out of here before you know it."

"I hope so. I'm sick of this place."

A few minutes later an OB/GYN, who often covered for my doctor, entered the room with a wheelchair. He shook John's hand. "Hi, I'm Dr. Grayber. I'm on call for Dr. Swensen." He turned to me. "Sorry to see you here again. Why don't you hop into the chair? We have a more comfortable examining room on the fifth floor. I'll take a look at you there."

On the fifth floor, Dr. Grayber prepared to examine me. I sucked in a deep breath, dreading the pain I'd experienced downstairs. His examination, however, caused me no discomfort.

His brow furrowed. "I don't think you have an infection in your uterus. I'm going to put you on an oral antibiotic and something to bring down the fever. Dr. Swensen can take a look in the morning. He'll call in your primary care doc, if nothing else presents itself."

***

The next morning, Dr. Swensen entered my room with a quick knock and smiled as he strolled toward my bed. "What are you doing here? You should be at home recovering. Let me take a look at your stitches."

I exposed the sutures. "What do you think is going on?"

"Sometimes women wind up with an infection from the C-section." He poked around at the sutures, then picked up my robe lying at the end of the bed and handed me the outer garment. "Let's take a walk down the hall, so I can examine you."

I donned my robe and slippers and followed the doctor into the corridor.

He looked down at me as we walked. "Your stitches are healing nicely, so that's not the problem."

In the examining room, I went through an encore examination from the night before. He took his time. "You don't feel any pain?"

"No. It's kind of odd. Last night in emergency, I nearly

broke through the roof, but when Dr. Grayber checked me out, I was fine. I think the ER doc might have been a bit miffed about something."

"You're a puzzle. There's an infection somewhere. I just don't know where. I'm ordering some tests and have your internist, Doc Atkin, check you out. Your fever hasn't come down much, so I'm putting you on IV antibiotics."

Storm clouds gathered over my heart.

A half hour later, someone from the IV team inserted the IV. A nurse's aide came soon after and wheeled me down for an ultrasound. That afternoon, they took me for a CAT scan, as well.

At dinnertime, Dr. Swensen returned. "You're a puzzle. The tests didn't show us anything."

I sighed. "Maybe it's all in my head. I have been under a lot of stress lately. It's not every day one gives birth to a preemie."

"No, it's not in your head. Fever says infection. There's no doubt. We just don't know what's affected. Odds are it has to do with the C-section. It's just not showing itself. The antibiotics should take care of it. Has Dr. Atkin been in to see you?"

"He came this morning."

"Good. I think we'll run another test."

***

The next morning, a nurse I didn't recognize entered my room carrying a small metal box. Affixed to the long sides of the rectangular container, the word *radioactive* blazed in prominent lettering.

I frowned.

The nurse set the receptacle on my bedside table. "Hi, Nancy. I'm from radiology. Your doctor ordered a gallium scan. I need to inject this so that when we do the scan your insides will light up."

"You're kidding. It says radioactive, and you're going to inject me with it? It's got to be toxic."

She opened the small chest exposing a syringe.

"It shouldn't hurt you." She then proceeded to plunge the needle into the port of the IV already in my arm.

"Shouldn't?"

Replacing the empty syringe into the metal box, she closed the lid and headed for the door. "You'll be fine. Lots of people go through these scans. The doctor can't help you if he doesn't know what's wrong."

As quick as she appeared, she left. She did have a point, but I wasn't pleased. Was I an experiment?

An hour later a nurse's aide rolled in a gurney, asked me to slide onto it, and wheeled me down to radiology for the scan. He left me lying alone in the hallway, just outside the door to radiology. What am I, a sideshow?

A steady stream of visitors passed, staring at me. Like a young virgin stripped naked before a crowd, I lay there, wanting to hide. Didn't he have a more private place to put me?

***

Later that evening, Dr. Swensen stood at the end of the bed. "The results of the gallium scan showed us nothing. We're pretty sure now the infection has nothing to do with the C-section. You've become quite a puzzle. Dr. Atkin will be taking your case from here. The antibiotics are bringing your fever down. Maybe we'll get you well and never know where the infection came from. Getting you well is the most important thing. I'll check on you from time to time. If you need me, let me know."

Dr. Swensen squeezed my foot and stepped toward the door. "Good luck."

What was I to think? I just wanted to be well, and wanted to get Brianna's room ready to bring her home. Why couldn't the two of us be healthy, so we could get on with the business of living? Would that day ever come? Things seemed hopeless. Only God could help us now.

Dear Lord, please help us both to get strong and healthy. The doctors don't have a clue what's wrong with me, but You do. Give them the piece to the puzzle to make me well. Brianna needs me.

John entered, pushing a wheelchair. "You ready to see the baby?"

"Yes, but I have to drag this IV pole with me."

Brianna was the only redeeming thing about my stay in the

hospital. She resided in the neonatal unit, three floors below.

John helped me thread the IV bag through the sleeve of my robe. I sat in the wheelchair, pushing the IV pole ahead of me as he pushed the chair, and off we went.

After we scrubbed and robed, Nurse Kim met us at the door of the ICN. She smiled. "Are you ready to give Brianna her first bottle feeding?"

I eyed her. "Really? I've been waiting forever. She sucked quite a bit on her pacifier earlier today, I noticed."

Kim strolled over to Brianna's isolette. A doll-sized baby bottle sat on top. "Yes, she's getting the sucking thing."

John pulled a chair over to where I sat in the wheelchair. "Let Nancy go first."

Kim brought Brianna to me, and for the first time, I fed her a bottle like a normal baby. I wanted to jump out of the wheelchair and dance a jig.

While I fed her, Brianna's eyes opened wide. This was something new.

I peered at my child's sweet face soaking in the moment.

Her dark hazel eyes returned the gaze and she seemed to be content.

John scooted close. "She's drunk half the bottle. Do I get a turn?"

Like a hungry animal devouring a long-awaited meal, I didn't want to give her up but after all, he was her father.

"Do you want to go to Daddy?" I asked Brianna, who was still fixated on downing her first real meal.

I gave her to John and smiled. All Brianna needed now was to gain weight, and we would take her home.

That is, if I could get well.

***

On the eighth morning of this hospital stay, Dr. Atkin entered my room and smiled. "Let me take a look at you."

After checking me over, he said, "Your fever has come down, so I think I'm going to allow you to go home today. We still don't know the source of the infection, but if the antibiotics are taking care of it, you should be good. You'll need to keep taking oral antibiotics, but we can get you home and back on your feet."

"Yeah, thank you. I'm ready to get out of here."

***

March 20, 1988

Only home for two days, I stood on the sidewalk in front of Faith Bible Chapel's main entrance. John pulled up in the car, opened the door for me, and I slid in. "It was good to be at church today," I said, "but I feel exhausted."

He pulled the car out into the street toward home. "Thought you were pushing it to come to church this soon."

"I needed to do something "normal" for once. But you're probably right. I feel all drugged out. I'm gonna nap on the way home."

With my elbow propped on the armrest, I cradled my head in my hand. As I touched my face, I sat up straight. "I think my fever's back. My face feels hot."

John felt my forehead with the back of his hand. "You do. Thought it was a bad idea for you to come to church today. You should've waited."

"You're probably right."

As we entered the house, the pleasant aroma of beef roast greeted us. Momma stepped from the kitchen. "How was church?"

"It was great and dinner sure smells good."

Momma wiped her hands on her apron. "It'll be ready in about half an hour."

I shared a glance with John. No need to throw a wrench into her meal, yet. "I'm going to change my clothes."

In the bedroom, I placed the thermometer under my tongue as I changed clothes. Once dressed in jeans and a sweater, I checked my temperature. One-hundred-two degrees. I sank to the bed as my vision blurred. *Really, Lord? I just want to be well. Please, heal me of this infection.*

John entered the room. I held out the thermometer for him to read.

He squinted to get a better look. "Again?"

"And that's *on* antibiotics. I shouldn't have a fever like that."

John shook the thermometer. "Here, take it again."

He stuck the gauge back into my mouth and proceeded to change into jeans and a T-shirt. After a time, we checked the reading again. One hundred two.

I sighed as I reached for the phone. "I'll call the doc."

Dr. Atkin instructed me to meet him at the emergency room waiting area right away. He told me to come expecting to be readmitted. I packed a few things to take along, and then entered the kitchen.

Momma bustled about putting the final touches on her meal. "I'm sorry, Momma. My fever's returned. Dr. Atkin wants me to meet him at the emergency room right away."

The color left her face. "Oh my. Surely you have time to eat. You have to eat."

"Sorry, Momma. We can't keep the doctor waiting. It smells good though. Maybe I can eat some leftovers later. The doc said to plan on being readmitted to the hospital, so pray that God will give them wisdom."

She frowned as I hugged her and Daddy good-bye. Her food begged to eaten as we left for the hospital and I never did get any of her luscious-smelling meal.

***

Dr. Atkin met us in the emergency room waiting area. He took us into a vacant room in the ER, and checked my vital signs.

He shook his head with a sigh. "You have me stumped. Obviously the antibiotic you're taking isn't working. We'll try another. The hospital is full. But I've scrounged up a bed for you. Someone will be down to get you. I'll have a breast pump sent to your room."

***

After I settled into my room, I sent John home. He needed his rest and a good meal. He would be starting a new job in the morning, and the last thing he needed was this extra stress. For the past several months he had been trying to get this job, and I wanted him to be able to focus and do well.

Not happy about having to share a room, I knew there weren't any other options. How much privacy would I get, even though I had the bed next to the window? And would I disturb my neighbor when I needed to use the breast pump in the middle of the night?

Not long after my admittance, someone from the IV team came in to get another IV antibiotic going. How many pricks and prods would it take to feel whole again, to feel normal, to be a mother able to care for her child? A dark cloud floated in and settled over me that night.

I just wanted to be well.

The next morning, my roommate received visitors before breakfast. I ate my meal hoping they would leave. It was necessary to use the breast pump, but I didn't relish the idea of using the machine with a room full of people. As the morning wore on, it became obvious they intended to spend the entire day.

I slipped into my robe, pulled the curtain farther around my bed for as much privacy as the drape would provide, and began to use the pump. I tried to relax, but the pump made considerable noise, and the conversation on the other side of the drape dropped to a whisper. I glanced over my shoulder. A strange man peered at me. He made a swift retreat behind the flimsy barrier when I eyed him.

Really? Am I a peep show? Where was human decency?

Half an hour later, Dr. Atkin poked his head around the curtain. "There you are. How are you feeling?"

"About the same."

"Your fever hasn't budged. Lie back and let me mash on you. Let me know if I'm hurting you."

"Yes, a little."

"Really?" He pressed on the other side of my abdomen. "How about here?"

"No."

"Your pain was over here yesterday, but it doesn't hurt here now?"

"No."

A nurse wandered in. The doctor turned toward her. "I thought this patient was going to be put into a private room. What happened with the room at the end of the hall?"

She shrugged. "Maintenance is storing furniture in there during the remodel."

"Call them and tell them to store the furniture elsewhere. And they need to do it now. This patient needs a private room. They informed me yesterday they had a room for her."

She turned on her heels and left.

Dr. Atkin crossed his arms. "Sorry, about this." He dropped his voice. "And then they're having a party next door."

An hour later, two nurses liberated me by stacking my things on the bed, and moving me, bed and all, down to the end of the hall to my own private room.

***

Later that morning, I underwent another ultrasound. That afternoon they gave me nasty-tasting stuff to drink for a CAT scan—another repeat test. Each time a nurse checked my vitals, my temperature remained the same, but I began to have a nagging pain in my abdomen.

The next morning Dr. Atkin examined me. "You sure are a mystery. Nothing showed up on the ultrasound or CAT scan. Your fever hasn't budged, so I think we'll try another antibiotic. I've invited a few other docs to take a look at you, so don't be surprised if some strangers come for a visit. How are you feeling?"

"The same, except the pain in my stomach is more nagging now."

"Really? Let me mash on you."

He pressed where the discomfort had been the day before and raised an eyebrow.

"It doesn't hurt there anymore. Maybe the pain is in my head."

He pressed at a different spot. "I doubt that."

"Ouch! Now it hurts there."

He stood up straight. "Like I said, you sure are a mystery, but other docs will be by." He patted my shoulder and smiled. "We're going to figure this out."

As he left the room, the cloud hanging over me grew dark

and heavy. It threatened to envelop me into its shadowy mist forever.

During the next few days, doctors came to visit. They ran more tests, but the outcomes were always the same. The source of my fever remained a mystery, even as the numbers edged gradually higher.

***

One morning a few days later, Doctor Atkin came for his daily visit. "How are you feeling?

"The same."

"The antibiotic we have you on now seems to be keeping your fever from rising."

"Well, at least it's doing something."

"Yes, just not enough." He paused a thoughtful moment. "Do you think you might have had an X-ray taken in the past few years that would show your lungs? There's a spot on your lung that concerns me. If we can come up with something to compare it with and see that it's not changing, then we won't have to worry about it."

Was he talking about cancer? My heart thundered in my ears like a herd of elephants. *He thinks I might have lung cancer.*

"A chiropractor took X-rays of my back a few years ago. They might show something. I'll have John check into that."

"Do you think it would be possible for John to get those X-rays today? I'd like to look at them this evening."

I inhaled a calming breath to slow my breathing. "Someone in my family should be able to get them."

"Good. My kids are on spring break, and I'm going to be gone for a few days. I've asked a number of doctors to keep an eye on you while I'm gone. You'll be in good hands." He patted my arm. "We're going to figure this out."

As he left, dark thunderclouds gathered. They had no clue what ailed me and weren't a smidgen closer to the answer. A storm amassed above me, threatening to thunder and rain. The tempest poured, and I lost all hope. For the first time in my life, I stared into the soulless eyes of death. I tried to pray but found myself incapable. My mind could not formulate words, and my focus frayed.

I needed to do something, so I reached for the phone and called someone in my family to get the X-rays.

Not long after that conversation, a black pit opened and sucked me in. I could no longer form words without a lisp. For some unknown reason my mouth no longer worked correctly.

My phone rang.

"Hello'ss."

"Nancy?"

"Yesss."

"This is Debbie. I'm calling to see how you're doing."

"Not sso good's. I can'tss speaks rights any's more's. Theys don't's knows whats wrongs with me sstill."

I went on to tell her about the conversation I had with the doctor that morning.

Her voice came over the line with a certain resolve. "Do you mind if I take things into my own hands? I want to talk to a doctor I work with at the surgery center. His wife is also an MD and is involved with a study on the kidney disease you have. I'm thinking they might have insight on what's going on with you. It's worth a try."

"Pleassse do. I'ms desperates. Can'ts even prays anymores."

"I'll pray for you. You just rest. I'm going to call them right away. Hang in there. I'll call as soon as I hear anything. Bye."

As I hung up the phone, an unfamiliar doctor entered my room. He introduced himself and examined me. Before leaving, he gave me his suspicion of what he thought my problem might be. An hour later, another doctor came in with a different scenario. Not long after, a third discounted the first two doctors' diagnoses, giving me one of his own.

It was obvious. I was the topic of discussion in the physicians' lunchroom, and without the help of God, I wouldn't be leaving the hospital anytime soon, if at all.

That evening, John brought in the X-rays, and we tried to pray. Brianna, our only bright spot, graduated from the oxygen hood. She now used a nasal cannula, and she gained weight steadily. Her future grew brighter, while mine only dimmed.

***

The next day was a revolving door of more doctors hoping to be the one to solve the "puzzle." One young, type-A personality doc, determined to be the one to uncover the mystery, listed all the reasons why the other doctors had to be wrong. They all ordered more tests I had to submit to.

Terror became an unwelcomed companion.

My fever rose. By bedtime, they told me not to get out of bed unless a nurse stood by. Freezing, at 11:00 p.m. I asked for more blankets. At 1:00 a.m. I used the restroom with the nurse's help

When I climbed back into bed, pain in my stomach paralyzed me. Doubled over, the nurse had to lift me into bed. She covered me with a freshly warmed blanket and took my temperature.

Her eyes widened with a gasp. "Oh shoot."

"What's it at?"

She headed for the door. "One-hundred-four degrees. Try to get some sleep."

Help, Lord.

At 2:00 a.m. A male lab tech awakened me. He held a little metal box marked "radioactive." Too weak to protest, he injected the vile stuff into my IV. "Someone will be in to take you down to radiology soon."

When 3:30 a.m. came, an orderly pushing a gurney awakened me again. He helped me onto the rolling bed and wheeled me to radiology. Then he left me in a hallway for a few minutes as he entered the radiology department.

He returned and wheeled the gurney closer to the door. "The gallium scan tech had to be called in and is on his way. He should be here in a bit."

Then he marched down the hall and disappeared, leaving me alone in the long, lightless and deserted corridor. Illuminated by a dim nightlight, a clock on the wall struck 4:00 a.m. I peered down the lonely passageway. Dense blackness enveloped me with a shroud.

Had God forsaken me?

Chapter 7
Breakthroughs

NANCY'S STORY

Late March 1988 – The next day

When would I feel better, I wondered, as I stared at the ceiling tiles above my bed. Would this nightmare ever end? The phone rang. "Hello?"

"Nancy?"

I recognized Debbie's voice. "How are you doing, Deb?"

"I'm fine. Your speech sounds better, but the real question is how are you doing?"

"They changed my antibiotic again. My fever hit one hundred four last night. They did another gallium scan in the middle of the night, but I haven't heard any results."

I heard her sigh. "I'm sorry. I think I know what's going on with you."

"Really?"

"Yes, I finally got a hold of the doctor I told you about. He gave me his wife's number, and she just called me back. She says she knows exactly what's wrong. When you had the C-section a cyst on your kidney probably got infected."

The stormy, dark cloud over me began to lift. "Really?"

"Yeah, she sees this kind of infection in a lot of patients who have PKD. Only 50 percent of the time will the infection show up on any scan. Sound familiar?"

"Sure does."

"Patients in your situation fly in from all over the country to be treated by her. She also said only two antibiotics have the ability to cross the cyst wall to get you well. One of those medications has fatal side effects, so there's really only one antibiotic that works."

"That has a familiar ring to it, too."

"It sure does. I'm to give you her number and have your doctor call her. The only thing she asks is you participate in the study at University Hospital, once you're well."

"Anything. I'll do anything to get back on my feet, but my doctor is on vacation right now."

"He had to leave you in the care of some other doctor. Give her number to him."

"He left me in the care of a host of doctors. I feel like I'm the subject of a big competition to find my cure."

"Sorry. Hopefully someone will take the time to give her a call."

"Thanks, Debbie, for stepping in. This is the first ray of hope I've seen in a long time."

When she gave me the name and number of the doctor at University Hospital, I viewed it like a pot of gold.

***

Two Days Later

"We want to get you well. We really do." Doctor A-personality stood over me. "Please be patient. We'll get you well. We don't need to call a doctor at another hospital."

A surgeon stood on the opposite side of my bed. "To say that only one or two antibiotics will work is ludicrous. We have hundreds of options."

If I hadn't been so weak, I might have strangled them both. "You don't think it's worth a call? What will it hurt?"

The surgeon headed for the door. "I don't have time for a doctor who suggests there's only one antibiotic that would work."

Doctor A-personality followed him. "Like I said, we want to get you well, just be patient. We'll figure it out."

Although it was snowing outside, I was as hot as a volcano, erupting lava and steam. My hopes dashed, the dark clouds gathered once again, hovering over me with an ominous glee. I attempted to give the information to every doctor who visited me. Not one was willing to contact the PKD-expert doc. I asked them to commit the unpardonable sin and break an unspoken code. If only Dr. Atkin was in town. He would have called without any reservation.

I sucked in a deep breath and tried to relax my straining muscles against the bed. *Dear Jesus, please move on someone to listen and make the call. All I need is one.*

***

John sat on the edge of my bed, fuming. We'd just returned from visiting Brianna. He shook his head. "I'm so angry. It's been two whole days, and not one doctor will even consider calling that woman."

I took his hand. "I know. If only Dr. Atkin was in town. I'll just sit here and rot until he gets back." I glanced at the clock. It read 11:05 p.m. "It's late. You probably should go home."

Doctor Grayber entered with a quick knock. "I thought I'd come in and check on you."

Surprised to see him after all this time, I sat up. "I wish I were better."

"Bet you do. I've heard in the wind that a doc at University Hospital says she can get you well."

"Yes, but no one's willing to contact her."

John entered the conversation. "It's a doctor involved with a PKD study. I'm pretty upset because I'm sure she knows what's up, but nobody here will call."

Dr. Grayber wiped his weary eyes and sighed. "This is ridiculous. Give me that name and number. My wife is a MD over there. I'm not afraid to step on anyone's toes to get you well."

I picked up the slip of paper and handed the information to him. "Thank you, thank you so much."

"You're welcome. I get tired of the politics that goes on in hospitals. Dr. Atkin would have called them in a heartbeat."

Thank You, Jesus.

John shook the doctor's hand. "We really appreciate your willingness to call, thank you."

Dr. Grayber turned toward the door, waving the slip of

paper. "I'll check into this."

The next morning, a doctor I didn't remember meeting came into my room before breakfast. "We're putting you on Bactrim. I hope this antibiotic gives us a better result."

I didn't recognize the name of the drug but hoped it to be the one recommended by the doctor at University Hospital.

A nurse followed him in and switched IV bags.

Later that afternoon, I felt better and each time the nurse took my vitals, my fever dropped. Clouds lifted and departed, and I had vision for the future. Dr. Grayber popped in just to make sure they had put me on the correct medication. I couldn't help but express my gratitude over and over, stunned at how quickly I began to improve.

***

The next day was Easter. Brianna's first. Through all my struggles, Brianna had continued to improve. We celebrated not only the Lord's resurrection but also the improvement I experienced by the second day on the correct medicine. My fever had dropped into the acceptable range, and Brianna had graduated from the isolette to an open crib. She still needed the oxygen cannula, but the future looked brighter by the hour.

A friend of mine had visited the day before, bringing Brianna her first Easter basket. It came with a small stuffed animal and an Easter bonnet.

Momma came in with Cabbage Patch doll clothes she'd borrowed from my two nieces. With clothes washed and pressed, we dressed Brianna up for her first Easter picture. The newborn Easter bonnet gaped around her little head, but that didn't matter. Momma snapped pictures with celebration and hope, and Brianna wore her wardrobe of doll clothes until a month after her release.

***

The next day Dr. Atkin returned. "Heard you had a difficult time in my absence."

"Yes, a little crazy."

"Your fever continues to drop, so we're pretty certain we've finally gotten you on the mend. I've spoken to the physician at University and think you would benefit seeing her after you're back on your feet. She can help us with your disease. By the way, that spot on your lung isn't anything to worry about. It hasn't changed at all since you had those X-rays taken. It's a good thing they were taken or we might have chased down that rabbit trail."

The bright morning sun spread its brilliant light within my heart.

"I'm so glad. That's good to hear. So when can I go home?"

"Not yet. You'll need two full weeks of IV antibiotics to kill the infection that has gone unchecked for so long."

"Two more weeks?" I groaned. "That seems like an eternity."

"I want you to dress every day and walk the halls. You need to get your strength back so you can take good care of your little one. How's she doing?"

"She's in an open crib now, but we'll probably take her home on oxygen and an apnea monitor."

"It's nice to see both of you are heading in the right direction." He laid his hand on my shoulder. "Finally, it's about time. Well, now that we have answers, all we have to do is stay the course, do the time, and you'll be back on your feet. I'll see you tomorrow."

***

Later that day, the surgeon who refused to contact the doctor with the PKD study entered my room. I stiffened at the sight of him.

He stood next to my bed. "Just wanted to come by and apologize. I was wrong. Turns out most antibiotics can't cross the wall of a kidney cyst. I'm sorry."

"Thank you for taking the time to do that. You're forgiven."

He shook my hand. "Sometimes we start to think we know it all."

I smiled as he left. Perhaps they weren't all as bad as they had seemed.

I stayed in the hospital for two more weeks, spending much

of that time with the precious little gift God had given me.

***

April 22, 1988

I sat in a rocking chair with Brianna as John entered the ICN. Brianna and I had spent the night together in a little room off the ICN. It served as my trial run for taking care of her oxygen and apnea monitor.

John beamed. "Are my girls ready to go home?"

"She's all dressed and ready to go."

Nurses bustled around us, bringing carts in to carry medical equipment and Brianna's stuffed animals and flowers.

One nurse, whose nickname for Brianna was "Little Pistol," moved the blanket away from Brianna's face. "I'm going to miss my 'Little Pistol.' Brianna had earned the name because she cried loud and long until she got what she wanted.

The nursing staff faced this bittersweet moment with smiles and tears. They had mothered Brianna as much, possibly more, than I had. After all, she had spent over two months in their care.

John shook each of their hands. "Thank you all for everything. We thought this day might never come. I'll get the car."

Several nurses helped Brianna and me to the hospital's front entrance. They helped load everything into the car and buckled Brianna into her car seat. As we drove off, they stood on the sidewalk waving good-bye.

The Lord had been so good. He had given us the desire of our hearts. On the drive home, I couldn't help looking toward the bright future ahead. Now that we had all the answers, I shouldn't have trouble getting pregnant with a second child. And I should never have to face such an aftermath again.

Chapter 8
Losing What I Love

KELLY'S STORY

1989

The summer after I turned thirteen, I learned about losing the things I loved. The end of the cold war and the fall of the Berlin Wall started a downward spiral in my life once again. Dad worked for Rocky Flats during this time, a government facility that dealt with nuclear weapons. As part of the peace negotiations, the US began the daunting process of eliminating part of its nuclear program. Rocky Flats began layoffs. We weathered layoffs, hoping my dad's job would be spared, but soon he was on the chopping block as well.

Unable to find work in Colorado, Dad found a job in Las Vegas, Nevada. At first this temporary job required him to stay for a few days and then fly home for a weekend. As airline prices rose, the cost of tickets became too expensive, and my dad opted to rent an apartment in Las Vegas. He then would drive back every couple of weeks for a weekend. Now for an alcohol/prescription drug addict, the combination of being away from family and the loose living of Las Vegas were not a good mix. Dad's steady decline became more apparent.

Molly held down the fort at home with Bethany, David, and me, while Dad came and went. I rode in Westernaires every Saturday and Monday night. Molly came week after week and encouraged me to continue.

After Dad had been commuting for six months, Molly declared either we all moved there, or he needed to find a job in

Colorado. After weeks of looking—and prospects were not favorable—we began the slow process of getting rid of things for a move. To my horror, my horses were first on the list.

The cost of feeding, shoeing, and vet bills were pretty high. Finding them new homes would help the household expenses, but knowing this didn't ease the pain in my heart.

I woke early the day the truck showed up to get the horses. The windows rattled as if even the weather seemed to echo my sentiments while massive billowing clouds moved in. Their dark menacing presence became the prelude for what would come later.

When I went outside, the wind nearly knocked me off my feet. It blew with a vengeance holding me back, telling me that Cloud and Teddy would soon no longer be mine. Both horses neighed as I got closer. After hoisting their hay onto my shoulders, I held on tight to my load, turning my back to the tempest building an invisible wall between us.

I leaned against the wall outside the stalls watching them eat, and a storm of tears clouded my vision. "Hey guys, this is the last time I'll get to feed you. I love you guys. I wish . . ."

I needed to keep it together, but the last remnants of my heart crumbled to dust. "You'll like . . . your new homes."

I looked at the sky. *Why God? What did I do wrong? You gave them to me, and now You are taking them away. I don't get it, I thought you loved me.*

The wind howled as I turned to leave, blowing my jacket off my sagging shoulders.

Once inside my room, I glanced at the clock. Only a few short hours remained until the woman who bought Teddy would arrive to take him. Cloud's new owner would pick her up an hour later. Sobs ripped through my chest, as I clutched a photo of me riding Cloud to my breast.

Why God? Why do I have to do this?

I curled into a fetal position on my bed and stared unseeing at the wall. When a knock came on my door, I remained motionless.

Molly walked in and sat on my bed. "I heard you get up to feed the horses."

I remained silent.

She tried to chuckle. "Just think, no more early morning feedings. No more plowing through snow to get to the barn."

My heart screamed that I had never minded feeding them.

She tried to lighten the mood, but I didn't respond.

She sighed. "Honey, I know this is hard. I wish we had found another way, but . . ."

Her voice wavered and I rolled over. I couldn't help the tears that streamed down my face.

Molly put her hand on my shoulder. "Please tell me you understand, Kelly. I didn't want to hurt you."

I wiped the tears, took a deep breath, and told her what she wanted to hear. "I do understand, Molly. I'll be okay. I know this is what we have to do. I'm gonna miss them, that's all." But how could she allow this and how could I forgive her for taking away the most important thing in my life?

She pulled me into a hug and whispered into my ear, "I'm going to miss them too. I'm so sorry"

It wasn't her fault. I just wanted to be angry with someone.

When the truck arrived later that day, my legs felt as if they were encased in lead as I made my way out to the horses. Teddy pranced up and down the fence line, almost as if he understood something major was about to happen. The wind wailed as the first raindrops pelted the horse. How could I make time stand still? But before I knew it, taillights on the horse trailer pulled away with my beautiful Teddy.

The rain bludgeoned the earth in torrents, as if all the angels in heaven were crying with me. Cloud refused to be caught and ran the length of the pasture keeping far away from Molly and me. I attempted to grab her as she ran past me, only to slip and fall the mud. Was there any way out of this mess? After ten minutes, we had her cornered, and I placed a halter on her. If only I could set her free.

The lump in my throat swelled as I led her to the waiting horse trailer. Horses sense human emotions, and Cloud knew she was leaving me that day. Each step I took, she resisted, pulling her head back and refusing to go forward.

I turned toward her. "Come on, pretty lady, you're going to like your new home."

She wouldn't budge.

"Please, Cloud, I don't want to do this either, but we have to." I pulled gently once again. "Come on, girl, it's not that bad. I'll always love you."

She walked forward a few steps. "That's right, girl, good job."

The wind moaned and swirled around us as the rain stung my face. But I continued talking her on. "Come on, girl, that's it."

How do I say good-bye?

Once I got her in the trailer, I hugged her neck. "I love you, girl. I'll never forget you."

My muscles protested as I closed the door to the trailer. I fell to my knees when Cloud's neighing faded as the truck drove down the driveway.

"Bye, girl."

The mud and pouring rain blurred the taillights and disappeared down the road. Wiping tears and rain from my face, I struggled to pull myself from the sucking mud. The tattered remains of my torn heart lay in pieces in my chest.

The next summer, after making what felt like the hundredth commute to see Dad in Vegas, we looked at houses while on summer break. Our Colorado house back home wasn't on the market yet, and Dad stalled on selling it. He didn't want to leave Ann and Ben. Then another obstacle we hadn't counted on rose when my mother refused to let me move out of state. Molly now faced two dilemmas: move and lose me, or not move and lose my dad to alcohol and drugs. She opted to pray and stay in Colorado for me.

Soon afterward Dad found a job in Colorado.

Now a freshman in high school, I was involved in sports and cheerleading. Molly decided to go back to school to get her cosmetology degree, often using Bethany and me as her test subjects. I went to school a few times with purple hair and my sister with orange as Molly practiced on us. I didn't mind the experiments, but Bethany was horrified.

Dad's steady drinking increased. David couldn't take it anymore and moved in with a friend. Molly watched as the household crumbled and insisted that Dad go into a treatment center once again. Still in school, Molly thought about quitting but decided to push on through and graduate. Her grades were high and she did well. The day she graduated, Dad got drunk and no one showed up to her graduation. Still too young to drive, I waited at home with Bethany after Dad passed out on the front lawn.

As Dad went in and out of treatment centers, the strain on his and Molly's marriage increased. In the back of my mind, I knew she didn't leave him because of me. Ben and Ann continued to visit every other weekend, and my dad decided to institute a Thursday night dinner with them as well. Both Ben and Ann were in band, and that meant adding their band concerts to our crazy schedules, too. I can't tell you how many times Bethany and I tried to get out of the dinners and concerts, but it became an unspoken, mandatory edict we attend.

Right before my sophomore year in high school, things escalated. I'll never forget the conversation leading up to the events that followed.

Molly waited up for me one night when I came home from babysitting.

My heart quickened when I saw her red eyes and tearstained cheeks. "Hey, Molly, what's wrong?"

"Honey, we need to talk."

Something bad was coming.

She clutched a Kleenex in her hand. "It's your dad. He went into a treatment center again today. The thing is . . ." She cleared her throat. "I just don't see a desire in him to quit drinking. I'm afraid it's going to kill him one day and harm the rest of us in the process."

Why did I feel like a *but* was coming?

Tears gathered in my eyes. "Okay, so what are you saying?"

"I can't take it anymore, I'm taking Bethany, and we're moving out. I'm going to file for separation."

"What about me?" I sensed my world was crumbling.

She enveloped me in her arms. "I'm sorry, honey, but I have to send you back to your mother. If I had any way around it or some other solution . . ."

I needed to be strong for her. I owed her that much after all the sacrifices she had made on my account. I managed to nod, though inside my heart splintered into a thousand tiny pieces.

I swallowed past the lump in my throat. "It's okay, Molly, I'll be all right." Wiping the tears away, I straightened my shoulders. "I'll call my mother and let her know."

As I walked away, Molly grabbed my shoulder and gently squeezed. "This is the hardest thing I have ever done, Kelly. I thought about taking you girls and running away to Canada, but we wouldn't have gotten far."

I nodded at her, while the tears streamed down my face. "I know you don't have a choice, Molly. I'll be okay."

Why couldn't we run away? I didn't understand why she was leaving me.

Her eyes seemed to plead with me. "I love you, Kelly. I'll be praying for you every day, and you can call me anytime day or night."

Again I asked, *Why, God? Why are You taking something else I love away?* Didn't He love me? I looked away from her piercing gaze. "I guess I better make that phone call now."

Alone in my room, I dialed the number I knew from memory, hoping my Mother wouldn't pick up. I just wanted to leave a message.

"This is Susan"

Great, I needed to sound upbeat. "Mom, it's Kelly, Dad is back in a treatment center and Molly is filing for a separation. I'm calling 'cause . . ."

I didn't want to ask the question. I swallowed the lump in my throat and took a deep breath. "Can I move in with you guys for a while?"

She sucked in air. "Oh honey, you have no idea how long I've waited for this day. Yes, you can move in with us."

I tried to sound cheerful as she went on and on, while inside I fell apart, hoping that things would change. Maybe things would be all right. Could they get worse? How much can one person lose? My home, school, horses, mother figure, and sister, that's all. It seemed I was Dorothy from the *Wizard of Oz* watching as a tornado ripped through my life, tearing away everything that mattered. I just wanted to click my heels and make everything go back to normal.

***

Fall 1991

The first couple of months at my mother's house went by quickly and with relative ease. In the beginning, she tried to make me feel welcome. But going from two to three teenagers would be an adjustment for any parent.

I didn't just change homes, but schools and made new friends as well. I tried to keep a positive. My mother enrolled me in a driver's education class, which began a couple weeks before school started. This allowed me to meet some students I would be going to school with.

The transition from being a guest in my mother's house to becoming a member of the household was difficult. For the past eight years, I had lived at my dad's house with a different set of rules, and this new life was a learning curve for me. In some ways my siblings resented me. Just one more person they had to share attention with. Lost, left behind, and a sacrificial lamb in limbo, I never really fit in anywhere.

~ ♦♦♦ ~

Chapter 9
Second Time Around

NANCY'S STORY

Three Years later - 1991

Dr. Swenson stood, stepped to the trashcan, peeled off surgical gloves, and tossed them into the garbage. "Lie there for thirty minutes. You know the drill. I think you're the bravest woman I've ever met, to pursue another pregnancy. After all you've been through."

I sighed. "I don't know if it's bravery or stupidity. We thought artificial insemination would be our ticket to getting pregnant the second time. But this is our fifth try. John and I decided to give it six months. If I don't get pregnant by next month, I guess we'll look into adoption."

He came and stood beside me. "Each couple must decide when enough is enough. I won't fault you for giving up." He patted my arm. "How's your little one?"

"She's three years old now. The pediatrician says she's a bit slow on her milestones, but it's normal for babies born two and a half months premature."

"No respiratory issues now that she's off the oxygen?"

"No, thankfully."

"That's good to hear." He picked up a periodical and handed it to me. "Do you want the magazine you were reading?"

"Yes. Thank you."

He motioned toward the clock on the wall. "After thirty minutes, you can leave." He opened the door, turned, and held up crossed fingers. "Let's keep hoping."

***

March 1992

John and I stepped through the glass entrance to the office building. Down the hall, we found a sign saying Adoption Services. John opened the door and held it open for me.

A brunette receptionist greeted us. "Are you here for the three-day Adoption Education Workshop?"

I fidgeted. "Yes."

"Good." She pointed to the left. "Take the hall. They're in the room on the right."

We entered a conference room. Four couples, well-spaced from each other, sat at a large table in the center of the room. Two men bounced nervous legs as we found seats. No one spoke as we waited for more couples to arrive.

I whispered to John. "Take a look at our competition."

We were well aware each couple attending this class had already submitted a written application for adoption and paid a sizable fee. They all had passed the home study and a background check, just as we had done.

I fiddled with my purse strap as more couples arrived. A wave of queasiness passed over me.

There were nine other hopeful couples. How would John and I stack up against them in the eyes of a birth mother? Were we good looking enough, rich enough, educated enough? Would our biological daughter be a strike against us? I studied the face of each woman and thought I detected the same questions in their eyes.

At last, a blonde woman with short hair took the place at the front of the class. "It looks like everyone is here, so we will begin. My name is Bonnie, and I will be your facilitator for the next three days. I'd like to start out by saying that if you stay with our program, eventually each one of you will receive a child."

Is that statement really true? In open adoptions, weren't the birth moms in charge?

She continued. "During the next three days we will explore our motivations, expectations, and misconceptions. We'll dig deep, and as an agency, we hope this group of parents will stay in touch, and perhaps each of your children will grow up knowing other kids who are adopted." She scanned her notes. "Before we get started, is everyone aware a fee is due upon completion of this class?"

A series of nods answered her question.

She made "the fee" sound minimal even though thousands of dollars was involved. I looked at John as an unspoken message passed between us.

Bonnie went on. "The first thing I'd like to do is to go around the room and have everyone tell the story that has brought them here today."

She started with the couple closest to her. As each couple relayed their quest for a child, tears were shed. We found the journey had been similar for each of us. John and I were happy to learn another couple also had a biological child.

Bonnie then covered what should be on the profile letter. "This letter will be placed in our Profile Books. It should be just over a half page with a nice picture of you and your children, if you have any." She handed sheets of paper to the people closest to her. "Pass these around. These are some examples of letters that have worked well."

"Since all of you are enrolled in our open adoption program, you will be writing directly to the birth moms. You'll want to give a lot of thought into what you say to the prospective moms. On the back, each of you should have a column listing your age, education, employment, religion, ethnic heritage, and interests. You also should include your child care plan, whether you will use day care, etc."

"The last thing you need to put down is what racial backgrounds you are willing to adopt. This is something you need to discuss with your spouse. You must realize that if you adopt a child of another race, you will be changing the racial makeup of your family. You need to decide if that is important to you."

John and I encountered many thought provoking discussions during those three days. By the end of the class, we looked at the other couples not as threats but as friends. As a class, we named ourselves the March Madness class, since we met in March and were mad for a baby. We decided as a class to get together every few months, at least until all of us adopted a child.

As we left, I still carried uncertainties. What if we were the last couple picked? Worse yet, what if no birthmom picked us?

***

Days Later

"This is frustrating." I glowered from the dining room table as I plunked out a letter on an old electric typewriter. "I've hit a wrong key, again."

I tugged the paper from the roller, wadded it up, and tossed the trash to the floor beside other crumpled attempts. Snagging a blank piece of paper, I turned the roller to insert the page into the typewriter. "I wish we owned a computer. This is crazy."

Working from my handwritten copy, I started typing slow and deliberate, one key at a time. Praying I'd not hit a wrong letter.

An hour later, I struck the last key. "Finally."

Breathing a sigh of relief, I removed, with care, the final copy from the typewriter and laid it on the table. "Perfect."

I sat back and thumbed through a package of photos. Removing three, I laid out each picture at the top of the letter.

"I think this one is best."

The picture showed my little family standing next to an old rustic nineteenth century cabin. John looked handsome in his deep aqua blue shirt. I wore red, and our now four-year-old daughter wore a *Little Mermaid* sweatshirt that blended all of our colors together. Her hair was done up in pigtails as she sat sandwiched between us.

At the kitchen bar, I snatched up a package of colored copy paper and returned to the dining room table. The top portion of the paper was aqua blue and faded to white at the bottom. Setting the photo atop the paper, I smiled. The color matched perfectly.

I planned to photocopy the letter onto the paper, glue the picture to it, place some heart and butterfly stickers to add interest, and mail it to the adoption agency. It was the best I could do. The rest was up to the Lord.

Please, bless my efforts.

Chapter 10
Attraction and Betrayal

KELLY'S STORY

Spring 1992

Jumping into a lake to get him to notice me might have been a little extreme. One warm spring day, during endurance training, the track team ran up and around a nearby lake. On that particular day we ran against a relentless wind. As we turned to go around the bend, Andrew's baseball cap flew into the lake. No one made a move to get it, as we stood there staring at the hat as it bobbed up and down in the ripples.

Andrew walked to the end of the dock running his fingers through his hair. "Man, that's my favorite hat."

He looked torn between jumping in after it or letting it go. Keyes found a large stick and joined Andrew on the dock, trying to grab the hat with the branch. After several attempts without success, he gave up.

Most of the runners laughed but continued running. That left the three of us there watching the floating hat.

The waves brought it closer to shore, and the solution seemed simple enough. Here was my chance. *Maybe Keyes will actually see me?* I stepped to the end of the dock, kicked off my shoes then dove in the water.

Coming up sputtering and coughing wasn't part of my plan. *Great Kelly, real graceful!* Who knew the water would be so cold? Probably everyone. I'm just too stupid to think about the temperature of the water. My muscles threatened to cramp in the frigid liquid. *Thank heavens I'm close to shore.*

Retrieving the hat, I called out as I got to shore. "I got it."

Andrew and Keyes stood there with gaping mouths.

Keyes recovered first. "I can't believe you just did that."

He actually talked to me. I needed to play it cool. Sloshing my way to the shore, I wrung out my shirt. "What? Andrew wanted the hat, and it seemed like the best plan."

"It's a little wet, but at least you have it."

"Ahhh, thanks."

I handed Andrew his hat, then made my way back to the dock and my discarded shoes.

My muscles were spring loaded, the cold water had them tighter than usual. I put my shoes back on. *Please don't cramp up yet, muscles*, I prayed as I tried to rub some heat into them. "Guess we better catch up to the team."

Keyes watched me. "Yeah, okay."

At least it was a warm day. I stood and squeezed as much water out of my shirt and shorts that I could. Hoping the wind would dry me by the time I got back to the school. Was the rest of the team back at the school by now?

Andrew and Keyes waited for me. I couldn't believe it. "You guys can go ahead. I know you run faster than I do."

Keyes glanced at Andrew and shook his head. Andrew shrugged. "That's okay, we'll run with you."

We took off running together. They could have left me in the dust, instead they slowed their pace to match mine. Should I say something? No, I'll wait for one of them to talk first. By the time the school came into view, no one had said anything the whole way back.

Coach waited for us as we ran onto the field. We went our separate ways and finished up some sprinting drills before he released us to go.

Stephanie found me as I got out of the shower. "What happened, Kelly? I thought you were with us until we got back to the school, and you weren't there. What's this I keep hearing about you jumping into the lake?"

I shrugged and opened my locker, pulling out my clothes. "Nothing. I waited to see if Andrew could get his hat."

Stephanie's eyebrow rose. "I saw him wearing his hat. So,

I'm guessing it went good with Keyes?"

Heat rushed to my cheeks. "He doesn't even know I exist."

"I don't know about that. He watched you do your sprint warm-ups."

"Really? I thought I saw him watching me, but was too afraid to look at him."

She winked. "Yep."

I pulled my shirt over my head. I shouldn't get my hopes up. "It's probably a fluke."

"Come on, Kelly, you've been mooning over him since February. This is good news."

I wrapped my wet hair in a towel. "I don't know. He's still into Jennifer Gyes."

"Didn't you hear what happened with them?"

Something happened? Could that be true? Hope flickered to life in my mind.

Stephanie bantered on. "I heard he asked her out, but she turned him down flat."

"No way."

Why would anyone turn him down? That couldn't be right. Keyes was hot.

Stephanie barely took a breath. "I heard her talking to Laurie afterwards, and she said the only reason she flirted with him was because she heard you were asking questions about him."

"What? When did this happen."

"This morning, silly. I hoped to tell you at practice, but you disappeared."

"This morning? Where was I? Oh no, please tell me she didn't tell him about me."

"Doubtful, she wouldn't have wanted the competition. Girls like her just like to play around with guys. Seriously though, Kelly, Keyes is an idiot if he can't see the way you look at him."

I buried my face in my hands. "I'm that obvious?"

"No, I don't mean it like that. I'm your friend, so of course I would have told you. I've only heard you mention his name about a couple hundred times in the past few months. I wanted to go knock him over the head and say, 'Wake up,' but he's a little clueless, I guess."

"You don't think he knows I like him, do you?"

"Nope, I don't think he's aware of much with Jennifer hanging all over him."

"I know, it bugged me like crazy, but I figured I didn't have a chance anyway."

She's so beautiful, why would he look twice at me if she's around?

"I don't get what you see in him, Kelly. You make it sound like it would be a downgrade for him if he went out with you. The truth is, it would be an upgrade, since you're a cheerleader and several guys want a chance with you."

I rolled my eyes. "Yeah, I'm so popular. I know you think I'm crazy. There's something about him that draws me. From the very beginning, I thought him special."

She rolled her eyes back. "Yeah, I thought you were a little nuts."

"As I recall, you told me Keyes's name was Jeremy."

"Yeah well, I thought he was someone else."

"He's beautiful, quiet, serious, yet playful, too."

She giggled. "You got all that the first time you laid eyes on him, did ya?"

"Okay, maybe not all of that, but he is beautiful."

"Yeah, I'm sure he can't wait to hear you think he's beautiful."

I stuck my tongue out at her. "You know what I mean."

"Nope, I don't get it, didn't get it then either, but love is a funny thing I guess."

I closed my locker and grabbed my bag and threw my arm over her shoulder. "One day you'll see, just wait."

Stephanie stopped. I glanced at her in surprise. "What's wrong?"

She nodded over her shoulder and winked. "I forgot a book in my locker, I'll catch up with you later."

"Uh, yeah, I'll see you later."

What's wrong with her? As she walked off, I strolled to the door leading to the parking lot.

"Hey, Kelly?"

I turned and found Keyes right behind me. *He knows my*

name? My heart exploded. "Yes?"

"I just wanted to say, it was a cool thing you did today." He shuffled his feet. "I mean with the hat and all."

Heat rushed to my cheeks. "Thanks, I didn't think the water would be so cold, though."

"Yeah well, I know Andrew appreciated it."

Oh right, Andrew. Why else would he talk to me?

He kicked a rock with his toe. "You wouldn't want to go to a movie or something with me sometime, would you?"

I froze. *Did he just ask me out?* "What?"

He laughed. "I asked if you would want to go to a movie or something sometime."

He did ask me out. "Um . . . yeah that would be nice."

A blush formed on his cheeks as he eyed at the ground. A smile formed at the corner of his mouth. "Good, I better get on home now."

I decided to go for it. "Do you need a ride?"

He put his hands in his pockets and shrugged. "That would be great, if it's not any trouble."

Trouble, is he kidding? I've only dreamed about this. I shook my head. "No trouble at all.

An awkward silence followed as we made our way to my car. Once we were both in the car, he directed me to his house. Neither of us said anything else during the drive.

When I pulled up in front of his house, he got out. But before he closed the door he looked down at me and smiled. "I'll see you tomorrow at the track meet, right?"

Wild horses couldn't stop me. I smiled. "I'll be there."

"Good"

He closed the door and entered his house.

Was I dreaming? Did that just happen? Life was looking up. Or was it? I still had to go home, back to my real life.

***

The phone rang the moment I entered my basement bedroom. Throwing my bag on the floor, I flopped down on my bed and grabbed it. "Hello?"

"Tell me what happened!"

I laughed and rolled over on my back. "Oh hey, Stephanie. What do you mean?"

"Oh no, you don't. You know exactly what I mean."

In a rush, I told her everything that had happened.

"No way! So, he like, asked you out?"

"Sort of, he asked if I would go to a movie or something with him sometime."

"That's awesome."

A light rap sounded on my bedroom door, I covered the mouthpiece with my hand. "Come in."

My mother entered. "I've been calling you to get off the phone. It's time for dinner. Look at your room. You need to clean this mess up."

I followed her gaze to the gym bag on the floor. "Okay, Mom, I'll get off the phone and clean my room."

She turned and left, leaving the door open. "Hey, Stephanie, I have to go."

"No problem, I'll see you at the meet tomorrow."

Hanging up the phone, I threw my track bag on the bed and removed my damp clothes. Scooping up a few of my other dirty clothes from my hamper, I put them in the washer.

Returning to my room, I scanned it over once more, making sure everything sat in the right place. Mother would inspect it later.

As I went upstairs the sweet aroma of bread and meat teased my nose and my mouth watered. Ravenous, I rounded the corner and saw everyone already seated. "Sorry, I didn't mean to make everyone wait."

I took my usual seat on the chair that didn't match the other four. It creaked under my weight. I sighed, grateful it didn't give way. The chair reminded me of my outsider status. Maybe they never thought about how I viewed it.

Joe cleared his throat. "Let's pray. Come, Lord Jesus, be our guest and Thy food from You be blessed. Amen."

Every night we said the same prayer for as long as I could remember, but the words were forced and not at all like the prayers we said at Dad's house. My stomach growled, and I couldn't wait to eat. "Wow, something sure smells good."

Mother eyed me before she began serving. "Really? Are you sure you're hungry?"

I glanced around the table and cringed, something must be up. "Uh yeah, I'm hungry."

She served my brother, sister, and Joe before she looked back at me. "I'm surprised to hear that, since all the cookies are gone, I figured you'd be full."

"What?" Cookies? I didn't eat any cookies. What is she talking about?

She narrowed her gaze. "When I left for work this morning, the cookies were unopened. Now they're gone. Would you like to explain why?"

I glanced around the table. My siblings' heads were down as they ate quietly.

"I don't know what you're talking about. I didn't eat any cookies."

She sighed as she filled her own plate. "So do you expect me to believe that the cookies just up and ran away?"

Really, I'm just supposed to fess up to something I didn't do? Heat rushed into my face as I glared at everyone. "I don't know what you are talking about, I didn't eat any cookies."

"So now, you're lying, too?"

"I'm not lying. I don't know what you're talking about." Of course she thinks I'm lying, why *would* she believe me?

She grabbed my plate and placed it on the counter. "Well, when you decide to confess and tell us the truth, you can eat."

Tears welled as I stared helplessly at them. Would no one come to my defense? My brother and sister wouldn't make eye contact with me. Even my stepdad refused to say anything in my defense. "I'm telling you the truth. I didn't do it. Why don't you ask Ann and Ben?"

Mother stared at me, her jaw tight. "Nothing like this ever happened before *you* moved in."

Would nothing I say convince her I told the truth? No, she had already made up her mind about me. I pushed my chair back. "May I be excused?"

"No, you will sit here until dinner is done."

With my hunger long forgotten, my mind raced with

thoughts of anger, betrayal, and sadness, as I watched the four of them eat during the next thirty minutes. Did they all hate me?

When they were done, I helped clear the table and load the dishwasher. As everyone talked around me, I remained silent. I feared I'd break down, and I couldn't let them see the pain they caused me and give them that satisfaction.

I escaped to my room, my one reprieve. Mother would be down at some point to inspect my room. But after the dinner fiasco, something would surely be wrong. I had a track meet the next day, and Keyes would be there. That thought kept me going.

I climbed into bed and punched in Molly's phone number. It rang twice before she answered.

"Hello?"

"It's me."

"What's wrong?"

I swallowed past the lump in my throat as tears began to run. "Nothing. I'm okay."

"Don't give me that. What happened?"

A click on the line made me pause. "Hello, is someone on the phone?"

Nothing, I knew someone listened in. Wiping the tears, I sniffed and willed my voice to sound cheerful. "So, I just wanted to let you know, the meet starts at ten."

There was a long pause on the other end. "Yes, I have it written down. I have to work tomorrow, but I'll be cheering you on."

Another click sounded, and the background noise disappeared. "Sorry, someone listened in again."

"I know. I could hear it too. Are you all right?"

Could I tell her that my mom hated me and thought I lied to her? No, she felt bad enough that I was there. "No, it's getting worse here."

Molly's voice wavered. "I'm sorry."

"I'll be okay. It's been a rough day." I couldn't tell her what happened. I stifled a sob.

When the line clicked again, I didn't even bother acknowledging it. "So, I'll talk to you later."

"Yes, all right. Good luck tomorrow, Kelly."

"Thanks, bye."

I hung up the phone and took a deep breath.

A knock sounded on my door, and I rolled my eyes. Here came round two.

Without waiting for a reply, Mother entered my room. I don't know what came over me, but tired of playing games, I took a deep breath and faced her. "Did you need the phone a few minutes ago?"

She glared at me. "What are you talking about?"

"I was on the phone and someone kept picking up."

Her eyes narrowed. "Are you accusing me?"

"No, I'm just telling you someone kept picking up."

She looked surprised. I had never stood up to her. She took a step closer to me. "I don't like your tone, young lady. You live in *my* house remember that. They are other people who live here too. Anyone could have picked up the phone."

"I'm sorry." My gaze fell to the floor.

She sucked in a breath and stepped back. "Yes, well I came down to say good night."

I glanced at my alarm clock. Six thirty glowed back. "It's a little early for bed."

"Oh, I'm not going to bed. Have you decided to come clean about the cookies yet?"

I balled my fists. "For the last time, I didn't do it!"

Her eyes widened. "Well then, good night."

"Wait, are you saying I have to stay in my room for the rest of the night?"

"That's exactly what I'm saying. However, if you come clean, you can join us."

She walked over to my nightstand and took my book that was sitting open. "I'm taking this with me. I know you don't mind not watching television, so I'll take your book."

Heat flooded into my face. "No, not my book. That's not fair"

"Then confess about the cookies, and I'll give it back."

I glared at her. "I didn't eat the cookies."

She sighed. "Okay, good night then."

As she turned and walked away, taking my book with her,

the urge to slam the door enveloped me, but I restrained myself. Most days it came as a relief to be forced to stay in my room. No one seemed to care about me, but I had my books. Now, I couldn't even escape into the land of fiction, a place where the characters became my family. Books were my only reprieve from pain and rejection.

Not until my sister became an adult did she confess to eating the cookies, as well as other deeds I had been blamed for.

***

My alarm clock went off early the next day. It couldn't be morning already? I stumbled into the bathroom. Splashing water on my face, I blinked a few times trying to clear my vision. Staring at my reflection in the mirror, I gasped. Dark rings under my eyes proclaimed my lack of sleep the night before. How long had I stayed up? It must have been later than I thought. How long can a person stare and the ceiling? I guess a long time.

Smiling at my reflection. "At least I get to see Keyes today. Perhaps it will be a turning point in my nonexistent dating life."

Seeing the clock through the mirror, I gasped. I better get a move on. Coach wanted us there early.

I broke my record for the shortest shower and put on my track uniform. Adding a little makeup to hide the circles, I left to go. Climbing the stairs, I was careful to make as little noise as possible, hoping not to see my mother after last night's drama.

After snagging a banana and filling my water bottle, I made my way to my car. Doubting anyone would be coming to my track meet, I tried not to let it bother me during the short distance to the school. There were only a few cars in the parking lot, so I selected a spot closest to the gym.

A few of my teammates arrived at the same time, and I waved as they passed by. Buses rolled in, filled with competitors from other schools. I searched the stands for my team, and found them on the end. Stephanie had saved a place for me and waved me over.

Sitting beside her I searched the stands for Keyes. Where was he? He said he would be here. Maybe he was with another girl and was just joking about a date. That would be my luck.

Enough about Keyes, I needed to get my head in the game. My relay team would run first, and I knew the importance of us qualifying for the State meet.

Stephanie leaned closer and whispered. "Keyes isn't here yet?"

I shook my head. I didn't want to go into it.

Coach told us the order of events for the day, and I wanted to hear them. Once the instructions were issued, we were excused to go warm up.

I latched onto Stephanie's arm. "Do you think he's coming?"

"I'm sure he's just late. Don't worry, he'll be here. He's a shoo-in for State with pole vaulting."

"Come on, let's practice the hand-off again."

As the anchor on the girls four-by-one relay team, Stephanie handed off the baton to me. Nervous about getting the timing, I took my position. "Ready, go."

After we had the timing right, we sat on the ground to stretch. I heard a noise and turned to look behind me. Keyes stepped onto the field with two other guys. I turned back, not wanting to be caught watching him.

He was here. I needed to play it cool and not let him see how he affected me.

Without looking at Keyes again, I stood. "Come on, Stephanie, we need to go get in place."

I pulled her to her feet. "We've got this."

She gave me a high five. "Dang right we do."

***

Hours later, when I had a long break before my next event, I went to the gym. It had been a great day so far, yet I wanted to be alone for a while. No one was in the small gym, so I went in. A tennis ball lay next to the wall and I scooped it up. I sat at the far end of the gym and sighed, taking in the silence.

My relay team qualified in two events, and we were going to State. My individual events were coming up. Unable to talk to Keyes, I had watched him during the pole-vaulting event and cheered with the rest of the school when he qualified for State. If he saw me, he made no attempt to come and find me after the event.

No one in my family showed up. Molly had to work, and who knew where Dad was. I tossed the tennis ball against the wall and caught it as it bounced back into my hand. Would I be stuck in my room again tonight? Maybe confessing to eating the stupid cookies was my best option. I didn't want to, but knowing my Mother, she wasn't going to let it go.

"Here you are. I've been looking for you all day." Keyes strolled toward me.

I jumped, missing the tennis ball as it hit me in the head.

Keyes stared down at me with a lopsided grin. "Sorry, didn't mean to sneak up on you."

Embarrassed, I wanted the ground open up and swallow me whole. "Guess I was lost in thought."

"Mind if I join you?"

Really? He wants to join me. "Sure, pull up a seat."

He sat next to me. I threw the ball at the wall, fully intending on catching it, but Keyes beat me to it.

He threw the ball up and caught it. "This looks like fun."

"Um . . . I was bored."

He tossed the ball, and I caught it.

His brows arched. "Nice catch."

I should say something . . . "I watched you pole vault today. Congrats on making it to State."

"Thanks, I saw your relay team win too, great job."

"You watched?"

"Yeah, thought that redheaded girl would overtake you at the end, but you pulled it off."

"Tell me about it. I was running for my life to keep a stride on her."

I pitched the ball for him to catch. "Do you get nervous when you pole vault?"

Oh my gosh. Did I just ask him that? What a stupid question.

He shrugged. "No, not anymore. I did when I first started, but now I like the adrenaline rush."

"I guess I'm like that about some things. I've never met a

roller coaster I didn't like." That was stupid too. I need to keep quiet.

"Oh yeah?" He smiled. "Maybe we could go to Elitch's sometime and ride all the roller coasters."

Wow, did he just ask me out again? Maybe I said the right thing after all. "That would be fun."

He glanced at the clock. "We should head back to the field. The individual events will be starting soon."

"I'm sure Coach is looking for us."

We walked silently back to the field. Stephanie ran over when she spotted us. "Hey guys, Coach is looking for everyone."

"We figured that."

Keyes moved closer to me and leaned over to whisper in my ear. "I'll see you later."

My heart leapt. "Okay, see ya." *Maybe he does like me.*

He walked off.

Stephanie stared at me with her mouth open. "What did I miss?"

"Nothing, we were just talking, that's all."

***

I didn't see Keyes again until after I had run both of my individual events. He walked toward me with a woman and a dog. Once they were close, I bent down to pet the dog, who promptly licked my face.

I laughed, enjoying the affection and attention, even if it came from a dog. "She's sweet."

The woman's eyes lit up. "Thank you. We love her don't we, Keyes?"

"She's all right. Mom, this is Kelly, the girl I told you about."

The woman was his mom, and he had told her about me. Wow.

I put out my hand. "Nice to meet you, ma'am."

She clasped my hand and seemed surprised. "It's so nice to know manners aren't lost on the youth today. It is truly my pleasure to meet you, Kelly."

Stephanie and my other teammates called out to me. They

huddled together watching me.

"I better go see what they need. It was nice to meet you, ma'am."

I turned to look at Keyes. "Are you coming out with the team for pizza?"

He looked at his mom, and she nodded back.

"Yeah, I guess I am."

"Okay, I'll see you later then."

I walked toward my teammates. I wonder what his mom must have thought of me? She had a nice smile that reached her eyes.

I pulled Stephanie aside to tell her. "I met Keyes's mom."

"I wondered who you were talking with."

I couldn't help but smile. "She seemed nice."

"Shh . . . Keyes is coming."

I prayed he hadn't heard me.

Stephanie winked at me. "I'll catch up with you later."

I tried to compose myself.

Keyes stood beside me. "Hi, again."

I gazed into his aqua eyes. "Hi, yourself."

"My mom liked you."

I smiled. "I liked her, too."

"Do you think you could give me a ride home after the pizza thing?"

"Sure." Did he not realize how in love I was with him?

His eyes lit up. "Thanks."

We joined the rest of the team gathered together on the bleachers. To our surprise, Coach arrived carrying at least fifteen pizzas.

I whispered to Keyes. "I thought we were going out for pizza."

He shrugged. "I guess not."

My stomach growled and I laughed. I hadn't eaten anything other than the banana since lunch the day before. "I'll take whatever. I'm starving."

Waiting till all the pizzas were lined up on the tables near the stands, Keyes got plates for the two of us.

I smiled as he handed one to me. "Thanks."

"I don't want you to starve to death."

Great, does he think I eat too much? Maybe he thinks I'm fat like my mother does. He's probably not into me then? Tears threatened spill, and I turned away so he wouldn't see. "Sorry to burst your bubble if you're thinking I'm one of those girls that won't eat in front of a guy. I'm not a Barbie doll. I know that."

"I didn't mean . . ."

I turned back to him. The sincerity in his eyes had my spirit soaring. Maybe I overreacted a bit. "I'm sorry. I just get so tired of people watching everything I eat. I'm going to eat if I'm hungry. I won't apologize for it."

He grinned. "I like that about you. You speak your mind. I didn't mean anything by the other comment. I'm saying . . . I just like you."

Heat flooded my cheeks. "I like you, too."

We took our pizza slices to the stands and ate. Other teammates joined us, and we laughed and joked with one another.

My hunger pains eased after eating three slices of pizza. Keyes ate another piece as I lounged back against the bleachers.

He stood up and stretched. "Guess we should probably get going."

Already? No, not yet. "Yeah, I wonder what time it is?"

"I'm guessing close to eight p.m."

Could it be that late? "Really? No wonder I felt starved."

"It's been a long day."

"Yeah, I guess so."

"Do you need to get anything from your locker?"

I was giddy. "Nope, I just have to go grab my warm-up pants on the field. My keys are in the pocket. You?"

"No, I'm good."

He held out his hand to me, and I clasped it.

When we got to the warm-up area, I let go to retrieve my pants. Nervous, I stared up at the sky. The first stars had begun to light the night. "It's beautiful, isn't it?"

Keyes looked up. "Yeah, amazing."

"I guess we better get going then."

He looked back at me. "All right."

He held out his hand once again, and I took hold of it. I

could barely control my elation. What did this mean? Were we together now? We walked hand in hand to my car.

We fell into silence in the car. The drive to Keyes house seemed way too quick. I wanted the night to go on forever. I couldn't contain my disappointment as I pulled up in his driveway.

He unlatched his seat belt and opened the door then turned back to me. "Do you want to go to a movie next weekend?"

I thought my heart would fly out of my chest. "That would be great. I'll have to ask my parents."

"Okay, just let me know."

"I will."

"Good night, thanks again for the ride."

His back muscles rippled and strained against his shirt, as he walked up the driveway and disappeared inside his house. As I backed up the car, worry threatened to spoil the memory. Would Mother even let me go on a date? Or would she say no and steal my chance at happiness?

Chapter 11
Changes

KELLY'S STORY

I pulled alongside the curb in front of the house. If only no one was home. Sweat dripped down my back as I opened the door, waiting for the cookie onslaught to resume. Several seconds ticked by, and nothing happened.

The television blared from the family room, and Ben and Ann were spread out on the couches.

"Hey guys."

They both glanced over at me and then back at the TV.

"Where's Mom and Joe?"

Ann shrugged still not looking at me. "They went out for the night. Mom said to tell you she'll see you tomorrow."

"Oh, all right, I'm beat. It was a long day, but I qualified for State."

Ann's focus remained on the television. "That's nice."

Her lack of interest irritated me. "It's a big deal."

"It's not all about you, you know."

"I didn't say it was. What did I ever do to you, anyway?"

Why did she hate me so much?

She turned to me with narrowed eyes. "Don't you get enough attention?"

Did she really say that? My mouth dropped open. "I don't know why I bother even talking to you. Why I thought we might have some sisterly connection is beyond me. You're just like Mom."

She smiled at me. "Mom got more cookies, in case you get

hungry again."

Tears pricked my eyes. "I didn't eat the other ones."

Ben watched us but said nothing.

I flew down the stairs toward my bedroom before the tears flowed in earnest. If only Bethany were here. She would have been excited for me. I didn't understand why Ann had to be so hateful.

After selecting a change of clothes, I showered and let the warm spray splash over me. Twenty minutes later, I emerged feeling refreshed and relaxed. Checking the clock on the wall to make sure Molly would still be up, I called her.

Molly answered on the second ring. "Hello."

I climbed into bed. "Hey Molly, it's me."

"Hi, how did it go?"

"I'm going to State."

Her squeal of delight had me holding the phone away from my ear. "I knew it, congrats. honey. I'm sorry I missed it."

"It's all right. I knew you had to work. Did you get a lot of clients today?"

"No, not as many as I would've liked."

She told me about a few of her clients. As she wound down, I debated telling her about Keyes. She knew I had a crush on him and had cautioned to let him come to me.

"Are you still there, Kelly?"

"Yes, I'm here. Sorry, I'm beat. Not to change the subject but guess who asked me out on a date?"

She chuckled. "Let me guess, Keyes?"

"Yes, he wants to take me to a movie."

"Oh honey, you must be so happy. I know you've been hoping for this for a long time."

"I don't know . . . if Mother will let me go, though."

"I don't know either, honey. I hope so. How's it going with her?"

"Not so good. She thinks I lie to her. Then she accuses me of doing stuff I don't do. She's out tonight or I'm sure she'd be listening in."

"I'm sorry. I talked to your dad today. He wants me and Beth to move home."

"Really?" Could that be true? My heart soared.

Her sigh muffled through the phone. "He's been going to meetings pretty steady and has a sponsor he likes. I don't know what to do. I'm tempted. But cautious."

"Wow. I don't know what to say." *Oh please, Lord. I want to go home.*

"Well, nothing's set in stone, but I'm thinking about it. Beth isn't so thrilled though."

"Yeah, I bet."

"You sound tired, honey, I'm going to let you get some sleep now."

"Okay, love you, Molly. I'll call you tomorrow."

"All right, love you too. Good night, sweetheart."

After I hung up, I lay there, staring at the wall. If they got back together, I could go home and back to my real life. *Oh please, Lord, let Dad have his stuff together, now. What about Keyes though? I can't think about him when I may have a chance of escaping.*

***

The next couple of days dragged by, and Mother surprised me. She said yes to a date with Keyes. I couldn't believe she actually would let me go and kept waiting for her to change her mind. I apologized for the cookies but not in a way that I actually admitted to eating them. I told her I was sorry they were missing, and I hoped I could earn her trust and faith in me once again. I bit my tongue through the whole thing, but she ungrounded me, and I figured confessing seemed the lesser of two evils.

I kept my head down and survived the week. When Keyes showed up on Saturday night to pick me up for our date, I worried about his first encounter with Mother. Since everyone I had introduced to her to so far this year came up short, I could only imagine what she would say to him.

Any hope of slipping out past her died when I found her standing by the door. She clucked her tongue. "He's late."

I prayed she wouldn't say that to him. "He doesn't know where I live. He might have gotten lost."

She turned and looked me over. "Is that what you're wearing?"

I looked down at the cotton button-up shirt and jeans I

wore. "We're just going to a movie, Mom."

She crossed her arms. "Tell me again why his mother is driving you?"

I looked at the floor. "He doesn't have his license yet, only his learner's permit."

"I thought you said he was older than you."

"He is. His parents wanted him to wait, that's all."

When headlights came up the driveway, I opened the door. "I'll see you later, Mom."

She closed it, preventing me from leaving. "Oh no, you don't. I want to meet him."

I faked a smile. "Okay. But please no third degree."

She sighed. "I find it amusing that you think its third degree. I'm merely looking out for the safety of my daughter. What kind of parent would I be if I didn't?"

Please don't embarrass me. Couldn't she see how much this meant to me?

A few seconds later, Keyes knocked on the door.

Mother opened it but blocked my exit. "So you're Keyes."

Keyes glanced back and forth between us. "Yes, ma'am."

"Kelly tells me your mother is going with you because you don't have your license yet."

If only the floor could swallow me whole. I wish we could have slipped out already.

Keyes looked down and shuffled his feet.

Heat burned my cheeks. "His mom is dropping us off at the movies and picking us back up."

Keyes gaze found mine. "That's right."

After skirting around my mother, I placed my hand on Keyes arm. "Mom, we have to go or we'll be late."

She didn't move, but I squeezed by nonetheless. I wanted out before she could embarrass him further. "Bye, Mom, I'll be home later."

"All right, I'll see you when you get back."

Oh great! She had that we'll talk when you get home tone, but I wasn't going to let it spoil my night. I waved over my shoulder as we walked to the car.

Dates for high school students meant maybe dinner and

most likely a movie. Keyes didn't disappoint, although the movie we had intended to see sold out. We went to see *Wayne's World*. We topped off the night with dinner at McDonald's.

In the car on the way home, his mother asked us about the movie, and as we laughed and talked, I wished the night would go on forever. When his mom pulled alongside the curb instead of onto the driveway in front of my house, a battalion of butterflies took flight in my stomach. Would he kiss me good night?

As Keyes opened the door, I turned to face his mother. "Good night, Mrs. Grayson, thank you for driving us."

"You're very welcome. Good night, Kelly."

As we walked up the driveway I glanced at Keyes. What was he thinking? Did he have a good time?

I lowered my eyes. "Thanks for tonight, I had fun."

"Me too."

At the door we stood in silence. My heart raced as I watched him step closer then back away. Was he going to kiss me? That would make this the best night ever. He moved forward again only to be stopped in his tracks as my mother flung open the door.

"Oh good, you're home. Say good night, Kelly."

I clenched my teeth. "I'll be right there, in a minute, Mom."

Heat flamed into my cheeks as my mother just remained at the door watching us. I turned toward Keyes and tried to smile. "Thanks again, good night."

He looked awkward as he glanced back and forth between my mother and me. "I'll see you around at school."

I stood just inside the door and watched him walk back down the driveway and out of sight without a backwards glance. *Yep, can't blame him. I'd want out of here as quick as I could, too.* Sighing, I turned and leaned up against the door and faced my mother.

Here we go. Round two.

Mother waved her arms. "I don't like him, Kelly. I don't want you to see him again."

I clenched my teeth as she rattled on. "I like him, Mom, but after that crazy scene, don't worry. I doubt he'll want anything to do with me again."

"I don't know what you're talking about."

"Really, Mom? So standing at the door and giving him the third degree wasn't part of your plan?"

The vein in her neck pulsed. "Plan? I didn't have a plan. I allowed you to go out with him tonight, against my better judgment, and now you're accusing me of some ulterior motive. That hurts, Kelly."

I hung my head and mumbled an apology. I couldn't win against her. Why did I even try?

Mother nodded, excusing me. As my foot touched the first step toward my room, she stopped me. "I meant what I said, Kelly. You're not to see that boy again. Do you understand?"

I glared at her but said nothing and went down to my room. Sitting on my bed hugging my stuffed bear, I cried. What was wrong with me? Why didn't she try to understand?

I hated my life. I couldn't live like this anymore. If only Molly were there. Sometimes, I wished that I would die.

***

The next couple of days were filled with cheerleading practice and track. I only saw Keyes from a distance and doubted he noticed me at all, especially after the scene with my mother. Our schedules kept us apart.

I tried to stay as busy as possible and came home as late as I could each night. Exhausted, I would crash as soon as dinner ended. This helped me avoid everyone at home. I didn't even call Molly for a few days. I knew she would pick up on how miserable I felt, and that would hurt her.

I think I could have rolled with things until the end of the school year if it weren't for another confrontation with my mother.

Running a little late for school, I hurried into the kitchen, reached into the cabinet for a pop tart, and pulled out an empty box.

Mother came in at that moment. "I caught you red-handed this time, Kelly."

"What?"

"You ate the whole box of pop tarts, didn't you? I just bought that."

I stared back. "No, I went to grab one but found an empty box. I haven't even had one."

Mother grabbed her stomach and winced. "Not again, first it was the cookies and now this. All this stress is giving me an ulcer."

I tried to reason with her. "Really, Mom, I didn't eat any of them. Are you all right?"

She latched onto the counter closing her eyes. "I'll be fine. I'm just so tired of your lying."

"I didn't do it. I swear." I couldn't help the tears as I looked back at her speechless. *Why does she always accuse me? Other people live here too.*

She held her hand out. "Where are your keys to the car?"

"On the counter. Why?" Was she going to take the car away?

She scooped them up and put them in her pocket. "Your driving privileges are revoked."

I glanced at the clock. "Please, Mom. I'm going to be late for class."

Ann chose that moment to walk into the kitchen. "What's going on?"

"I caught your sister red-handed and she's denying it."

Ann glanced back and forth between us. A faint blush crept into her cheeks. She glanced in the direction of the empty pop tart box and spun on her heels to leave the room.

Mom filled a glass with water and opened an aspirin bottle by the sink. Taking the pills she turned back to me. "Stop denying it, Kelly."

Ann yelled from the foyer. "I need to get to school. Are we going, Kelly?"

Mother called back. "Kelly has lost her driving privileges. I'll take you."

I hung my head and followed Mother out of the kitchen. I snatched my backpack from the stair railing, and we exited out the door.

As I reached for the car door, Mother's words stopped me. "What do you think you're doing?"

"Getting into the car."

"Oh no, you don't. I'm driving your sister to school. Not you."

What? Was she serious? She couldn't be. "I need to go to school too."

"Start walking. You can walk off all those pop tarts you ate."

The tears I held back burst free. "I'll be late, Mom. Please, don't do this."

She climbed into the car, closed the door, and rolled down the window. "I guess you should have thought about that before eating the entire box."

They backed out of the driveway and left. A black cloud of despair and helplessness devoured me as the last remnants of my life collapsed. If only I could just disappear into nothingness.

I reentered the house and dropped my backpack by the door. It didn't matter now. Even if I ran, I couldn't make it to school on time. I sat on the couch and stared out the window as tears fell. I decided to call Molly.

She answered on the first ring.

"Hi, Molly."

"Kelly? Is that you? Oh sweetheart, I've been so worried about you. This morning the Lord told me to pray for you."

I sobbed. "I hate it here, Molly."

I went on to tell her what had transpired, crying the whole time.

"That's it. I'm coming."

"What?"

"I said I'm coming. I'll be there in twenty minutes. Don't worry about school. I'll call and tell them you're out sick today."

"No. It's okay, Molly, you don't have to do that."

"Yes, I do. That woman is . . ." She sighed into the phone. "No, it's done. I'm coming, and we're going to pack your things and bring you home."

"What about Dad?"

"Don't you worry about that. I'll take care of it. Now sit tight and I'll be there soon. I love you. Bye."

The line went dead. I stared at the phone stunned. Could I really go home?

An hour later, in the car surrounded by my clothes and meager belongings, I breathed my first real breath of freedom as the car turned down my old familiar street.

Molly and I spent the next couple of hours unpacking and putting my things away in my room. It felt like coming home to an old friend. Bethany at school, and Dad at work, I relished my time alone with Molly.

I didn't know how my departure would affect my mother, and inside I feared I would have to go back. I voiced those concerns to Molly at lunch.

"Will Dad make me go back?"

"No, I've already told your dad there's no way you're going back."

I hope I hadn't gotten her in trouble. I looked at my sandwich. "What did he say?"

"He was surprised at first. Then I told him about what happened and he agreed. You needed to come home. He's calling your mother later today."

"Is he still sober?"

"Going on ninety days now."

"Wow. That's great."

She took my hand in hers. "Baby steps. We'll see."

"Can I finish the school year at Centaurus?"

"I don't see why not. You only have a couple weeks left. I don't know about next year though. You might have to transfer to a school in our district."

I looked up at her. "I made the varsity cheerleading squad, but I'll do whatever I have to."

"I'm sure there are squads here you can try out for."

"Yeah, I guess. Before I forget, thank you for coming to get me."

Standing, she pulled me to my feet and embraced me. "I wish I could have come sooner."

"I know."

"You're home now, and that's what counts."

Wrapped in her arms, I looked up to the ceiling. *Thank you, God, for saving me again. Please, let everything work out.*

***

Molly let me use her car to get to school the next morning. I gave myself plenty of time for the added commute. Once I got to school I went to find my cheer coach and track coach to explain the situation to both of them. Then I headed to my first class.

Stephanie met me at the door. "Hey, where were you yesterday?"

"I'll tell you about it later."

"Okay."

The rest of the day passed in a blur. Before I knew it, I needed to go to track practice. The State meet would be the next day, and Coach wanted to go over everything with us. We were shocked to hear that there would be no practice at all that day. Coach wanted us to rest up.

Cheers followed the announcement, but I was disappointed that I wouldn't get to see Keyes. Stephanie and I, along with the other girls from our relay team, sat together discussing our strategy for the next day. I saw Keyes sat with some guys, and I waved at him. He waved back, and I couldn't help but smile. Perhaps it wasn't over with him.

***

The next day, as I sat on the bus waiting for the rest of the team, I couldn't contain my excitement. We were going to the State meet. Having been excused from my classes for the rest of the day, I sighed in relief. I pulled on my headphones and rocked along with the music on my CD player. Keyes approached the bus. Would he sit by me? As he passed my seat he nodded to me, and I smiled back. I was disappointed that he didn't sit next to me and turned back to the window. I guess it was just as well.

Stephanie walked down the aisle with another team member, and I waved to them. They took the seat across from me and continued their conversation. Once everyone boarded the bus, we set off.

Lost in my music, I failed to see movement to my left. The seat moved, and I turned to find Keyes now sitting next to me. He had grin lighting up his face.

I wasn't certain what to say, so I pretended to listen to my music, but my heart began to race.

He removed my headphone. "Hey, do you want to go out?"

My throat went dry. "Sure, when?"

"No, not that kind of going out. I meant would you be my girlfriend?"

I couldn't believe it. Did he just ask me to be his girlfriend as in everyone would know? Music blared out of one earpiece, as I stared back at him. I couldn't come up with a single response. I just nodded yes and smiled.

He smiled back, and the world got a little brighter. We didn't speak the rest of the way to the meet. It's pretty silly now, looking back on it, but in that moment I finally felt wanted.

I didn't place that day at the meet, and I never did run with my relay team again. I finished off the year at Centaurus and transferred to a school near my dad's house.

Keyes and I continued our summer romance, despite the distance between our houses. We talked for hours on the phone, and unlike my mother, Molly and Dad seemed to like him. We saw each other as often as we could. I made the cheerleading squad at my new school, and although practice took up much of my time throughout the summer, Keyes and I managed to see each other. Our families hit it off too and we planned a joint camping trip for the Fourth of July.

***

"Dad, come on, we need to get going."

He laughed as he grabbed his fishing pole. "We have reserved spots. It's not as if we won't get one."

I rolled my eyes. "But Dad, we told Keyes and his family we would be there by three o'clock, and it's already two."

Molly came out with more bags to load in the van. "I think we have everything, I'm worried about the weather though. I just heard a storm is coming in this weekend."

Dad waved her off. "It's July. Rain is all we'll get."

Molly frowned. "We better pack some jackets just in case."

I ran inside. "Come on, everyone. We need to go."

Ben made googly eyes at me. "You just want to see your boyfriend."

Heat flooded my cheeks. "Sooo, come on."

I ran to my room and pulled my jacket from the closet. Molly was right, better safe than sorry.

The whole family piled into the van a few minutes later, and we headed to Rainbow Lakes. Our trusty pop-up camper in tow behind us, we made the hour and a half journey.

The campground was alive with activity. Every spot was filled except Keyes's and ours when we arrived. Our campsite was right next to the one Keyes and his family had reserved.

Once we unhooked the camper and began setting up, Keyes's family arrived with their pop-up trailer. I felt a bit jittery about both families together. But Molly and Keyes's mom hit it off. His dad was quiet and kept to himself once we were all set up.

Keyes and I sat by each other at the fire later that night. The temperature had fallen and we could see our breath in the air.

Viewing my family and his together, I pictured more upcoming trips with them. At about 9:30, Dad called it a night for everyone.

Keyes and I tried to stall for time.

Dad came over to us. "All right you two, say good night."

Keyes blushed and gave me a quick hug. "Night."

I laughed. "Night, see you in the morning."

He went to his camper and I to mine.

Around two in the morning, Molly and Dad's talking woke me.

"Is everything all right?" I asked.

Molly shook her head. "It's snowing."

I looked out the camper screen. "What?"

No wonder I was cold.

Dad laughed. "It's not going to snow much, don't worry. Take the kids to the van if you want, Molly."

I snuggled into my sleeping bag. "I'm okay."

My brother and sisters went to the van while Dad and I toughed it out.

Dad was wrong. We ended up with three inches of snow. In the morning, Molly announced we would be going home.

I was so disappointed. This trip had not gone according to plan. Keyes's family decided to stay. "When I went to say goodbye to them, his parents asked me if I wanted to stay with them."

I ran back to Molly. "Keyes's parents want to know if I can stay with them."

She looked at Dad. "I don't know."

I clutched her arm. "Please. They said I would have my own bed, and they are right there."

Dad smiled. "Sure, I don't see why not."

Molly frowned.

I ran over and gave my dad a hug. "Thanks, Dad."

Keyes's eyes lit up when I told him I could stay.

When my family was all packed up and left, nervous energy went through me. I felt jittery again. I was all alone with his family now. But his mom said she was glad for some female company. At night when everyone went to bed, Keyes and I stayed up whispering and holding hands. My bed was right next to his. When his lips pressed up against mine briefly, I thought I had only imagined it. He kissed me. What did that mean? We held hands as we fell asleep that night. I had a great time with his family. They were different from mine, yet a lot of fun.

It wasn't until the end of the summer, that Keyes and I began to deal with the physical attraction in our relationship.

Like most young couples, we started kissing and hand-holding. However, pretty soon the kissing stirred up more emotions and chemistry. We couldn't seem to keep our hands off each other. I didn't think about the "what happens next" stage. Being naive, I just felt beautiful and loved for the first time in my entire life, and I didn't want to ever lose that feeling.

One afternoon, Keyes and I huddled up next to each other on the sofa. His arm draped across my shoulders as we tried to watch a movie. His parents had left for the day, and we had the house to ourselves.

It seemed innocent enough. A few casual glances and nudges, but we soon forgot the movie. Keyes tickled me. I tried to move away, but he held my arms pinning me to the couch.

I laughed. "All right. You win. I give up. You're stronger than me."

He leaned his face down close to mine. "I am. I think you owe me a kiss."

"Will you let me up, if I do?"

"Maybe, if it's a good kiss."

I smiled. "I'll make it good."

Heat surged through my body as our lips met.

He pulled me up. "Come here. I want to show you something."

Where are we going? He tugged me down the hall to his room. I hesitated before entering. "Are you sure we should go in there?"

"Are you afraid?"

"No, I just . . . I don't know." Yes, my parents told me never to go into a boy's room if his parents weren't home. *What do I do? I don't want him to think less of me.*

Posters hung on the walls, clothes were piled on the floor, and a big stereo system sat on his dresser. "So, what did you want to show me?"

He blushed. "Actually, I lied. I just wanted to come in here. Come here."

Alarm bells screamed in my head as he pulled me toward him and kissed me gently. "Have I told you how beautiful you are?"

He thinks I'm beautiful? "You're not so bad yourself."

He kissed my cheek and then my neck. His hands went for the buttons on my shirt. I pulled back, and brushed his hands away. "What are you doing?" I wasn't ready for this.

He pulled me close again, nibbling my neck. "You're so beautiful."

"I believe you told me that already."

I looked at the door, wanting to retreat, and then back at him. If I left I might lose him. If only we had stayed in the other room. My heart leaped into my throat, but I reluctantly yielded to his embrace.

He tugged me toward the bed. As I sat down, he turned and took something off his nightstand.

He tore open a condom. Had he been planning this? Who kept condoms in their nightstand?

"Um . . . wait. I'm not so sure about this, Keyes."

"Come on, we love each other, don't we?"

He loves me? I swallowed. "Yes, I love you, but . . ."

He kissed me again and all rational thoughts evaporated.

I gave myself away. The realization of what I had done overwhelmed me. It wasn't just a physical pain, but a spiritual tearing away of something that I would never recover from.

Keyes expressed jubilation, as I brushed a lone tear from my cheek and turned on my side. The magnitude of what we'd done, hit me. Guilt and shame enveloped me as I pulled the sheet up to cover myself. *Oh Lord, what have I done?*

A car door slammed outside, Keyes jolted up and raced toward the window. "Oh, shoot! My parents are here. They were supposed to be gone all day."

Oh my gosh! His parents are here. We're dead. What were we thinking?

I jumped from the bed, grabbed my clothes, and ran into the bathroom. My heart thudded in my ears as I quickly dressed.

Once dressed, I opened the door fearing his mother would be outside waiting for me. The door to Keyes room had been closed, so I walked down the hall toward the family room. Keyes sat on the couch watching the abandoned movie, looking calm and collected like everything was normal.

His mother came in a few seconds later. "Hi, Kelly. How's the movie?"

"Good, Mrs. Grayson."

His mother sat down across from us. "I've wanted to see this movie for a while."

A few minutes later, with his mother engrossed in the movie, Keyes leaned down and whispered in my ear. "It's all right, they don't know. Relax."

Relax? Why was I the only one feeling guilty? I was afraid that if his mother looked closely at me she would see the guilt written on my face. I took a deep breath and looked at the clock. "I think I should get going."

His mother frowned. "Don't you want to see the end of the movie? Don't let me run you off."

"Oh, no. It's not you. I have a headache, and I'm pretty tired from all the cheerleading practice this week." Actually, I wished they could have been home an hour ago.

"I bet. It sounds like you have a really busy schedule this

summer."

I stood, reached for my purse, and glanced over my shoulder at Keyes. "Do you want to walk me out?"

"Sure."

We walked down the driveway together, and I opened the car door. "I'll see you later."

"Hey, wait." He tilted my chin up. "You don't have to leave. My parents don't suspect a thing."

"I know, I'm a little tired and sore."

He brushed my hair back from my cheek. "That was just the first time. It'll be better next time. Hey, I love you, Kelly."

Avoiding his gaze, I climbed in the car. "I love you, too."

As I sped away my thoughts were jumbled. Next time? I don't think so . . . that was horrible. I couldn't understand why anyone would want to do that. Maybe Mother saw something in Keyes and had tried to warn me, but I didn't want to believe it. What I wanted to believe was that Keyes loved me.

If only things could be that simple.

Chapter 12
Burned by Fire

KELLY'S STORY

Webster's Dictionary defines *fire* as "a rapid, persistent chemical change that releases heat and light and is accompanied by flame." It's so elemental and yet all-consuming when conditions are right.

In 1871, Chicago was hit by a massive fire that almost destroyed it. It was reported that a cow knocked over a lantern and changed the course of history, bringing a powerful city to its knees. It only took three days. A single act can alter the course of one's life and bring one's entire world crashing down.

I paced the floor. *They're going to kill me. Or they'll kick me out.*

I slammed shut the outdated medical journal, dust particles filtered into the air. My worst fear seemed confirmed. Trembling, I placed the book back on the shelf and walked to the window. Storm clouds had gathered, but they did little to relieve the August heat. The pitter-patter against the window made me wish the rain would wash away my problem. No, this situation wouldn't be easily remedied. I placed my hands on my still flat abdomen and feared for the life I might now be carrying. Tears streamed down my cheeks. Is this how my birth mother felt sixteen years ago?

When I was nine, I broke my arm falling from my horse. That night my dad came home with a big bunch of balloons and admired my cast. It was too painful to sleep, and the cast felt like a block of cement attached to my arm. Molly stayed up reading me stories, while I tossed and turned in bed. There would be no balloons or casts this time.

I wiped away the tears as Molly came into the room bearing groceries.

She frowned when she saw me. "What are you doing here? I thought you had cheerleading practice."

I relieved her of some of the bags and followed her into the kitchen. "I wasn't feeling well and decided to come home."

I stood across from her as I helped unpack the groceries. Her steady gaze followed me.

She frowned causing my heart to leap into my throat. Could she tell by looking at me? What was I going to do?

I tried to remain calm as I continued to unload the bags without making eye contact. I had never kept anything from Molly before, and the emotions inside me boiled up like a giant volcano.

She paused. "Is something wrong?"

Like a dam breaking, tears broke loose and ran in torrents down my face. "I . . . I have to tell you something, but I don't know how."

Molly rushed over to me. "What is it, honey?"

I stared back at her trying to form words. How could I tell her?

She touched my forehead with the back of her hand. "Are you sick?"

"No. Yes. I don't know." If only it were just a cold.

She sighed and placed her arm across my shoulders. "Did you and Keyes have a fight?"

With clouded vision, I forced the words past the lump in my throat. "No, I think . . . I think . . . I might be pregnant."

There. I had said it.

An uncomfortable silence filled the kitchen. I couldn't look at her. After what seemed like an eternity, she took in a deep breath and exhaled. "Why do you think that?"

I hung my head keeping my eyes on the floor. "I'm late."

"I didn't know you and Keyes were . . . um . . ."

"We're not. It was just a mistake. I never intended for it to go that far. I'm so sorry. I know I've disappointed you."

She reached her hand out to grasp mine. "How late are you?"

"A few days, but I'm never late."

She sighed and smiled at me. "Only a few days? That could mean nothing. Did you use protection?"

I looked up but couldn't hold her gaze. "A condom."

Molly waved her hand as if to shoo away the problem. "It's most likely stress. We'll give it a couple of weeks. If your cycle hasn't started by then, we'll see the doctor."

"Do you hate me?"

Molly squeezed my hand and shook her head. "No, of course not. But sex isn't something to be taken lightly. God created it to be shared between a husband and wife. I wish things were different, but I still love you."

Please Lord, let her words be true, I can't make it through life without her. I wrapped my arms around her. "I love you, Molly. Thanks for loving me."

We stood that way for a while, not talking.

"Soooo . . . Do we have to tell Dad?"

"I don't think we need to tell him right now. However, at some point, even if nothing comes of it, you might want to tell him. We'll cross that bridge if we must. For now, we'll pray and hope all this worry is for nothing."

***

A Month Later . . .

Dr. Whitman opened the door and entered the examination room. "Hello, ladies. What's the problem?"

I glanced at Molly then down at the floor. Could a person die from embarrassment? "My period's late."

"I see. Intense sports activity can cause a woman to miss a cycle. Rapid weight loss can also affect it, but looking at your chart your weight's the same as it was last time."

Molly interjected. "Actually, Dr. Whitman, we're afraid that Kelly's pregnant."

The room fell silent.

Dr. Whitman cleared her throat. "I see. Let's get a urine sample, and then we'll know for sure."

After collecting the sample, I returned to the examining

room to wait for the results. I feared the worst and prayed for a negative result. If I ever wanted a magic wand, now would be that moment.

"How long does it take, Molly?" The waiting was excruciating.

Molly paced in front of me with her hands clenched together. "We should know any minute now."

The ticking of the clock grew louder. "It seems like an eternity."

"I know. I'm praying it's negative."

"Me, too."

The door finally opened. The doctor's jaw was tense, and the grave look in her eyes told me the result was positive.

I cleared my throat and met her gaze. "I'm pregnant, aren't I?"

Sighing she nodded. "Yes, and we ran the test twice to make sure. I'm sorry."

"We only had sex once. We used protection. How is it possible?"

"Sometimes, once is all it takes." The doctor grasped my hand. "No birth control is 100 percent effective, except abstinence."

I struggled to hold back another flood of tears, but they escaped. *Abstinence*, the big A-word I had pledged to uphold by not making the same mistake my birth mother had made. I had failed. We all sat in silence for a moment. Molly came and stood next to me her face drenched in tears.

Dr. Whitman sighed. "Part of my job is to tell you there are options. I'm not a supporter of abortion, but I can provide you with names of doctors who are. There is also adoption. Since you're adopted, I'm sure you've thought of it. It's important to set up an appointment with an OB/GYN as soon as you can. I'll write you a script for prenatal vitamins."

She lifted the prescription pad from the pocket of her white lab coat.

If only this wasn't real. During the past month, I'd pushed the terrible thought aside; now the weight of the world rested on my shoulders.

Molly squeezed my hand. This was real for her as well. In that moment, I knew my life would be forever changed.

***

As Molly steered the car down our street, I broke the silence. "I guess I have to tell Dad and my mother now. Don't I?"

She nodded. "I can't save you from that, Kelly, as much as I'd love to."

"I know. I appreciate your support. Guess I'll ask them to meet me for dinner tomorrow at a restaurant. Thanks for not saying anything to Dad. How do you think they'll react?"

We rolled into the driveway, and she put the car in park then turned to me. "I really don't know. They'll be angry for sure. They might yell, but I pray they'll support you, too."

"Will Dad kick me out?"

I stared at my childhood home, fearing her answer.

She sighed. "I'll fight tooth and nail not to let that happen."

I wiped a tear away. "I better go call Keyes. I know he's waiting to hear."

I climbed out of the car, walked into the house, and picked up the phone.

He answered on the first ring. "So, are you?"

He must be going crazy too. "Hello to you too."

Silence.

The dead air in my ear signaled that my attempt at humor had been wasted on him. "Yes, I'm pregnant."

He exhaled. "What are you going to do?"

"I was under the impression, this was a *we* thing."

"You know what I mean."

My heart stopped. "No, I guess I don't. Are we in this together? Tell me now, if you're planning on bailing."

"I'm not bailing. I'll do whatever you want."

I sighed with relief, hoping he told me the truth. "I have to tell my parents, but I'll do that tomorrow. Molly knows."

Keyes breathed heavily into the phone. "She must hate me."

"No, she doesn't. It's not like she's thrilled with us right now, though."

"No, I guess not. So . . . what do you want to do about the whole pregnant thing?"

"It's a little late to do much. I'm thinking adoption. I mean . . . my birth mom gave me up, and I think it's the right thing. I won't do the other."

"All right, I'll support you in whatever you decide."

Why did "whatever I decide" sound like, "I don't really care"? Maybe I was reading into it too much. I closed my eyes. "I better go now. I'm pretty tired. It's been an emotional day. I love you, Keyes. I'm sorry about this."

"Why are you sorry? I was there too, you know. I better figure out a way to tell my parents too. Love you, we'll get through this."

"Yeah, I hope so. Bye."

I sat in silence after I placed the phone on the receiver. Was this going to get any easier?

***

I fumbled with my shirt and bounced my knee, as I waited for Dad and Mother. I'd practiced my speech a dozen times in my head, but it had done little to tame the herd of elephants trampling my stomach. The Chinese restaurant I'd chosen was a favorite of mine, but right now the thought of eating made me want to vomit.

As the hostess led my father to the table, I glanced out the window. Mother pulled into the parking lot. My hands trembled as I waved and tried to smile at Dad.

He sat across from me. "So, what's this about?"

I diverted my gaze only to find my mother rushing toward the table. Our waiter was right behind her with water and green tea.

She sat next to Dad across from me. "Is everything all right? I cancelled an appointment for this."

Dad raised his eyebrows. "Yes, Kelly, what's going on?"

I couldn't hold his gaze. I was saved by the waiter as he sat water glasses in front of us.

Clearing my throat, I said. "Let's go ahead and order first."

Without looking at the menu I rattled off my favorite meal to the waiter. My parents reviewed their menus and ordered too.

The room felt hot and stuffy as sweat poured down my back, and I looked back and forth between them. "Mom, Dad . . . I have something I need to tell you."

Dad reached for my hand. "What is it?"

"I . . . just want to let you know . . . I'm . . ."

I couldn't say it. The words wouldn't come out. I reached for my water glass and took a long drink.

Mom seemed annoyed. "Spit it out. Do you realize I cancelled an appointment for your brother that took me a month to book? If you have something to say, say it."

"I'm pregnant."

Silence.

The room seemed to stand still as if time itself had stopped.

Dad let go of my hand and finally found his voice. "That's ridiculous, Kelly."

Mother's face reddened. "This had better be a bad joke."

I looked down and lowered my voice. "It's not."

The veins on Dad's neck bulged as he gripped the edge of the table. "I'll kill him!"

Mother's eyes blazed. "How could you do this? You're a varsity cheerleader, for Pete's sake, and a good student. Do you realize what you've done to your reputation? What about your brother and sister? I can't even think right now. I'm so mad." Her face turned fire engine red. "What are you planning on doing?"

Dad pounded the table. "I'll tell you what she's going to do. We're going to have this taken care of. I'll call to schedule the procedure tomorrow."

Mother looked at him, her mouth wide open.

Anger rose within me. I looked at them both face on. "I'm not having an abortion."

She opened her mouth to say something, but the waiter arrived with our soup, and we all fell silent as we stared at it disinterested.

Dad leaned over the table and lowered his voice. "The sooner we have this problem taken care of, the better off you'll be."

I trembled, not from fear, but from anger. I gripped the table and leaned toward them. "I won't do it!"

His eyes got big. "Now Kelly, you've chosen this path and with it comes consequences."

"I know I made a mistake, but no one is going to make me do something I don't want to do. My birth mom was the same age I am now when she had me." I stared back at him. "What if she had been made to have an abortion?"

He reached across the table, took my hand in his, and squeezed. His eyes softened a little. "We're grateful your birth mom made the choice she did. I'm just concerned about you. An abortion would be best in the long run."

I pulled my hand out of his grasp. "An abortion would be best for who? You? Certainly not me. I'd have to live with that decision for the rest of my life. I'm having this baby."

Mother's eyes narrowed. "And then what? You're sixteen. How are you going to support a baby?"

"I . . . I'm thinking about adoption."

My parents shared a glance.

Dad cleared his throat and shook his head. "Adoption is a noble thing. Believe me; I commend women who choose it. However, it's not the best choice for you. Think of all you've accomplished in cheerleading and track, plus all your friends. Do you really want to see all that washed away?"

Why couldn't he understand? An abortion was not an option for me. "Dad . . ."

Mom's voice cut across the space. "What does the father of the baby think of this? I assume he knows, doesn't he?"

"Yes, he knows. He has a name, Mother. It's Keyes. He's fine with whatever choice I make."

She snorted. "Oh, that's rich. He's fine with whatever you choose because it's your problem, not his. That boy will walk away. I warned you about him and now look what happened. You have that baby, and he'll drop you so fast, your head will spin."

I clenched my teeth and glared back at her. "You're wrong about him." She didn't know him like I did. He loved me and I loved him.

"Am I? Let me guess. He's okay with an abortion too. Right?"

My throat tightened. "He said he'll support me in whatever

I choose to do."

She snickered "Yes, and that means he's there for you as long as you take care of the problem."

Dad stared at the table twiddling his thumbs.

"Dad, you know Keyes. He isn't that way."

He looked over at my mother. "It doesn't matter. Kelly won't be seeing him again."

"He's the father of my baby." I couldn't lose Keyes now. Dad would calm down, and everything would be all right. Wouldn't it?

He leaned forward. "I'm not sugarcoating this. He's not welcome in my home. In fact, you might want to reconsider an abortion or find somewhere else to live."

Mother glared at him with venom in her eyes. "She's not living with me. I can't deal with this right now."

I struggled to find my voice as the tears flowed. "So my choice is an abortion or I'm homeless?"

Dad stared at the table again. The veins in his neck no longer bulged. "I'm not saying that. It's just a lot to take in."

He cupped his face in his hands. "I'll have to talk to Molly. Then I'll decide."

Through my own blurred vision, I saw tears in both their eyes. Dad's arms were crossed in front of his chest, and Mother clenched her hands.

"I'm so sorry. I never wanted anything like this to happen. I hope in time you both will forgive me." I took a deep breath and leaned forward.

I had once again failed them. I didn't measure up, but then I never really had, had I?

I didn't wait for a response. I snatched my purse and fled.

Back at home, I sat in the car in front of my house and sobbed. I mourned the loss of my previous life. One thing was certain: I would remember this horrible day forever.

***

October . . . two months pregnant

Panels of ceiling lights flickered above me, illuminating

the entire adoption center floor. To the right was an immense reception area.

The receptionist eyed me thoughtfully. "Hi, can I help you?"

"Yes, I have an appointment with um . . . I'm not sure, actually. My name is Kelly Frank." My pretense of maturity was blown by my quivering voice.

"Yes, of course. You're meeting with Jeanie Watkins. Here's some paperwork to fill out." She handed me an enormous stack of papers on a clipboard.

I took a seat in front of a large, glass-topped coffee table. The base of the table was made of an enormous piece of polished driftwood. *Wow, how did they make it look so pristine?*

"That's beautiful," I said as I took a closer look running a finger along its smooth surface.

The receptionist smiled as she walked over to me. "Would you like something to drink? Water, soda, or tea?"

"I'm good, thanks." I couldn't drink anything if I had wanted too. I hoped that I'd made the right choice coming there.

She turned back to me. "If you change your mind, let me know."

I thumbed through the papers and looked up at her. "This is a ton of paperwork,"

She flashed a smile and went back to her desk. "It's daunting, but necessary."

When I finished the last form, I returned the pile to her. She took them and walked down the hall.

When she returned, she smiled. "You can go in now."

As I made my way down the hallway, the phone on the receptionist's desk buzzed, sending a jolt through my nervous system. With my heart in my throat I approached Jeanie Watkins's door. How would I make it through this? The responsibility felt like a boulder tied to my back.

A woman wearing a crisp navy blue suit with a white ascot-style blouse smiled at me and held out a hand. "Come in."

Her blonde hair was caught up in a clip, with soft tendrils framing her face. "You must be Kelly."

I shook her hand. "Yes, Ms. Watkins."

"Please, call me Jeanie. We're pretty informal around here."

I glanced around the office and observed the photos lining the walls. Many were of newborns but also toddlers. "Are all these kids adopted?"

"Yes, they are. I didn't work with all of them, but some were my cases. The counselor before me started this picture wall, and when she retired, I kept up the tradition."

I raised an eyebrow. "Why would you want pictures of cases that aren't yours?"

"They remind me that lots of kids out there have a better life because of adoption. Why don't we sit down and talk for a while?" She pointed to the sofa against the back wall. "All we're going to do is talk."

"I'm okay with talking. Where do you want to start?" What did she want me to do, lie down on the couch and spill my guts? I sat on the end of the couch.

Jeanie smiled and placed her notebook on her lap as she sat across from me. "How far along are you?"

"Um . . . about two months, give or take."

She jotted something in her notebook. I placed my hands on my flat stomach amazed at the life within me.

"Are you feeling all right?"

"A little tired now and then but no morning sickness."

"You're lucky."

I shrugged. "I guess."

"So why are you here?"

Why does she think I'm here? Hello.

She laid the pen on the pad of paper and looked at me. "I mean why did you choose this adoption agency?"

"It's the same one my birth mother used."

Her eyes widened. "You're adopted?"

"Yes."

"That's wonderful." She leaned forward in her chair. "Well, this is what we do here. You'll meet with me every other week and mostly we'll just talk."

"Do I get to pick out the parents?"

"Eventually, but you have a long way to go before that.

First, I'd like to answer any questions you may have."

I clasped my hands together in my lap as my gaze took in the floor. "Um . . . well, do all the women that come here go through with it?"

"Excellent question. The truth is, no. Sometimes it's just too hard. We understand this is one of the hardest decisions a person must make. This is why we will meet twice a month. We really want to understand what it is you're thinking and be up front with information."

Tears blurred my vision as I looked up at her. "What if I can't go through with it?"

"We'll cross that bridge if we need to."

***

December . . . four months pregnant

Like in Webster's definition of *fire*, when conditions are right, gossip burns hot and fast.

The news of a pregnant varsity cheerleader spread to four high schools at a rapid speed. Teammates I trusted betrayed me. I knew eventually the secret would come out, but my so-called friends were the ones leaking it.

A couple of days before winter break, the whispers and stares from classmates took their toll on me. When the school principal requested a meeting with my parents and me, I knew it would only get worse. I tried to keep positive but was unable to shake the feeling of dread.

My parents had hung in there with me. Though Dad struggled with my condition, he was now more open to continuing the pregnancy. It might have had something to do with Molly's fury when she found out he wanted me to have an abortion. I knew he wanted something better for me, and that I had disappointed him, but he seemed to be coming around.

On the morning of the meeting with the principal, I awoke to an overcast sky. Dad hadn't told Mother about the meeting, which was a good thing. He and Molly followed behind me in another car. The principal requested that we come in before school started. I felt like a prisoner facing execution and was grateful few would be there to witness it.

My breath billowed out in the frigid air as we walked into the main office. We found Principal Danner waiting.

He led the way to his spacious office. Three chairs were positioned around his desk. As we sat, tension rose in the room.

Principal Danner cleared his throat. "I've asked you to come in today because it has been brought to my attention that, ah . . . how should I say this? Ah . . . that Kelly is in a rather delicate situation."

Dad's agitation was evident in his eyes. "Are you asking us?"

Mr. Danner shifted in his chair as his face flushed. "Well, some of the students have alluded to her . . . being pregnant."

Dad's face reddened. "And?"

Mr. Danner avoided making eye contact with me by looking just over my shoulder. "And well, I need to know if those rumors are true."

Dad shook his head. "You made us *all* come in this early so you could ask that? She's sitting right there. Ask her yourself."

Mr. Danner seemed uncomfortable as he shifted his position in his chair again.

I decided to help him out. "Yes, Mr. Danner, I'm pregnant. I'm looking into adoption."

He smiled. I imagined he was grateful he didn't have to pose the question. His eyes seemed tinged with sadness, though they only briefly found mine. He looked away and began stacking papers on his desk. "Yes, well . . . you see, Kelly, we have a little problem. The school district doesn't allow girls who are pregnant to attend school, at least not at regular schools. We have a special school for girls in your situation."

I wiggled in my chair. "I have to switch schools?"

Special school? *What am I now, part of the black plague?*

"Yes, that is, if you choose to continue the pregnancy. You know it's not too late to change your mind. Several girls that attend this school chose . . . how should I say this? . . . another path."

"Are you telling me that in order to continue going to school here, I need to have an abortion?" Was he asking or implying that I should get an abortion? Seriously?

"I'm just telling you the policy. It isn't too late. You're a popular cheerleader and have a lot going for you. Just think about it. You'll be excused from your classes and will be able to resume them as if nothing happened. However, if you're still in the same condition after the winter break, well . . . you'll then need to start attending the other school. You should consider all your options."

Options. It seemed as if everyone thought I had them, but mine had disappeared when I chose sex with Keyes. If only . . .

***

The lights from the Christmas tree cast a glow illuminating the family room as we all sat waiting to open our presents.

Keyes and I were snuggled up on the sofa. His arm wrapped around behind me. The snow fell gently in the night as Christmas carols played in the background.

Molly handed out gifts to each of us. As I reached for mine I was startled by the nudge in my stomach.

"Oh my goodness! I think the baby just moved."

Everyone stared at me as I tried to see if the baby would move again. I didn't want to even breathe as I waited.

Keyes eyes bored into mine as he waited with me. After a few seconds, and no movement, everyone went back to opening their gifts.

Settling back into the couch, I sighed. "I guess I just thought I felt something."

Keyes snuggled me close and his arm tightened around me. "Whoa, I felt that."

Beth raced over to feel my stomach. The nudges were getting stronger.

Beth's eyes widened. "I felt it too. Does it hurt, Kelly?"

"No, it doesn't hurt. It just feels really weird."

Beth pulled her hand back when the baby moved again. "That's so creepy."

Molly came and gently placed her hand on mine, and the baby moved again. "It's not creepy, Beth, it's amazing. You have an active little person in there."

Everyone took turns trying to see if they could feel the

baby move and after a few minutes all movement stopped.

Smiling, I waited. "Guess the baby is sleeping now."

The night went back to Christmas festivities. When everything started winding down, Keyes leaned in and whispered in my ear. "Can we go somewhere private for a second? I need to talk to you and don't want everyone to hear."

I pulled back and my heart thundered like stampede of cattle. Was he breaking up with me? Tears pooled as I looked away. "Um . . . yeah, okay."

My legs wobbled as I stood.

Molly frowned. "You okay, Kelly?"

"Yeah, just need to move around a bit. I'm going to go get some more milk from downstairs. Keyes, you want to come too?"

He scrambled off the couch. "Sure."

Dad's gaze bored into us. "Hey, no monkey business."

Beth laughed. "Don't you think it's a little late, Dad?"

I could feel the heat rush into my cheeks. "We're just getting milk."

The basement was colder than the rest of the house and each step down I could feel my heart pound harder into my ears.

I walked to the fridge and pulled out a gallon of milk, trying to look unconcerned.

Keyes said nothing and only watched me, I panicked.

This is it. It's going to be the worst possible Christmas for me, isn't it? Silence brought the longing in my chest to a crescendo. "So, um . . . you wanted to talk to me?"

He took a deep breath. "Yes, . . . I . . ."

A tear broke free. "Okay."

His eyes widened. "Hey, what's wrong?"

I looked at the ground. "Are you breaking up with me?"

"What? No, of course not."

I wiped the tears away. "You're not?"

"No. I just wanted to give you your Christmas gift in private."

I smiled. "Oh."

He got down on one knee as he withdrew a small box from his back pocket. "Here, this is for you."

He's down on one knee with a small box, that can't mean

what I think it means right? My hands trembled as I reached for the box. "Um . . . it's not a . . . you know . . . ?"

"Open it and see."

I tore open the delicate wrapping paper, took a deep breath, and opened the jewelry box. Inside, nestled in black velvet, was a beautiful ring with an emerald sparkling in the light. Two small diamonds graced each side. "Keyes, it's beautiful. It's too much though, I only got you a watch."

Keyes took my hand and gently placed it in both of his. "It's not an engagement ring but a promise ring. I love you and want to marry you one day."

Tears streamed down my cheeks. "You do?"

"Yes, that is if you say yes."

"Yes, I want that, too."

The baby gave me a sound kick to my rib. "Ouch, I guess he agrees too."

Sadness came into his eyes. "We'll do the kid thing right, next time."

I placed my hand on my stomach. "Yeah, I hope so."

Chapter 13
New Challenges

NANCY'S STORY

January 1993

We searched for the correct building as a cold January wind blew over us. Stepping into a foyer, we found a handwritten sign, directing us to the meeting on Chinese adoption.

We still had our letter in the profile books at Adoption Services, but ten months had passed with no interest. So we decided to explore more options. As we sat down, a small crowd of couples gathered at the front of the room.

A Chinese woman in her thirties stood up. "Thank you for coming tonight," she said in broken English. "My husband and I work with foreign adoptions. We are Christians who are desperate to find homes for thousands of abandoned babies. Since China has outlawed couples having more than one child, many Chinese couples have discarded their girls. In the Chinese culture, boys are more valued than girls are. This is the unfortunate reality."

I was appalled. Perhaps it was God's will we rescue one of these forsaken but precious little girls. The woman continued, explaining that at least one adoptive person from each couple must plan to spend ten to twelve weeks in China. This, I knew, would pose great challenges both in the financial and logistical realms. I would be the one spending weeks in China because John had to work. Finding someone to watch Brianna for that long would be another issue. Dark fingers of fear entered my thoughts. Did I have the guts to do it alone? We left that evening with an application in hand and planned to seek God for His guidance.

***

Days Later

Sitting cross-legged on the bed, I opened my eyes to examine a list of prayer requests I'd received at church the past Sunday. Since I had prayed for requests, I closed my eyes again.

"Lord, I pray for a child to adopt and for wisdom. Show us if we are to rescue a Chinese little girl. If not, help a birth mother to pick us, someone from a Christian home, if possible. In fact, it would be really cool, Lord, if she came from our large church. We'd then have our faith in common with the birth mother."

Pray for Kelly and Keyes.

Words from a still, small voice entered my mind. I frowned and shrugged. I didn't know anyone by either name. What an odd name. Keyes. Or was it Kelly Ann Keyes? No, I felt confident. I had received two names. Kelly and Keyes.

"Lord, I pray for these people, Kelly and Keyes. They obviously need Your help. Give them wisdom if a decision must be made. Bring them help if they need it. If they need physical provision, I pray for You to provide it. Dear Lord, You know their needs. May my feeble prayer release Your hand to do the work in their lives You want to do. In Jesus' name I pray, Amen."

From that day forward, during each of my quiet times, I felt impressed to pray for Kelly and Keyes. Time went on. Would I ever get the chance to meet them and learn what it was I was praying them through?

***

KELLY'S STORY

January 1993

Five months pregnant . . .

My first day at the Jefferson County Adolescent Pregnancy Program (JCAPP), I found myself surrounded by other pregnant teens. I felt part of a club others frowned upon, a sorority of girls in the same situation, a sisterhood of misfits, outcasts by society.

My class schedule, similar to the one I took at my old high

school, had a few added requirements. In addition to my regular high school curriculum, I spent an hour a day in the nursery taking care of babies born to mothers the semester before. The goal was to train teen mothers to look after babies in a monitored environment. Because I didn't want to fall behind in school, I made sure to take all the required courses for high school graduation. Most of the girls looked pregnant, but my stomach was nearly flat.

Fifty-three girls attended the school when I enrolled. With the youngest being the shocking age of eleven and the oldest at eighteen. I fell into the oldest category at seventeen. The average age of the girls attending the school happened to be fifteen. Since I opted to take more of the advanced courses, they assigned a teacher to me who monitored all my classwork. It felt like independent study. I did most of the work myself and then went over it with my teacher.

As I sat at a table going over my schedule, a girl approached me.

"Hi, can I sit with you?"

She looked about the same age as me. I hoped she was friendly. "Sure."

She smiled and took a seat. "My name's Neelie, what's yours?"

"Kelly."

"How far along are you?"

What a weird thing to ask. I scrunched up my face. "What?"

She chuckled and patted her stomach. "You know, how far along are you in your pregnancy? You don't look very pregnant, so I'm guessing around two months?"

I frowned. "No, about five months actually, I guess. You?"

She smiled. "Really? I'm twenty-two weeks. I just found out I'm having a boy."

Why does she sound so excited? "That's great. What high school did you come from?"

"Stanley Lake. I'm a junior."

Interesting. I didn't think I had seen her before though. "Me too."

"I thought you looked familiar. You were a cheerleader, right?"

Oh great, is that all people will remember about me? I looked down. "Yep, that's me."

She touched my arm. "Hey, it's okay. Who cares what people think?"

I looked up at her. "I guess."

"Do you know the sex of your baby yet?"

"Yeah, it's a boy."

She smiled. "Like me. I already have a name picked out. So what classes are you taking?"

I handed her my schedule. "Math, English, history, and science. I need to keep my credits up to have a hope of still getting into college when I graduate next year."

She looked taken aback. "You're thinking about college?"

I raised an eyebrow. "Of course, aren't you?" Wasn't that what we were supposed to be thinking about?

She laughed. "No, not with a baby on the way. It will be hard enough keeping up with him let alone classes."

She was keeping her baby. Was I the only one not keeping mine?

"I'm going the adoption route."

Her eyes widened. "You are? Wow, I think you are the only one here that is."

"Yep, that's what I hear."

I figured she would get up and leave and go sit with some of the other girls. Instead, she pulled out her lunch and started to eat. I pulled mine out of my backpack and joined her.

We changed the subject to due dates. It turned out hers came three weeks before mine. She talked about her boyfriend and her parents' reaction to the pregnancy. I told her about my parents' reaction, and a little about Keyes. I was pleased to find out we shared two classes. We also were the same age and had similar interests. I was happy to have a new friend.

You would think with fifty-three girls occupying three outbuildings, it would have been crowded, but with girls heading to doctors' appointments, and others bringing babies to and fro, it worked. On the rare occasions when we all were in attendance, for guest speakers or what not, it did get a little crowded.

I met several students I liked. One girl even hooked me up with a job as a telemarketer offering free lawn evaluations for a local landscaping company. With decent pay and being able to sit down the whole time, it seemed perfect. School and work became the focus of my life. Keyes found a job at a local Safeway in order to help support me, if I needed clothes or something. We still saw each other as often as we could, though not a lot, but we talked every night on the phone.

Dad became a little more accepting of Keyes after he got a job, even going as far as commending him on staying with me and supporting me. Not an ideal situation, but at least he allowed me to see him.

***

"Kicking again?"

"No, he's good today. I'm just sad, I guess."

She moved closer. "Neelie's shower is today, right?"

"Yep, in about an hour."

She leaned up against the table. "What are you sad about?"

More tears pricked the corners of my eyes. "I'm not having a shower for my baby. I guess I'm feeling a little left out."

Molly rested her hand on my shoulder. "Are you thinking of changing your mind?"

Tears rolled down my cheeks. I looked down at my stomach just starting to protrude. "I don't know anymore. I know what my head says, but my heart is a different matter. I love this baby so much. He's the only biological link to me that I have."

"I know, honey. I told you I would support you in any decision you make, and I will."

I looked up at her. "You mean, I can keep him? I didn't even think that was an option."

She closed her eyes. "Yes, if that's what you want. We could turn David's old room into a nursery for you and the baby. We would have a lot to do, if that was what you wanted. I guess we could throw you a shower, too."

I brushed away the last tear traveling down my cheek. "I don't know what to do anymore. I'm the only girl at school even considering adoption. I didn't think it would be this hard."

She wiped the tears from her face. "I can't begin to imagine what you're going through. I'm so proud of you, though. You have risen to the occasion, and I know God has a plan for your baby."

If only He would tell me what those plans were.

I hugged her. "Thanks, Molly, for always being there and for giving me options. I better get going or I'll be late. I love you."

On the drive to Neelie's house, I gripped the steering wheel. Hope flooded me. I could keep Alex? I had taken to calling him that since I found out I carried a boy. It sounded better than just referring to it as *the baby*. As I thought about what it would mean for me to keep him, I felt uncertain.

I need you God, now more than ever. I don't know what to do. I know you understand. You gave up a Son, too. The pain is so great when I think of parting with him. I don't know if I can do it.

Chapter 14
Divine Appointments

KELLY'S STORY

End of April 1993

I closed another binder full of pictures of hopeful parents, and sat back and looked over at Jeanie. "I don't know how I'm supposed to decide who to pick."

It had been a rough month. I went back and forth between deciding to keep Alex or give him up. Jeanie suggested I proceed with looking at the potential parents and see if any of them caught my eye.

There were several books full of profiles, some I dismissed right away and others I marked with a bookmark to look at closer. From the beginning I was adamant. I didn't want Alex to go to a family with a biological child. Given my childhood history, I refused to even consider a family with one. I finally narrowed my choice down to two couples whose profiles seemed interesting.

The first couple agreed to meet with me the next week. They were nice and made a decent living, Alex would want for nothing, but they only wanted me to have contact with him for the first two years. Not open to that, I ended the meeting soon afterward.

The next couple rubbed me the wrong way, right from the start. I couldn't put my finger on what nagged me. I just knew they were not the parents for Alex. I dismissed them as well.

Discouraged and anxious, I decided to make a deal with God. I wanted Alex to go to a Christian family who held similar beliefs to mine, so I told Jeanie I would agree to meet with any potential parents who could answer one question. Were they born again? If no family could answer that question, then I would have my answer and keep the baby.

She asked what it meant, and I told her to just ask the parents. I knew if they were born again they would know the meaning. She agreed to call each family in the profile books and ask them the question. After a few hours passed with no word, I figured I had my answer. Little Alex would be mine.

***

NANCY'S STORY

Friday, Late April 1993

As Brianna took a nap, I sat at the dining room table scrapbooking her baby pictures. The phone rang on the kitchen wall.

"Hello?"

"Hi. This is Jeanie at Adoption Services. Is this Nancy?"

My heart skipped a beat. "Yes. How are you?"

"I'm fine. I have an odd question that a birth mom wants me to ask you."

"Okay."

"I'm not sure what this means, but she wanted me to ask you, 'Are you and John born again?'"

My heart raced. "Yes. We definitely are."

"Oh, I'm so glad! None of the other couples I've talked to understood what that means. Since you are, I think Kelly would like to meet you and John."

My heart thumped loud in my ears. *Kelly? Have I been praying for the birth mom of our child?* "Uh, that sounds great. We'd love to meet her."

"I have to speak with Kelly and Keyes and see if you can meet sometime this week."

My heart hammered against my chest. "Tha . . . that would be great. We'd love to meet Kelly, and did you say Keyes?"

"Yes, Keyes."

"We'll look forward to meeting Kelly and Keyes."

"I'll check with them and get back with you."

"Sounds good."

Weak in the knees, I hung the phone up on the wall and sank to the floor. Tears welled as the conversation sank in. "Wow, Lord! You've had me praying for the birth parents of our child! I'm so awed. John's not going to believe this."

***

KELLY'S STORY

When the phone rang, I ran for it thinking it was Keyes. "Hello?"

"Kelly?"

"Yes."

"It's Jeanie."

My heart skipped a beat. Was she calling to tell me she couldn't find anyone? "Hi Jeanie. Any news?"

She sighed. I took that as a sign that she couldn't find anyone. I smiled placing my hand on my belly.

"I did as you asked and called everyone in both books. Pretty much everyone had no clue what you were asking."

"Okay." My heart sped up. Was Alex going to be mine?

Jeanie cleared her throat. "I almost gave up, but then I had one woman say yes. Now Kelly, I know you said you didn't want to consider anyone with a biological child. They have a daughter who is five. I can bring you their profile if you want to read about them."

"Wow, only one couple in two books full of people?" I did say I'd meet anyone who answered yes. *Why did I do that?*

Jeanie went on. "I was so happy they said yes, that I asked if they would be willing to set up an appointment to meet you, before I realized they had a biological child.

"It's okay. I said I'd meet anyone who said yes to my question."

"I'm so glad that you are willing to meet them. I read their profile, and I really think you might like them. I'll bring their profile over in the morning."

"Okay, no promises though."

"I know. I'll talk to you tomorrow."

"Yep, have a good night."

Okay, Lord, I made a deal with you, but you know how I feel about the biological part. I'll agree to meet them. But I'm not promising anything.

The next day, after I got home from school, the profile waited for me on the counter. Molly said Jeanie brought it by on her lunch hour. Curious, I picked it up and scanned the picture. It listed their names as John and Nancy. Their little girl, named Brianna sat between them with her hair in pigtails.

As I read through their information, I grappled with the daughter issue. *I don't know, Lord. I guess they look like a nice family.* Would they make a good family for Alex though? Would they treat their daughter differently than him? I guessed they must want another child if they were considering adoption, so that would be different than my experience. Right?

I scanned the rest of the information then picked up the phone to call Jeanie. She answered on the first ring. "This is Jeanie."

I swallowed. "Hi, it's Kelly. I read the profile you brought over."

"And?"

"I'll still meet with them, but I'm not promising anything."

She exhaled. "Great, I'll set it up."

I left the profile on the counter knowing Molly and Dad would want to read it as well.

***

On Saturday, I had to work, so I pushed aside all thoughts about adoption and concentrated on my job. That night, Keyes stopped by and I showed him the profile. His nonchalant attitude in regards to picking parents wasn't lost on me, and it made me angry. Didn't he care that these could be the potential parents of our child? Was it all up to me? *Lord, please help me choose the right parents if it comes down to it.*

The next morning, Dad told me he had a dream that the couple in the profile picture went to our church. I wasn't sure I believed him and laughed it off.

***

Dad, never on time, took forever to get into the car. We arrived late to church as always. Amazed at how many cars filled the parking lot, I wondered as I walked toward the door, if one of them belonged to the family whose profile lay on my counter at home. Not that I really believed my dad. Even if I had, the church was too big to have any hope of locating them.

As we made our way into the sanctuary, I looked down at my pregnant belly. I often received interesting stares from people at church. I lost any hope of sneaking into the back and sitting near the door when an usher led us to the front. *Great, so if I have to go pee during service everyone will look at me.*

At least we arrived during the praise and worship portion. As we sang, Dad leaned down and whispered in my ear. "I see the couple from the paper you got from the adoption agency."

My jaw dropped. "What? Where?"

He nodded to his right. I scanned the rows but couldn't make out anyone resembling them. Dad only looked at the picture once, and there was no way he would be able to pick them out.

He leaned closer. "Third row from the front, ten people in."

I quickly counted the rows and the people. Sure enough, Dad was right. I finally believed his story about his dream.

He grinned triumphantly. "Let's see if we can talk to them after the service."

"Dad, there's no way we're going to catch up to them. They're clear across the church. It's not going to happen."

He winked. "We'll see about that."

For the next hour, I found myself glancing over to where they sat, wondering about them. Was it really them? When Pastor George released us, Dad made a beeline for them. I struggled to keep up with his fast pace. At eight months pregnant I lagged behind.

When I finally caught up to Dad, I found him searching the throngs of people. We had missed them, but Dad wasn't about to give up. "Wait, they have a daughter. They'll be in the Sunday school section."

He turned and strode toward the stairs leading to the Sunday school wing. I struggled to keep up with him as he weaved in and out between people, because my baby bump got in the way.

I caught up to him as he entered the Sunday school corridor. "Dad, wait. Are you sure this is a good idea?"

"Sure, why not? You're going to meet with them next week anyhow."

"I don't know about this."

***

NANCY'S STORY

Sunday, April 1993

The Sunday morning worship service ended with a song. As the meeting broke up, John and I wove through the crowd and made our way down the stairs and through a hallway. We came to the classroom where Brianna's Sunday school class met. John opened the door for me to enter and as I crossed the threshold, a man's voice from behind us, called out.

"Excuse me, John. Nancy?"

I turned to find a balding man rushing toward us. Breathless, he stuck out his hand. "My name is Travis Frank. You are the John and Nancy who are trying to adopt, are you not?"

"Yes." John shook his hand.

A pregnant teenage girl sidled up beside Travis.

He pointed with his other hand toward the girl. "This is my daughter Kelly. I believe you have plans to meet her and Keyes this week."

John glanced toward me with an eyebrow raised. "Yes, that's right."

Speechless, goose bumps ran up my spine. I shook hands with both father and daughter.

Travis spoke on. "I recognized the two of you, from your profile letter, even though you sat clear across the sanctuary from us. Kelly thought I was crazy, but I was sure it was you."

I finally found my tongue. "You attend this church?"

He smiled with an affirmative nod.

"This is amazing." I struggled to believe what was happening.

He shrugged. "Quite a coincidence."

I smiled. "More of a God thing, I would think."

Kelly smiled and gave an occasional polite nod.

Travis went on. "Did the adoption agency tell you she's having a boy?"

I looked at John and smiled. This news would make him happy.

John grinned. "No, they didn't tell us that piece of news."

Travis turned toward the door. "I won't keep you, just wanted to meet the two of you."

I smiled at Kelly. "I'm glad to meet you. We're looking forward to meeting Keyes."

She smiled, giving no hint of the turmoil that I felt sure brewed within her. "We'll be there. It's been nice meeting you."

As they disappeared through the door, the working of God's hand once again awed me. He answered my personal request that the birth mom would come from our church.

***

KELLY'S STORY

Dad moved closer to me as we walked down the hallway. "That went well, I think."

I nodded. "A little awkward but yeah. I still can't believe you found them after only seeing their picture once."

He smiled. "I'm good, besides I did tell you I had a dream about it last night."

He placed his arm around my shoulder as we made our way over to Molly and Bethany. Molly looked anxious. "Did you find them?"

I nodded. "Yes, they're pretty nice."

She smiled. "Oh good. We'll see how your meeting goes with them this week."

In the car on the way home, I stared out the window. A million thoughts ran through my mind. Could they be the parents for Alex? How do I feel about them having a daughter? As these thoughts rolled around in my head, I finally allowed myself to be optimistic about giving Alex up.

***

Sitting in my car in front of the adoption agency, I glanced at the clock on the dash, happy to see I got there early. I scanned the parking lot for Nancy and John. I wished Keyes had been able to meet them with me tonight, but he had to work. Since I already met them, the meeting became just a formality.

Tired of waiting, I climbed out of my car and entered the building. Jeanie waited for me in the reception area.

"Hi, Kelly, I'm glad you could make it tonight."

"Thanks, me too. Are Nancy and John here yet?"

"No, not yet. We can wait back in the conference area, if you'd like."

"Okay."

We walked down the hallway past her office to a conference room. I expected a big table, but instead found comfortable chairs positioned in a circle.

Jeanie gestured to the chairs. "Sit wherever you'd like."

I chose the chair closest to her. "So, what are we going to discuss?"

She smiled. "Anything you'd like. This is the time for you to get to know them and ask them questions and vice versa."

I tried to think of some questions. "I like them. I don't know if I told you, but we met at church this weekend. Actually, my dad picked them out and we sort of followed them. They're really nice."

Her eyes widened. "No, I didn't know. Wow, didn't you say you went to a large church?"

"Yep, huge. I think it's a miracle. What are the odds they attend there, too?"

"Amazing. Normally, this would be your first time meeting them, but since you've met them already, it will be easier."

"I guess. I'm not sure what I should ask them." I didn't know if it would be easier. What if they didn't like me? What if they pictured someone completely different?

"Well, they may have some questions for you."

When a knock sounded on the door, I looked up to see Nancy and John being let into the room. I smiled and waved. "Hi again."

Nancy smiled back. "Hi. It's good to see you too."

Jeanie made the formal introductions, and we spent the next hour talking about anything and everything. They had several questions for me, from how the pregnancy went to what made me choose adoption. They also asked how my parents and Keyes felt about it. As the night went on, I found I had several questions for them as well. I wondered why they were choosing adoption, since I knew they had a biological daughter already.

My back hurt so I leaned forward in my chair. "Nancy, will you take a leave of absence when the baby comes?"

She looked confused. "A leave of absence? Oh, no. I'm a stay-at-home mom."

"I'm sorry. I think I remember reading that now."

She took John's hand. "It's all right. John and I felt it's important to have me stay home."

When it came time to leave, I felt good about the meeting. I liked that she didn't work. We arranged to meet again for dinner, and I hoped Keyes would be able to make it.

As they left, I stayed behind to talk to Jeanie for a few minutes.

She waited until they were down the hall. "Well, how do you think that went?"

"Good, I like them. I forgot how short they are. Keyes is really tall and I'm above average too. Poor kid will tower over them."

She laughed. "Well, that wouldn't be for a long time. You do like them though, right?"

Did I? Tonight had gone really well, better than I expected. "Yes, I guess I do."

"Well, nothing's set in stone. So if you go home and change your mind, that's okay. This is a big decision."

I nodded, letting her know I understood. "I guess I better get going. I'll see you next week. Same time?"

"I'll be here."

With my purse and jacket in hand I opened the door. "Thanks, Jeanie . . . for making this a little easier."

She smiled. "Anytime."

As I drove home, I replayed the meeting in my head.

Thank you, Lord for making me meet them. Getting to know them a little more helped. I really hope I can do this.

Chapter 15
Practice Run

KELLY'S STORY

The phone rang when we entered the house. Bethany made a mad dash for it. "Hello. Hi Grandma. Mom, it's for you."

Molly took the phone. I couldn't hear what Grandma said, but Molly began to cry. She turned back toward us, the color drained from her face. "My father is in the hospital. He needs a quadruple bypass. I need to get to Arizona as soon as I can."

Dad put his arms around her. "Do you want us all to go?"

She shook her head. "No, Kelly is too far along. She has a doctor's appointment tomorrow. I'll take Bethany, and we'll fly out as soon as we can."

Dad frowned. "I guess I can take Kelly to the appointment. Call the airlines and see when the first available flight is."

Molly and Bethany flew out the next morning. Dad and I took them to the airport on the way to my doctor's appointment. Molly promised to call as often as she could, and I promised to pray for Grandpa.

At the doctor's I began to feel a little queasy. A sharp pain stabbed my stomach as I went to lie down on the examining table. Soon afterward, another pain hit. When Doctor Berry came in, I told him about the pain. He called for his nurse.

When she entered he turned to her. "Hook her up to the fetal monitor. I'm wondering if she doesn't have some contractions going on."

Contractions? I wasn't ready for that. I still had one more prenatal class. How could this happen? I looked over at the nurse.

"It's too early, right?"

Dr. Berry clasped my hand. "Let's see what's going on."

They hooked me up to a fetal monitor. A few minutes later, another pain hit.

Dr. Berry frowned. "I was afraid of that. You kiddo, are in labor. We need to get you to the hospital and see if we can stop it. It's too early."

Dad moved over to me. "What? How can that be?"

The doctor turned toward him. "Kelly has preeclampsia. It's common in first time pregnancies. Sometimes it can cause preterm labor. We'll get her over to the hospital and give her some meds to try and stop it."

My body shook as I processed the news. This wasn't right. Molly was supposed to be with me. What happens if they can't stop the labor? What happens to my baby?

An hour later, I sat on a hospital bed with an IV inserted into my wrist, pumping me full of medication to stop the contractions. Nurses came and went, taking my temperature and monitoring the baby's heartbeat. Lying against the pillows, I turned to Dad. "Did you call Molly yet?"

He sat off to my right in a rocking chair. "No, she and Bethany should be landing soon. I'll let her know when she calls."

I figured he must be nervous because he kept rubbing his face. Did he think I did this on purpose? He watched everything and asked the nurses questions each time they came in.

I hoped this wasn't too much stress for him. "Do you need to go to work today, Dad?"

He shook his head. "No, I'll call them in a bit. I'll just take a vacation day."

Twisting the sheet in my hands, I frowned. I hated that he had to take a vacation day for me. "I'm sorry, Dad. I know you didn't plan on this today."

He came and stood next to me. "Hey, kiddo, you didn't plan on this either. It's going to be all right."

As the hours went by, the contractions subsided. I hoped I could go home, but I found out I would be staying overnight for observation.

My dad looked tired and worn out. I smiled at him. "Why

don't you go home? Keyes and his mother will be stopping by in a couple hours. You should go and get some rest."

Dad sighed and smiled. "Yes, I should go home and let the dog out. Do you want me to pack a bag for you?"

"That'd be great. Could you call Jeanie and tell her I'm here and won't be able to make dinner tonight with the Faltermeiers? Her number is on the refrigerator."

"I'll call her when I get home."

"I'll be fine, Dad. Don't worry."

He hesitated, then gave me a hug and promised to return as soon as he could.

After he left, I prayed he would bring me something that matched and fit. My belly had grown a bit in the past couple of weeks, not enough for me to wear maternity clothes, but I needed to wear bigger T-shirts.

When Keyes and his mother arrived later that night, Keyes showed me a new T-shirt he bought for me.

I held it up. "I think this will fit. In fact it might just swallow me whole."

He blushed. "I told the guy you were pregnant and he recommended this size."

I laughed as I looked down at the sports shirt. "Did you tell him I was having triplets?"

He tried to grab it away. "I can take it back."

I shook my head and hugged it close. "No, it's fine. When this is over, I can use it as PJs."

"Is there room enough for me to lie on the bed next to you?"

I moved over to make room pointing to the tubes. "Sure, just watch all the wires and what not."

We watched TV the next several hours until Dad came back again.

I waved as he came in. "Hi, Dad, is everything all right at home?"

He leaned down and kissed my forehead. "Everything is fine at home. Molly called and Grandpa Claude is out of surgery and doing fine. She told me to tell you she's praying for you and will call you here later tonight, if she can."

Keyes got off the bed and stretched. "I guess my mom and I should get going."

I frowned. "I wish you didn't have to go."

He leaned over and kissed my cheek. "I'll be back tomorrow. That is, if you're still here. Hopefully, you'll be able to go home. Call me and let me know what happens."

As he walked toward the door, I felt abandoned. What if this is just too much for him? He might just leave and never come back. Keyes paused and looked back over his shoulder. I tried not to cry.

He came back to me and placed his hands on my cheeks and kissed my lips. It was brief at first, then deeper. Pulling back he looked into my eyes. "I love you, Kelly. That's never going to change."

Dad cleared his throat, reminding us we weren't alone, but I held Keyes's gaze. "I love you, too."

This time as Keyes walked toward the door, I felt better. He loved me and I loved him, together we could face anything. Right?

***

I stayed in the hospital for two days before being released, happy they had stopped the contractions. I couldn't wait to leave. My doctor restricted my activities until the baby came for safety reasons. I could go to school, but I needed to quit working. I also had to stay off my feet as much as possible.

Dad promised to bring me back in on Friday for another checkup. He seemed to be taking it all in stride. Molly would be back in a few days, but Dad hovered over me. It was nice to know he cared.

I caught up on my schoolwork and managed to still get straight As. I needed to take the tests I missed, so I arrived early at school the next day. Neelie met me as soon as I walked through the door.

She pulled me to the side as other girls filtered in behind me. "When I heard you were in the hospital, I almost lost it. I knew it was too soon. Is everything okay with you and the baby?"

I nodded while patting my stomach. "Yes, I'm fine and the

baby is too. Just a little scare, it's all good now."

Leaning up against the wall she sighed. "Oh good. I was so worried when I heard."

I touched her arm. "I should have called you. I didn't realize the teachers here would tell everyone."

"Don't be mad at them. I asked Mrs. Pattison if she knew anything about you when you didn't show up on Monday and Tuesday." Neelie looked agitated, as if I thought she did something wrong. "She knows we're friends."

I smiled back to reassure her that I wasn't mad. "It's all right, I'm glad she told you."

She smiled. "You can't have your baby before me. I'm due before you."

Laughing I looked down at my belly. "I don't have anymore control over this than you do."

I found it hard to believe we had only met a few months earlier. It seemed like we'd been in the trenches together for years. Now with both of our bellies protruding, we looked like a matched pair. Along with Keyes, she became my last remaining friend. The others had long forgotten me and didn't bother to see how I was doing.

The rest of the week flew by. Before I knew it I returned to the doctor's office for another checkup.

~ ♦♦♦ ~

Chapter 16
The Valley of Death

KELLY'S STORY

Sara, Doctor Berry's nurse, weighed me and took my blood pressure then left. A few minutes later, Dr. Berry walked in with a chart. "How's my favorite patient doing today?"

Heat rushed into my cheeks. "I bet you say that to everyone."

He winked. "Only the ones I like. Let's see how you're doing today, kiddo."

Lying back on the table he ran the Doppler over my stomach. "Nice steady heartbeat there."

After helping me sit up, he thumbed through my chart. He frowned as he flipped back and forth between two pages. "I want you to lie back again on your left side. I'm going to have Sara take your blood pressure again."

My heart raced. I didn't like his tone. "Is something wrong?"

He patted my arm. "No, kiddo, I just want to double-check something. Is Molly out in the waiting room?"

"Yes."

He left the room. I watched the clock, feeling time slow down. When Sara returned, she smiled at me and placed the cuff on my arm. "Hey, don't worry we're just checking it again. It's a little high but that's common after walking from your car."

She chatted on and on, but the word *high* concerned me. *Now what did I do wrong?* As the cuff tightened around my arm, I prayed it would be normal.

When she removed the cuff and jotted the numbers down but made no move to help me sit up.

Sweat dripped down my back. "Is it all right?"

She bit her lip. "I'll let Dr. Berry tell you."

"It's bad?" I couldn't keep the waver out of my voice.

She didn't respond before she left the room. When Dr. Berry returned a few seconds later, I felt like crying. "What is it, Doc? Is the baby all right?"

The grim look on his face had me stuttering. "Is . . . is it bad?"

He smiled at me before folding his hands. "Well, kiddo, your blood pressure is pretty high and you gained seven pounds this past week. What that means is we need to deliver the baby. I've already called the hospital, and you're heading over there now to be induced."

Induced? Hadn't we stopped labor a few weeks ago? Now they want to start it again? A lump formed in my throat. "Isn't it still too early? I'm not due until June sixteenth; it's still May."

He helped me sit up. "I'm not worried about that. I'm more concerned about your health right now, young lady. Toxemia is not something we want to mess around with. The baby has a strong heartbeat, and he should be fine. Now you go and get settled over at the hospital. I'll be over soon."

I returned to the waiting room where Molly waited for me. "I guess Dr. Berry told you?"

She nodded and took my arm. "It's going to be fine, honey."

***

It seemed like déjà vu, when I returned to the hospital. True to his word, Dr. Berry came to see me in my hospital room.

"How you doing, kiddo?"

"All right, I guess."

He checked my pulse. "In a few hours, a nurse is going to come in and add Pitocin to your IV. It's going to put you into labor and hopefully if everything goes right, by this time tomorrow you'll see your baby."

"This is all happening so fast." *Was I ready for this?* I

didn't think so. Tears welled up.

He squeezed my hand. "The Pitocin works quick. It'll kick you into hard labor pretty fast. I want you to try and remain calm, and keep lying on your left side."

I tried to laugh. "Oh sure, I'm seventeen and having a baby. I have no idea what I'm doing, even though I'm choosing adoption. I haven't settled anything, and you want me to be calm?"

"Well, when you put it like that, kid, I guess calm is not the right word."

Wiping a tear, I shrugged. "I just wish I could close my eyes and pretend this was just a dream."

"Sorry, kid, it'll be over soon enough."

After he left, Molly moved a chair closer to my bed. She rubbed my back and neck while keeping up a constant chatter. When a nurse came in to hang the bag of Pitocin, I squeezed her hand.

Watching the drops flow down into my IV, I closed my eyes expecting a contraction to hit. When nothing happened after a few seconds, I opened my eyes and looked back at Molly. "It's not working."

She grinned. "I don't think it's going to happen that fast, honey."

I bit my lip. "I guess not."

The contractions did start a little over an hour later. When the first one hit, it caught me off guard. It felt like a punch to the gut. Panting, I breathed through it

As the contractions kept coming, their intensity and frequency increased late into the night. Molly suggested Dad inform my mother that my labor had started. She arrived at the hospital soon after. I worried how everyone would get along. Would they yell at each other? Or would they be civil? I didn't worry long. Each contraction took all my concentration. They continued through the night with the pain intensifying as each hour passed.

Keyes arrived with his mother early the next morning He helped me with Lamaze breathing, coaching me as best as he could. Molly hovered nearby, holding my other hand and squeezing with each contraction. My mother had left in the early hours before dawn to make sure everything was all right at home but promised to return as soon as she could.

I barely had time to think about anything with the contractions coming every five to seven minutes. Exhausted and spent, I came off the tail end of a contraction and hit the call button for a nurse.

When the nurse entered the room, I told her through pants that I wanted an epidural. She promised to send in the anesthesiologist as soon as she could.

A few minutes later, a man pushed a cart into the room. Never had I been so happy to see someone before. I could've kissed him, but another contraction hit me hard.

He grinned as he watched me thrash in pain. "Havin' a big one, huh? An epidural will help."

Keyes propped me up as the anesthesiologist prepped me for the needle he would be inserting into my back. He handed me a form to sign and told me all about the risks involved with the procedure.

I signed the form as quick as I could and handed it to Dad to sign as well. Once done, a nurse pulled the curtain around the bed to give me some privacy.

Taking a deep breath, I felt the needle prick and a burning sensation. Soon the pain began to fade as the medicine went to work.

As I leaned back against the pillows on my bed, I took a deep breath and closed my eyes. "Thank you so much, Doctor."

He smiled. "Yeah, most pregnant women love me."

I didn't open my eyes. "I bet. Wow, I feel so much better now."

"Good, that's what the medicine is supposed to do. It will wear off in a couple hours."

Wear off? Hopefully, not before I had the baby. I opened my eyes when he pulled the curtain back. Molly waited on the other side and my mother stood next to her.

When Dr. Berry came in, I sighed hoping to hear I was getting closer.

"How's that epidural, kid?"

Smiling, I let out a deep breath of air. "Wonderful."

He chuckled and pulled the curtain closed again. "I need to see what progress you've made. The contractions are coming pretty steady."

He put on gloves, checked me, and frowned. "Well, this changes things."

I raised an eyebrow. "Is everything all right?"

He shook his head and walked over to the machine monitoring my contractions. "You're not progressing. I think we have no choice but to do a C-section."

"I need surgery?" I hadn't even thought about that. What was wrong with me that I couldn't have a normal birth?

"Yes, you do." He said as he pulled the curtain back and announced he would return as soon as he checked the operating room schedule.

Molly took my hand as my mother turned to him. "What do you mean?"

Dr. Berry glanced back at me and raised an eyebrow in question. I shrugged back. "I will be performing a C-section. She isn't progressing."

Mother stared open mouthed at him. "What? Wait, I hardly think she needs surgery."

Dad stepped forward. "Now, Susan, I think Dr. Berry knows what he's doing."

Dr. Berry looked at them and then back and me, shaking his head. Then he walked out of the room.

Mother and Dad argued after he left. Keyes, Molly, and I watched as an uncomfortable atmosphere settled over the room. When the doctor and his nurse returned, they walked right past them and straight to me.

"Okay, kid, we have an O.R. scheduled for nine thirty."

I let the tears fall.

The steady rhythm of the fetal monitor oddly brought me peace. Dr. Berry assured me everything would be fine, and a C-section on someone my age was but a hiccup in the long run. He informed me I could have two people in the operating room with me.

Molly and Keyes hovered nearby listening. When the nurse checked my blood pressure, the room fell silent. The fetal monitor which moments before had tapped a steady rhythm now sat silent. Dr. Berry stopped talking, looked at the monitor, and then at his nurse. Within seconds, the room became a blur of activity. Somewhere in the distance I heard my dad and mother arguing about who would be going into the operating room with me. I heard something about a coin toss before Dr. Berry and a couple of nurses ran with me out of the room. They pushed my bed down the hall as quick as they could. What was going on? It wasn't 9:30 yet.

The overhead lights lining the hallway flew by as we went. Someone dumped an orange brown liquid over my stomach as another used a razor blade to shave me. The next thing I knew I lay in the operating room and Dr. Berry leaned over me with a scalpel in his hand.

Someone called. "She's not draped."

I recognized Dr. Berry's voice. "No time, we have to do it now."

"She doesn't have any anesthesia yet."

"I hope the epidural hasn't worn off."

"Her blood pressure is rising."

What was happening? Why was I in the operating room? I searched the room for clues. Why wouldn't anyone tell me what was going on? I felt pulling and tugging as I closed my eyes tight.

"Kelly, we need to deliver you right now. There's no time."

Tears flowed freely down my cheeks. People talked somewhere in the room. I kept waiting for a cry, but nothing came. "Is my baby all right?"

Nothing. No one said anything. Alarms started sounding. The room blurred, darkened.

Molly stood next to me touching my face with tears streaming down. The room focused for a second, Keyes looked pale like he was ready to pass out.

Alarms still sounded in the distance. "Please, is my baby okay?"

The room blurred again.

I tried to get up but hands held me down. "You need to lie still, Kelly."

"My baby. What's wrong with my baby?"

I couldn't breathe. I needed to know what was going on. What weren't they telling me? I searched the room, frantic for a glimpse of my baby. I saw a group of nurses huddled around a black and blue object. "Tell me."

Another monitor started to scream. "Get that in her now."

I screamed, clawing at the tubes, and tried to get up again. "No, tell me."

Just then, in the midst of alarms screeching, the shrill scream of a newborn baby reached my ears. I stilled on the table and softly uttered, "Thank you, God."

Blackness crept over me as a seizure took me.

Someone said, "We're losing her."

~ ♦♦♦ ~

Chapter 17
The Decision

KELLYS' STORY

I awoke groggy and confused. What had happened? I tried to recall as much as I could. My throat hurt, and I could barely swallow. Blinking, I tried to clear my vision. Without my glasses, everything stayed blurry. Somewhere a monitor held a steady rhythm. Feelings of nausea overwhelmed me. I brought my hand up to my head and felt the tug on the tubes going into my arm.

The movement must have alerted Keyes because suddenly he stood at my side. He placed my glasses on my face. "How do you feel?"

I closed my eyes. Could I even talk? "Thirs . . . ty"

My voice seemed hoarse and it hurt to speak.

Keyes nodded, left the room, and returned with a nurse. She smiled. "I hear you're thirsty, that's good. I'll be back with some ice chips."

I looked over at Keyes afraid to ask, but I needed to know. "Ba . . . by o . . . kay?"

He sat on the bed. "I hear he's doing fine. I haven't seen him yet."

Was something wrong with him? I searched his face for answers. "Wh . . . y?"

My throat felt like I swallowed a cactus. I closed my eyes against the pain, grinding my jaw.

I felt his hand on my arm. "Don't talk. The doctor said your throat would be sore for a while. The baby's fine, I promise. I didn't go see him yet, because I wanted to see him with you."

I pointed to the clock.

He raised an eyebrow with a shrug. I gestured sleep with my hands and then pointed back to the clock.

His eyes lit up. "Oh. How long were you out?"

I nodded.

He scrunched up his face. "It's been about two and half hours now, maybe more."

The nurse came back in with a cup of ice chips. I smiled my thanks, as I popped one into my mouth. It felt wonderful on my throat. I reached for another.

She held my wrist and checked my pulse. She eyed me while I scooped more ice. "Not too fast, you need to go slow at first. I'll give you some pain medication through your IV in just a second."

I nodded as I swallowed the melt off from the ice shavings. The nurse plunged a needle into the IV. My eyelids felt heavy. I fought against it, frantically searching for Keyes.

He took my hand. "I'm here, don't fight it. I'm not going anywhere."

I took a deep breath and smiled as darkness fell over me.

I awoke again sometime later and found Keyes sitting with his head leaning up against the wall, his eyes closed. I swallowed and tested to see if the pain remained. It hurt, only not as bad as before. I found myself in a different room now, the blinds were drawn shut, but I could still see a stream of light filter through them.

A knock sounded on the door. Dr. Berry stared at me with a strange little smile on his face. "Well, kid, I think you scared ten years off my life. I'll tell you one thing. Someone above must be looking down on you because you and that baby shouldn't be here."

I just stared back at him, afraid to say anything.

He stepped closer. "You'll be sore for a bit. I had to put a tube down your throat. It was touch and go there for a while when you seized on the table and your baby wasn't breathing. I honestly didn't think you were going to make it, let alone the baby."

He squeezed my hand. "Yet, here you are."

The baby wasn't breathing? Tears poured. "Ba . . . by ok . . . ay?"

He nodded and pressed my call button. "Bring the Frank baby in, please."

He moved over to my monitor. "I need to check your incision real quick."

Moving my gown and blanket aside he pulled back the bandage and nodded. "Looks good, I'm going to send you down to X-ray though, to make sure we didn't leave anything inside. We had to do everything in a hurry. I'll be in to check on you again later."

Keyes woke up just as he left. He came and sat next to me holding my hand. A nurse came in a minute later with our baby.

I cried when the nurse handed him to me and teardrops fell on his arm. How could this little man be mine? He was perfect. As his tiny little face peered out from the blanket, I knew instantly I had never loved something as much as I loved him. I carefully unwound his blanket and inspected him from head to toe. I counted ten tiny toes and fingers, a patch of dark hair and a face too beautiful to be real. How could I ever let him go?

When the nurse returned to take him back to the nursery to be fed, I asked if I could feed him. She glanced at me and then away. "I'm not sure it's a good idea for you to spend too much time with him."

"Why?" He was my baby, and I had waited nine months to meet him.

She sucked in a deep breath before looking at me. "We try to discourage new mothers who are choosing adoption from spending a lot of time with their babies. It helps them not to get too attached."

I glanced at Keyes. He shrugged his shoulders. How dare they tell me what I could and couldn't do with my baby?

"I want to feed my baby."

My parents entered the room at the right moment. Dad glanced between me and the nurse. "What's going on?"

I turned toward him. "They won't let me feed him."

The nurse tried to take my baby from me, but I pulled him tight against my chest causing him to cry. "I want to feed my baby."

Dad stepped forward. "I don't see why she can't feed her own baby."

The nurse pulled back and rolled her eyes. "Fine, but you'll be sorry later."

She muttered something under her breath as she left the room. I could only make out teenage mother.

Alex began to cry in earnest now, and I pushed the call button. "Can I please have a bottle, so I can feed my baby?"

A few moments later, a different nurse entered the room with a bottle in her hand. She smiled, and I liked her right away. After nine months of people looking down their noses at me, I felt glad I had stood up to the other nurse.

Taking the bottle, I tried to get more comfortable. The pain from my incision hurt, but I wasn't about to pass up a chance to feed my baby. The nurse found me a pillow to lay him on while I scooted back against the tilted bed. Finally comfortable, I gently placed the nipple of the bottle in his mouth. It took a few tries, but he caught on quick.

When he finished, I placed him up against my shoulder and gently patted his back. When he let out a loud belch, I smiled triumphantly back at Keyes. I could do this. I couldn't walk yet, so I handed him to Keyes to change his diaper. Soon afterward, the baby rested back in my arms, sound asleep. My parents hovered around me snapping photos of us and salivating at a chance to hold him. Finally, when I felt too fatigued to continue holding him, I handed him off to Dad.

Dad's eyes lit up as he held my tiny baby. He cooed at him and held him close. Molly wiped tears away as she snapped photos of them. When a nurse came in to take him back to the nursery, I shook my head no.

Keyes cleared his throat. "Maybe we should let him go there for a while. You need to recover."

I shook my head again. "No, I want Alex to stay with me."

Dad moved closer still holding him. "Honey, do you think that's a good idea?"

"I want him to stay, so that I know what kind of work I will be in for, if I change my mind." How come they didn't get it?

I had to do this my way.

Dad tried again. "No one doubts you love this child, Kelly. We're all just trying to help. It's going to be harder if he is here all the time."

Molly piped in. "I agree with your dad, honey."

Tears streamed down my cheeks. "Please, I have to do this my way. I know you guys don't understand. You have to trust me."

Dad opened his mouth but hesitated. "All right, we'll do it your way."

I smiled at him as he handed Alex back to me.

Later that night, after everyone had left, I stared down at my sleeping child in wonder. Glancing at the clock, I knew the nurses would be in to get me up walking in a while. Each time I stood up, searing pain ricocheted through my body. Seeing Alex in the bassinet cart kept me going. Pushing through the pain, I walked around and around the hallway keeping him with me always.

***

NANCY'S STORY

Late May 1993

Drying my dishpan hands on a towel, I reached for the ringing phone. "Hello?"

"Nancy, this is Jeanie from Adoption Services. How are you today?"

"Fine. What's up?"

"Well, I'm calling to inform you that Kelly gave birth to a baby boy yesterday."

"Really? I didn't think she was due yet."

"Guess the baby thought it was time. Both baby and mother are doing fine and are still in the hospital. The plan is the baby will go into cradle care when the birth mom leaves the hospital. That's a foster care situation. If it looks like the birth mom is going to go through with the adoption plan, you will be allowed to visit the baby."

"Okay."

"We'll let you know if she relinquishes the child to cradle care."

"Okay. We'll be waiting on pins and needles."

"I'll talk to you later, hopefully with good news. Bye."

I hung up the phone and strolled down the hall. A mixture of feelings hit me. I squelched a pang of excitement, telling myself the baby boy was not mine, yet. I looked into the den that would be his room and panicked. I hadn't turned it into a baby's room yet. Should I get busy? I decided against it. It would be an unbearable disappointment if she kept the baby. No, I'd wait until the baby was in cradle care.

A twinge of guilt passed over me as Kelly's smiling face came to mind. Why should our joy come forth from her sorrow? *Lord, please be with Kelly. Give her wisdom with the decision ahead of her and give her the strength to do your will, whatever that may be. I pray for Your will to be done. Not mine.*

Wiping tears, I turned away from the "would-be nursery." An imagined scene of someone whisking away from me my infant daughter tore at my heart. I shook the unimaginable scenario from my mind. *If Kelly gives us her son, help me, Lord, to be always mindful of her pain.*

***

KELLY'S STORY

Over the following three days in the hospital, I fed and changed Alex, while keeping him in the room with me. When I had to get an X-ray, I reluctantly left him in the nursery but asked for him as soon as I returned. I knew the hospital staff thought I must have been crazy, but deep down I knew it needed to be that way.

The hospital administrator came to see me on the second day. She smiled when she entered my room. "Hi, Kelly, my name is Angie, and I need to file your paperwork. I know this is a difficult time for you, but I need a name for the birth certificate."

Why were they asking me? "I thought the adoptive parents would name him."

"Well, they do, but we need a name now for his original

birth certificate."

There was only one name for him. "Alexander Aaron."

She raised an eyebrow. "You don't want to think about it?"

"No, it's the name I picked for him when I found out I was having a boy."

She smiled. "It's a good name. I've got it down and will file the paperwork now. I'll let you rest."

"Thanks."

After she left, I looked down at Alex sleeping in his bassinet. "I hope if I do this that you'll understand one day. I'm doing this for you. I just want you to have everything that I can't give you right now. I hope you won't hate me for it."

The nights were the hardest. Walking the halls, I grappled with what I should do. The floor took on a ghostly quiet. Most of the new mothers had gone home with their babies. In some ways it helped knowing there were no new mothers in the rooms next to mine, cooing over their newborns waiting to take them home. Being isolated kept me alone with my thoughts, and those thoughts kept me awake. Feelings of guilt and betrayal followed me wherever I went. How could I do this? Would the baby understand why? Would I regret this for the rest of my life?

One night, I called Molly at two in the morning hysterical. She drove to the hospital to be with me.

I was helpless as she walked in the door. "I don't know. I don't know if I can do this."

She wiped tears away. "I know, honey. I'll support you in whatever you decide."

She wrapped her arms around me and let me sob into her shoulder. When Alex stirred, she picked him up from his bassinet. I pushed the call button and requested a bottle. Watching her look down at him made me sigh. I had her support. When the nurse came in with the bottle, I handed it to Molly. "Would you feed him? I need to go to the bathroom."

She resisted at first but then reached for the bottle. She spoke soft words to him as I made my way to the bathroom. I hadn't had any pain medicine for a while and each movement hurt.

When I returned, Alex had practically inhaled his bottle and rested up against Molly's shoulder. "He's a good eater, that's for sure."

After he let out a couple of good burps, she handed him to me so that I could change his diaper. He soon fell asleep once again.

Molly frowned as she helped me back into bed. "You look dead on your feet. Why don't you get some sleep? I'll stay and watch over Alex."

I fought against my sagging eyelids. "Thanks . . . Molly."

Alex cried a few hours later, jarring me awake. Molly changed him and talked to him.

I asked. "How long did I sleep?"

"A few hours, don't worry, Alex is fine. I fed him and changed him. You needed some rest."

How lucky was I, that I had Molly? I yawned. "Thanks, Molly."

She placed him into my arms. "He stared up at me for a while before going back to sleep."

Molly sat next to me staring at us. "I have to get going. Do you want me to come by later when you're discharged today?"

I shook my head but kept staring at Alex. "Keyes is coming to get me, with a friend. I think it's better to not have anyone else here."

"Okay, I'll be waiting at home for you."

I glanced up at her. "Thanks, Molly, for coming and for . . . everything."

She brushed away a tear. "Of course, you're my daughter. I wouldn't be anywhere else."

A lone tear trailed down my cheek. If only I could be somewhere else.

After she left, I stared out my window, watching raindrops pelt against the glass. Today my heart would be shattered into a million pieces. Keyes would be here soon, so I dressed and I relished the time alone with Alex. I fed him and changed him once again, only this time I changed him into an outfit I had bought for him. Tiny blue airplanes were scattered all over it. I found it a few months back and knew I must buy it for him. I hoped the new parents would keep the outfit.

It took a while for me to figure out what I thought would

be the best plan. I agreed to place Alex in cradle care for two weeks, so that I could be completely sure of my decision.

When the social worker called early that morning to tell me what time she would arrive, I grew nauseated. Could I give my child to a stranger? Or to anyone?

I held Alex close, kissing and hugging him, hoping to leave some part of me with him. Does he know how much I love him? Could he feel that love?

I dreaded the moment the social worker would arrive. Keyes showed up right before she did.

When a woman walked in with a car seat in her arms, I wanted to run away as fast as I could with Alex. I pulled him closer.

"Hi, Kelly. I'm Amy from Social Services." She showed me her badge. "I'll be taking your baby to a foster mother."

A lump in my throat forced tears to flood over. I looked down at Alex sleeping in my arms. *How do I make myself walk to her?* Each step toward her felt like my feet were encased in lead. My chest ached as I struggled to breathe. My heart began to fracture like thin ice cracking under my weight. She reached for Alex. I just couldn't let him go. I pulled back. *I can't do this, Lord, help me, please.*

I stood there paralyzed by grief. Openly weeping I looked to Keyes for comfort. He too fought tears as he stepped forward and put his arm around my shoulders, giving me strength. I tried handing Alex to Amy once again, but my arms wouldn't let go.

She watched and waited. "It's okay, Kelly. Take your time. I know this is hard."

What a horrible job she had! How could she stand taking babies away from their mothers? I closed my eyes as I held Alex out for her to take. *I can do this, I think.* When she took him from me, my arms felt empty and I longed to snatch him back. I fought the urge to yell at her to give him back.

Amy placed Alex in the car seat and buckled him in. He looked too tiny. I felt the light of life leave me, and I thought I would die.

Amy handed me papers. "You need to sign on this line."

My hand trembled so bad I barely held onto the pen. The

pen shook in my hand as the ink bled with my tears on the paper. *How do you expect me to hold a pen let alone sign my name?* Somehow I signed something close to my name, and Amy took the paper. She grabbed the car seat and swiftly left the room.

I collapsed.

The cold floor enveloped me as I heard her footsteps echo away. *What have I done?*

Keyes patted my back, lost for words. Finally, he said. "It will be all right."

He lied.

How could he think it was going to be all right? Anger welled up with in me, and I longed to lash out at him. He couldn't possibly understand how I felt. The other part of me knew he was just trying to be supportive. Didn't he realize a huge piece of my heart had just been ripped out and carried away? It would never be okay.

They released me soon after Alex left. I took the long walk down the hall, passing other new mothers holding their babies. I hated their happiness. My arms were empty while theirs were full. Keyes led the way, and I trailed behind him, not caring where I was going. Before Alex's birth, he had been the one person I loved most in the world. Because of that love, I now lived the worst possible day of my life.

***

I wanted to die.

My swollen abdomen ached in emptiness. My soul shattered like a thousand shards of glass, cutting deep as they pierced my inner core. The child I sheltered in my womb for the past nine months was gone. Life held little meaning to me now. The hollowness within engulfed me into a dark void. I wept for a dream that couldn't be. The roar of blood pulsed through my ears beating a mantra I didn't want to hear.

My breasts, heavy and laden with milk, protested against the ace bandage that bound them. There would no longer be a baby to relieve them of their heavy burden. I stood before the window of my bedroom and the images outside blurred.

So this was loss. How did anyone survive this?

My hand trembled as I reached for the phone on my desk. The number I knew by heart. I tried to dial, only to fumble and dial the wrong number. Over and over again I attempted the call that must be made. Against my will the familiar voice on the other end of the line crackled forth.

"This is Jeanie."

I swallowed past the mountain lodged in my throat. "It's me."

"Kelly? I've been so worried about you, how are you?"

"Not good."

"Is there anything I can do?"

"Yes." The words fell out in a constricted voice. "Call Nancy . . . and . . . John. Tell them . . . they have a son."

"Are you sure?"

Holding back sobs, I forced the word I didn't want to say. "Yes."

"If you need time to think about it . . ."

My whole body trembled. I closed my eyes to form the words. "No, it's right, he's their son now. I have to go."

I hung up before she could say another word. I curled into a fetal position on my bed and sobbed. The hollow feeling in my chest hurt beyond words, yet I knew in my heart I'd done the right thing. Alex deserved a life I couldn't give him, and if I truly loved him, I had to let him go. I would not bring him into my own life of rejection. No, I had to let him go.

Perhaps it was those moments of truth that began to mend my broken heart. Looking back twenty-two years now, I know I did the right thing. I'll never regret giving Alex (renamed Bryan) up. I have been fortunate enough to be a part of his life these past years. I didn't raise him, but he'll always hold a place in my heart. I'm grateful to his parents for raising him to be the man he is today.

Keyes and I broke up not long after the adoption became finalized. I finished high school and then graduated from college where I met my husband. God's hand surrounded me. Looking back now, I can see fully just how much God has intervened in my life.

Chapter 18
Doubt

NANCY'S STORY

May 31, 1993

John drove slowly down the street as we searched houses for the address written on a slip of paper.

I pointed to a middle-class home with a manicured lawn. "There it is."

He parked in front of the home.

I sucked in a deep breath and smiled at him as a swarm of butterflies invaded my tummy. "Are you ready for this?"

He gave a nod. "Ready as I'll ever be."

"Shall we go meet our son?"

Opening his door, he said. "Let's go."

I turned to Brianna in the backseat. "Want to meet your baby brother?"

She grinned and shook her head vigorously.

We made our way to the front door and rang the doorbell.

A middle-aged woman answered the door and smiled. "You must be John and Nancy.

We nodded. "Yes."

"Come in. It's about time for the baby's feeding. In fact, his diaper probably needs changing."

We followed her into the entryway and down a short hall. She stopped at a double door closet where the door stood half ajar and pointed inside. "It looks like he's waking up."

I peered inside to find the closet twice as deep as a normal closet. A wooden cradle sat against the wall and a short chest of drawers sat next to the tiny bed. A newborn squirmed in the cradle.

"Oh, Brianna, there he is."

The cradle care mom motioned for me to enter the tiny makeshift room. "You can pick him up, and I've set up the laundry room where you can change him."

I gently picked up the baby. He opened his sleepy eyes and peered at me as if he understood I was someone special.

The cradle mom moved toward the end of the hall. "Come this way."

She led us into a large kitchen and to a room on the left, a large laundry room with a good-sized bank of windows to one side. She had turned the countertop into a changing table. The woman pointed to the counter. "You can change his diaper and give him a bottle. Everything you need is next to the sink. I'll leave you to get acquainted."

As she left, I laid the baby on the towels she'd laid out for him. "Hi, little one. I'm your new mommy." I motioned toward John. "This is your new daddy." John picked up Brianna so she could see. "And this is your big sister Brianna."

The baby yawned but studied my face. John sidled up beside me and slipped his index finger into his tiny hand. As the baby clutched his finger, John wiggled it. "Hello there, I'm your dad."

I removed the blanket from around him. "Do you need your diaper changed?"

The baby fussed a bit.

"I guess so. Or are you hungry?"

John snapped a picture as I changed him.

After changing his diaper, I handed him to John, who cooed at him. I snapped a picture of them before making a bottle of formula. A love seat awaited us just outside the laundry room. I sat down and grinned up at John. "Okay, hand him over. I get to feed him first."

John laid him into my arms. "No fair, you always get to go first."

"That's because I'm the mom."

Brianna climbed up beside me. "He's cute."

The baby drank the bottle with eyes fixed on my face.

I examined his small round face. "I thought he would be bigger. Kelly and Keyes are both tall."

John took a seat on a kitchen chair beside me and peered at the baby. "I'm sure he'll outgrow us both someday."

I rocked the baby. "Probably so. We need to decide on a name. What do you think about Skylar?"

"No way. I'm not naming my kid some offbeat name like that. Do I get to feed him?"

Hesitant, I handed him the baby, and we changed places.

I squeezed the baby's little foot poking out from under the blanket. "He seems like a mellow baby. He's only whimpered once since we arrived."

John gave a wide grin. "Yeah, Brianna would've wailed the moment she woke up."

Brianna tugged at my leg. "I want to hold him."

John gave me the baby, and I held him on her lap as John snapped a picture. Then I held the baby until he fell asleep, wanting to sit and hold him forever. I certainly didn't want to put him back into the closet turned nursery. Struggling to give him up, I argued with myself that a few more days would be nothing. After all, I'd waited two and a half months to bring Brianna home from the hospital.

I scooted to the edge of the couch and sighed. "Guess we probably should go. This little guy's nursery needs to be put together, so we'll be ready for him at the end of the week."

John stood. "I'll get the cradle mom."

Brianna and I kissed the baby and laid him back into his cradle. The moment was bittersweet, but we would bring our new baby home on Friday.

***

Friday, June 4, 1993

We rose early. Who could sleep in on a day such as this? We would be bringing our new baby boy home this afternoon. After much discussion, we'd settled on a name just the evening before.

After breakfast, I rushed around making last minute touches to the nursery as the phone rang.

John answered the phone. "Hello? . . . Hi Bonnie . . . This morning? I think we can arrange a sitter for our daughter. At ten o'clock? We'll be there."

He hung up and made his way into the nursery. He shrugged. "The adoption agency wants us to come in for a meeting this morning."

I frowned. "Did they say why?"

"No. Do you think your sister will watch Brianna this morning?"

"I'll call her. Do you think Kelly has changed her mind?"

***

At the adoption agency, they ushered us into a conference room and closed the door. The room was thick with tension. Several social workers sat with Bonnie.

After an uncomfortable pause, Bonnie spoke. "We don't think you are ready to adopt."

A semitruck hit me head-on. A host of sudden tears readied themselves to escape. My heart pummeled my chest as my throat constricted tight enough to cut off air. "What?"

"We don't think you are ready to adopt."

I looked dumbfounded at John, who sat quite collected next to me.

He cleared his throat. "I . . . I don't understand."

~ ♦♦♦ ~

Chapter 19
Entwined

NANCY'S STORY

June 4, 1993 continued . . .

We sat in silence. Uneasiness dominated the room at Adoption Services. I struggled against the urge to sob. What did she mean they didn't think we were ready to adopt? Was this an affront to our Christianity? Anger welled to a fevered pitch, but I held onto my composure like a pit bull.

John's calm voice broke the awkward silence. "Who has concerns about us? The cradle mom?"

Bonnie nodded in the affirmative. "Yes."

He sat back in his chair. "We aren't demonstrative people. Nancy didn't show a lot of emotion when we left the baby, but you need to understand, we waited two and a half months to bring Brianna home from the hospital. A good share of that time, we weren't certain we would be bringing her home at all. We've had to wait a mere ten days for this baby. Besides, he's healthy. Ten days is nothing compared to what we've been through."

A collective sigh of relief and understanding passed throughout the room.

Bonnie's face softened. "We didn't think of that. I see your perspective now. I apologize for the anxiety we've put you through. We just had to be sure. Since that's settled, we'll see you back here at two o'clock to pick up your son. What are you naming him?

I wiped away tears of release. "We're naming him Bryan

Aaron."

Bonnie smiled as she stood. "I like that name. We'll see you in a few hours."

***

At two o'clock we arrived at the adoption agency once again. Everyone was all smiles this time. They instructed us to sit and wait in the very room we had been in earlier that day. I fiddled with the outfit for Bryan they had instructed us to bring.

Brianna crawled into John's lap. "Where's the baby?"

I shared her impatience. "They'll bring him in soon. I'm sure."

After fifteen long minutes, people from the agency filed in and sat around a low table in the middle of the room. Finally, Bonnie entered carrying the baby. "Let's get a picture of this little family."

John sat in a rocking chair and Bonnie gave him baby Bryan. Brianna climbed into his lap next to her baby brother, and I sat next to John. Everyone awed and cooed as someone snapped a picture.

Bonnie laid a folded blanket over the coffee table in the center of the room. "Change him into the clothes you brought, and you can take him home."

I took Bryan from John, laid him on the table, and knelt down. Everyone watched as I removed the pajamas he wore and dressed him in a blue and white outfit with white booties. Everyone laughed and cooed over him, forgetting the rigid meeting that had taken place earlier in the day.

I looked at John as I picked little Bryan up. "He's ready to go home, Papa."

After shaking hands with everyone and saying our good-byes, we walked away and into our new life with our son.

***

As we pulled up in front of our house, my sister and her family had mounted two banners in our picture window. One said, *Welcome Home Bryan,* the other said, *Big Sister Day, Brianna.* We were greeted by extended family as we brought our new son home. Even a neighborhood cat snuck in to take a peek at him. We all sat around smiling.

Our little family was complete.

***

Mid-June

I fiddled with the present I held on my lap. Inside the box and colored paper, lay a white teddy bear donned with a gold necklace. One half of a Mizpah coin hung from the gold chain. Bryan's name, engraved on the back, seemed like the most meaningful "Thank you" gift I could come up with. I would keep a similar necklace with the other half of the gold coin for Bryan. Kelly's name graced the back of his necklace. When the two halves were put together, a verse from Genesis could be read: *The Lord watch between me and thee while we are absent from one another.*

I hoped the gift would bring some measure of comfort to Kelly as we pulled into the parking lot of the restaurant. We had arranged to meet Kelly and Keyes for dinner, since we hadn't had the chance to do it before Bryan's birth. As we strolled across the parking lot, we found Kelly closing the door to her car.

I waved a hello to her. "Looks like perfect timing."

She smiled and glanced at the tall and handsome, teenage boy standing on the opposite side of the car.

John stepped forward and gave the young man his hand.

Keyes seemed uncomfortable with our handshakes as his eyes shifted to Kelly. "Nice to meet you." I looked up at him. "It's a nice evening, isn't it?"

John motioned to the restaurant. "Why don't we go on inside?"

Once seated, John turned to Keyes. "Are you still in high school?"

"Yeah."

Kelly broke in. "Yes, we're both seniors now. We used to go to the same school, until I had to attend a school for unwed mothers." A waitress brought menus. I opened mine and gazed at Kelly. "So tell us about yourselves. We didn't get a lot of time to talk about you the last time we met."

"Well, I'm adopted."

"Really, I had no idea."

"Yes, I am. But I look like my family. Nobody knows I'm adopted. I have a bunch of sisters and brothers. Sometimes people think my sister is the adopted one, instead of me."

John entered the conversation. "You're the only one who is adopted?"

"Yes, right after they adopted me my mother got pregnant."

Kelly smiled and talked on, giving no hint of the emotion I suspected lay beneath the surface. She seemed content with the decision to give us her baby. Did she grasp the permanent nature of her choice?

I handed Kelly the present. "I'd like to give this to you. It's a small token to show our gratitude."

She opened the gift and pulled out the teddy bear wearing the necklace. "Thank you. How sweet."

I showed her the other necklace. "I'm keeping the other half of the Mizpah coin with your name inscribed on the back, for Bryan."

She examined the necklace I would keep for Bryan. "That's nice."

"Did I spell your name right?"

"No, but that's all right."

"Really? I'm so sorry. I didn't think about that there were multiple spellings until now."

"Don't worry. I run into that all the time."

The rest of the evening, we shared a pleasant conversation with Kelly as Keyes sat quietly by. He gave only the short answer to our questions, content to let Kelly do most of the talking. I was amazed at how composed and cheerful Kelly presented herself. Her demeanor mystified me.

Would she change her mind when she grasped the finality of what she was about to do?

***

Father's Day – 1993

John held Bryan as we sat toward the back of the sanctuary. I'd dressed Bryan in a little white summer outfit, light blue socks, and tiny white shoes.

I eyed the people coming into the church, looking for Kelly and Keyes. We would be dedicating Bryan today, and had invited them to stand with us for his dedication. It was important to John and me that Bryan would have the heritage of both sets of parents dedicating him to the Lord.

Finally, I spotted them as they entered. I waved at them as they found seats nearby. As we stood together in front of the congregation, Pastor George shared that this was the first time in the history of Faith Bible Chapel that both the birth and adoptive parents stood together to dedicate a baby.

We stood in unity and dedicated Bryan to the Lord. I couldn't help but reflect on the goodness of God. Even today, He deals in the affairs of men. And if we trust Him with our broken lives, He will take our pain, sorrow, and mistakes and turn them into a thing of beauty, joy, and praise

PART TWO
White Diamonds

Study Journal

On Infertility and Adoption

Isaiah 54:1—3

"Shout for joy, O barren one, you who have borne no child;
Break forth into joyful shouting and cry aloud,
you who have not travailed;
For the sons of the desolate one will be more numerous
Than the sons of the married woman," says the Lord.
Enlarge the place of your tent;
Stretch out the curtains of your dwellings, spare not;
Lengthen your cords and strengthen your pegs.
For you will spread abroad to the right and to the left.
And your descendants will possess nations . . .

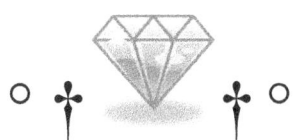

White Diamonds

Introduction

A few years ago, John and I were privileged to vacation in Great Britain. One of the places we visited was the London Tower. We both love history and the London Tower was filled with stories of bygone days. As we explored the compound, sparse groups of visitors milled about. We entered the Waterloo Barracks and came upon a large group of people standing in "queue," as the Brits call it. We took our place in line wondering what was so intriguing that such a crowd had gathered there. After time in line we came upon a sign stating "The Crown Jewel Exhibit."

John was not thrilled. The line moved at a snail's pace, and he wanted to skip the display, but my interest was piqued. After all, being a woman who loves jewelry, we couldn't be this close to the Crown Jewels and not see them. Finally, we entered the darkened room with lighted glass cases housing the precious ornaments of the British Monarchy. We then understood why the line moved so slowly.

Glorious gold and silver, jewel-encrusted pieces gleamed and sparkled in the light. Jewel studded swords, ceremonial maces, orbs, scepters, trumpets and tunics, along with the coronation spoon dazzled us. Then we came to the diamond covered crowns. Thousands of diamonds glittered, reflecting the light with prisms of color. What a magnificent sight! Each stone was fit for a king.

Then it hit me. God desires us to be like diamonds. His goal for us is to be pure brilliance, reflecting His light to a dark world.

In this study, we are going to use the analogy of diamonds as we explore what God has for us concerning infertility and adoption. So prepare yourself to get down and dirty. Grab your pickax and shovel, and let's go mining for the gems the Lord wants to unearth in our lives. Dig deep. His wondrous world of precious diamonds awaits.

~ ♦♦♦ ~

Lesson One
Graphite:
The Stuff of Diamonds

*Consider it all joy, my brethren, when you encounter various trials,
knowing that the testing of your faith produces endurance.
And let endurance have its perfect result,
so that you may be perfect and complete, lacking in nothing.*
James 1:2–4

The Story of Diamonds

Do you have a diamond ring, a pair of diamond earrings, or another piece of jewelry with a diamond? If you do, go get the gem, along with a lead pencil.

Do you have the items?

Take a good look at the diamond. Does the diamond sparkle and reflect the light with glints of color here and there? Look at the lead in the pencil. Does the lead look anything like the diamond? Of course not. Graphite is dull, black, and absorbs light.

Can one write a letter with a diamond? No, because the diamond is the hardest natural substance on earth and does not leave part of itself on the paper. However, graphite is soft and pliable, and it leaves its mark wherever it is put to paper. So, you may be thinking, what's the point?

Did you know graphite and diamonds are made of the same stuff? They are both composed of carbon atoms.[1] So what's up?

This is the difference. Through great hardship, the carbon atoms of the diamond are rearranged into cubic structures or a lattice type framework.[2] This gives the diamond the opposite characteristics of graphite.

The word diamond comes from the ancient Greek word *adamas*, which means unbreakable or invincible.[3] Because of Adam and Eve's sin, each one of us are born with a graphite heart, darkened and broken by sin, but the Lord wants to develop in us hearts like diamonds. He wants our hearts hard and unbreakable toward disobedience and full of his light. Just like the carbon atoms must be rearranged to be turned to diamond, the Lord rearranges our perspectives, priorities, and values. How does He do this? One of the tools He uses is pressure.

Every natural diamond was once a lump of ordinary carbon or graphite. As God formed the earth, deposits of carbon or graphite was laid deep beneath the earth's crust, down in the mantle, eighty-seven to one hundred twenty miles below the surface of the earth.[4] The weight of all that rock and earth causes at least 435,113 pounds per square inch of pressure.[5] Can we even imagine what that would feel like?

Have you experienced a time in your life when it seemed like tons of pressure bore down upon you?

Another tool God uses to transform our hearts from carbon or graphite to diamonds is heat. Not only did a diamond experience great pressure, but it also was exposed to heat—extreme heat.[6] They believe that heat to be somewhere from 900°C to 1300°C. Those numbers convert to a scorching 1,652 to 2,372 degrees Fahrenheit![7]

Have you encountered a trial where you felt you were under extreme pressure and heat? The best way to get the most out of this study is to have a notebook handy to write down your answers.

Avoiding the Blame Game

When we encounter intense situations, we wonder if God has forgotten us. In those times we wonder if God still deals in the affairs of mankind. Does He care? Often times, our adversary the devil tries to convince us God cares for others, but He is not mindful of us. I can assure you everyone entertains these feelings at some point in their lives.

Does God use infertility for His purposes? What does the Bible say about adoption? Are these feelings and questions valid? Let's see if they are. We're going to mine for the diamond facets of truth. Let's ask the Lord to guide our search.

Please lead us, Lord, to the treasure trove of Your truth. Help us discover diamond facets of understanding for the paths we walk. Give us insight to see Your hand moving in our lives and to discover Your love, grace, and mercy. May our hearts be willing to accept the direction You are leading us. Fill us with joy and strength for the journey.

Can you remember a time in your life when you didn't understand what the Lord was doing, but in the end you now can see His gracious hand?

1. Does that experience remind you He is at work in your life? Write about that experience.
2. In chapter four of our story, Nancy wrestled with many feelings regarding her infertility. What were the struggles and pressures she felt?
3. In Genesis 1:28 God gives mankind His first commandment. He said to Adam and Eve to "be fruitful and multiply, and fill the earth." If you are dealing with infertility, how does that verse make you feel? Does that command put you under pressure?
4. Often childless couples must work through feelings of inferiority, hurt, and wondering if they fit into a world of friends with children. Be honest. How do you feel when the heat of infertility is turned up?
5. Read Genesis 3:16–19. When Adam and Eve bit into the apple, they brought sin into the entire world. What was the consequence of Eve's sin?
6. What was the consequence of Adam's sin?
7. Continue reading Genesis 3:20–24. What other consequences come to both of them because of their sin?

This is the truth of the matter. Romans 3:23 tells us, "For all have sinned and fall short of the glory of God."

How many sinned? That's right: **ALL**.

We must remember that all those couples with children are guilty of sinning just as you and I do. Many unwanted consequences such as illnesses, barrenness, and death have befallen us because sin exists in the world. Not all consequences of sin are related to a person's own failings. For example, innocent babies are born with genetic diseases and deformities, yet have not yet sinned. Terrible things happen because sin has entered our world. The same can be true for a couple seeking a child.

Diamond Facet of Truth
If God punished sin with barrenness, where would we be?
There would be no mankind. Adam and Eve
would have remained childless.

8. In John 8:44 Jesus tells us the devil is a liar and is the father of lies. Based on this Scripture, what lies does the enemy tell us about our infertility? Do you think the enemy would like us to blame our spouses? If so, what can the enemy accomplish by you blaming your spouse?
9. What lies did Nancy believe?
10. What lies has the enemy tried to defeat you with?

Diamond Facet of Truth
Jesus tells us Satan is a liar.

There are, however, a few personal sins connected to barrenness in the Old Testament. Leviticus 20:20–21 tells us that if a man takes his uncle's wife or a man takes his brother's wife, they shall die childless. This excluded the custom of the day, that if one's brother died, he held an obligation to marry his brother's wife, but if he engaged in an adulterous affair with his sister-in-law or his uncle's wife, they would bear the penalty.

The Lord also gave Moses an "adultery test" for a priest to administer if a man suspected his wife of unfaithfulness. It is spelled out in Numbers 5:11–28. The wife would be taken to the priest to drink water mixed with dust from the tabernacle floor. If this bitter water did not make her generative parts (they called them the *thigh*) waste away and her abdomen to swell, then she would be proved innocent. She would be able to conceive children. These Scriptures are the only mentions of personal sin implying a barrenness connection.

You may be asking yourself, "What if I'm guilty of one of the sins mentioned in the Old Testament? Is there no hope for me?"

I have good news. Galatians 3:13 says, "Christ redeemed us from the curse of the Law, having become a curse for us." If you have repented of your sin and given your life to Christ, you are no longer under the curse of the Law. Thank You, Jesus!

If you are saying to yourself, "I'm not sure I'm right with God," there is still a great hope. First John 1:9 says this: "If we confess our sins, He is faithful and righteous to forgive us our sins and to cleanse us from all unrighteousness." That is what Jesus' death on the cross was all about. I encourage you to give yourself wholly and completely to Jesus and turn away from sin. Write a prayer from your heart. Ask forgiveness, and embark on a relationship with Christ that will last forever.

There is only one instance in Scripture where God used infertility as a judgment. Israel was worshiping an idol called Baal-peor in Hosea 9:10–17. Part of their judgment included infertility issues. The worship of this idol consisted of rites of sexual immorality, self-torture, and human sacrifice. The curses that came upon them appear—at least partially—the consequences of their promiscuous lifestyle.

What do you think are the consequences of such a lifestyle?

God is faithful to forgive us of our sins, yet we may still be dealing with the physical consequences of our sin. We must remind ourselves, however, that those consequences will not follow us into eternity. Remember, God is a merciful God. Thank You, Jesus!

> 11. Read Galatians 6:7–8. What did Kelly reap as an undesired consequence from her mistake?

Not Satisfied?

Nancy wanted God to take away her desire for a child. She struggled against a deep-seated longing that seemed illogical to her. Why couldn't she just go on with her life and forget having a baby? The Scripture below sheds light on this issue.

> 1. Proverbs 30:15–16 speaks of four things that will not be satisfied. How does this Scripture compare the barren womb to the grave, the dry earth, and to fire?
> 2. Can you relate to this? If so, how?

When God told us to be fruitful and multiply, He put within us the desire to do so. Just like the earth is never satisfied with water, so a barren woman will never be satisfied until she gives birth to the nurturing desire within her.

Not every infertile woman faces such intense yearning, and some are at peace to remain childless. These women may have found another avenue to expend their nurturing desire. If this is you, a childless couple is more available for ministry than a couple who must divide their attention between their family and God's service. Don't allow friends and family to pressure you into the status quo. If, however, you are like Nancy, seek those in your life you can love and nurture. Minister to and focus upon those people while you wait for God to unfold His will to you regarding children. Who are the people in your life you can minister to?

Michal, a Childless Woman

We find one woman mentioned in Scripture who never gave birth. We aren't given the whole story of Michal, but we find enough snippets of her life sprinkled through 1 Samuel to piece together what most likely happened.

Although Michal had her shortcomings, it's quite evident she was used as a pawn. Michal was King Saul's daughter. After God rejected her father from being king of Israel, King Saul recognized David could most likely be raised up in his place. King Saul gave Michal to David as a wife, hoping she would become a snare to him, but Michal helped David escape her father's plan for murder.

Then, while David was on the run for his life, spending years hiding in caves and different places, King Saul gave Michal to another man as a wife. After King Saul's death, Michal was returned to David as a peace agreement.

Michal seemed to have received the short end of the stick more than once. Unfortunately for her, because of Saul's disobedience, God took the kingship away from him and all his descendants. It seems King Saul tried to use Michal in the attempt to place one of his descendants back on the throne, in spite of God's judgment, and Scripture tells us Michal died childless.

Scripture supports the idea that God wants to bless most of us with children, but what if He has not in your life? Perhaps you join David's lament in Psalms 13:1, "How long, O LORD? Will You forget me forever? How long will You hide Your face from me?" While we don't have all the answers, this we know: Diamond crystals grow larger the longer they remain in the mantle deep below the earth's surface. God has not forgotten you and has planned something special with you in mind.

We need to recognize God is doing something special in our families, whether He leads us toward adoption or gives us children by birth. Pray, pray, pray; trust Him, and follow the door He opens to you. As we continue through our study, we will gain a greater understanding of how God uses infertility and adoption to announce His special workings.

Diamond Facet of Truth
It is in the heart of God to bless us with children.

~ ♦♦♦ ~

Lesson Two
The Hope Diamond

*And not only this, but we also exult in our tribulations,
knowing that tribulation brings about perseverance;
and perseverance, proven character; and proven character, hope;
and hope does not disappoint, because the love of God has been poured out
within our hearts through the Holy Spirit who was given to us.*
Romans 5:3–5

The Story of Diamonds
Journey to the Surface

If diamonds are formed at one hundred miles beneath the earth's crust, how do we find them at the surface? It is believed there were three ways surface diamonds were deposited on the earth. The first and most common way was by a rare type of volcano. This type of volcano we no longer see today.[8]

While there is no scientific consensus, many geologists believe that not all diamonds found on earth originated here. NASA researchers have detected large numbers of nanodiamonds in some asteroid and meteorites.[9] These diamonds may have been formed in space.[10]

The asteroid theory of diamond formation has been supported by the discovery of tiny diamonds around several asteroid and meteor impact sites.[11] They were formed at the moment of a high-speed impact, creating shock zones of high pressure and heat. We do not often find these nanodiamonds set in jewelry because they are so small.

No matter how or where diamonds have been formed, they

all must endure immense pressure and heat. For our purposes, we will focus our study on the diamonds that are of earthly origin.

The longer a diamond stays in the lithosphere or mantle of the earth, in the environment of pressure and heat, the larger the diamond crystals grow.[12] This, however, is only the beginning of their arduous journey to becoming a gem of great value and beauty.

As mentioned before, a rare and special volcano eruption must occur to bring the valuable gem to the surface. It happens so infrequently that there is no recorded instance of such an eruption. These deep-seated volcanoes must originate from three times the depth of the source magma for most volcanoes.[13]

Diamond-bearing molten rock must be transported violently and with extreme speed to the earth's surface. This must happen in a matter of a few short hours to ensure the diamonds are not converted back to graphite, which can happen under conditions of high heat and low pressure.[14]

Due to the speed of this supersonic eruption and reducing pressure, some of the molten magma expands to gas, causing an explosive effect. Diamond-bearing rocks shoot up with force rather than gushing out like volcanic lava from a normal volcano. This speedy delivery and cooling, ensures the diamond's survival by locking their atomic bonds into place.[15]

Have you ever felt like your life was out of control and you were surrounded by explosive chaos, or that your life's been hit by an asteroid or a meteorite? If so write about those times.

Now that diamonds have reached the surface, they must be found or mined. They are diamonds in the rough, uncut, and still have more to endure before becoming a gem of beauty.

The diamond crystal lattice is exceptionally strong and only atoms of boron, nitrogen, and hydrogen can be introduced into the diamond during the growth at significant concentrations. When this happens, something beautiful occurs. A natural colored diamond is formed. Only one in ten thousand natural diamonds have color, yet colored diamonds have been found in almost any color of the rainbow in twenty-seven different hues.[16]

Naturally colored diamonds are rare, very expensive, and highly sought after.[17] While the Lord wants each of us to possess a diamond heart, some are made into something special. This can be applied to those whose families include a different element, giving them a unique hue, brilliance, and calling.

The Hope Diamond

The Hope Diamond is a natural deep blue diamond and is a perfect symbol for the discussions in this lesson as we examine Abraham and Sarah, also known as Abram and Sarai, and their struggle to birth the nation God had promised them.

Blue diamonds are made when boron is present, replacing some of the nitrogen. Where the most concentration of boron exists, the more color will be seen.[18] Boron is often used as a cleaning agent and laundry brightener. This inclusion makes these unique blue diamonds, a color quality others do not have. Blue diamonds are natural semiconductors, while most other diamonds are excellent electrical insulators.[19]

We find another unique property when we examine the Hope Diamond under an ultraviolet light. When the light is turned off, the blue stone gives off a lingering emission of red light.[20] This blue diamond reminds us of Jesus, the Hope of the world, a descendant of Abraham who washes our sinful hearts clean.

The emanation of red light hints to His shed blood. But we have gotten ahead of our story. Let's go back and start at the beginning of one special family who was set apart for a unique calling.

As we study Your Word, dear Lord, we ask for eyes to see Your plans and purposes for our lives. If Your plans are not our hopes and dreams, help us to lay our agenda down to follow Your leading. Please give us peace and confidence in Your love, and may we find Your hope for the future.

Abraham and Sarah
A Promise of a Blue Diamond Family

The Lord told Abram to leave his country and relatives, and go to a land that He would show him. He also promised to make him into a great nation (Genesis 12:1–2).

Abram faced a big command. He was to uproot his wife,

servants, and his livestock to go where? To a place only God knew. Obedience took a lot of faith. Perhaps all who knew Abram thought he'd lost his mind. Maybe even Sarai did.

1. What kinds of heat and pressure do you think Abram felt in this situation? Has the Lord ever asked you to do something that didn't make sense? Did you do it? Write about what happened.
2. In Gen 12:2, God promised to make Abram into a great nation. What kind of heat and pressure do you think Sarai might have felt to conceive a child?
3. Do you believe the Lord has promised you a child? If so, write about it and tell why you believe it's a promise from the Lord.
4. Abram questioned God about his childlessness in Genesis 15:1–6. He wondered if he needed to provide an heir to make God's promise come to pass. What was God's answer?
5. What was Abram's response?

Abram no longer doubted God's word. The Scripture tells us he believed God would give him a son. Sarai, however, looked at what she thought was reality. She was already up in years and had not conceived a child, so she came up with a plan to bring God's promise to pass.

6. What was her plan? Read Genesis 16:1–4.
7. How did Sarai's plan seem to work out?
8. Have you ever felt pressure to make God's promise happen? If so, write a prayer of submission for your situation.

If you continue reading Genesis chapter sixteen, Hagar gave birth to a son, but this situation only brought rocks, heat, and lava into Abram's and Sarai's lives. Abram finally had a son, whom he named Ishmael. But unfortunately, this situation was plagued with problems that have followed the promised line of descent, even into the present time. Ishmael is the father of many Arab nations still in existence today. We see the tension between the Arab nations and the descendants of the promise, the Jews, on our television sets almost every week.

9. When Abram was ninety-nine years old, the Lord appeared to him. What did the Lord promise Abram? Genesis 17:15–19.
10. God promised a special call on Abraham's and Sarah's son. What is Isaac's calling?

In Genesis 18, God appeared to Abraham as three men, and promised Abraham that Sarah would have a son. In the tent Sarah overheard Abraham's conversation with God and laughed to herself. The Lord asked Abraham why she laughed, although Sarah tried to deny it.

11. What was God's response to Sarah's laughing or doubt in Gen 18:14?
12. When did God say she would have a son?

If you are discouraged, but believe God has promised you a child, hang on to verse 14. "Is anything too difficult for the LORD?"

In Genesis 21:1–3 God kept His promise to Abraham and Sarah and gave them a son named Isaac. God chose Abraham's family for a special purpose. He took a family from obscurity and turned them into His chosen people. Through this nation, God showed Himself to all mankind and brought forth the Messiah who saved the world from sin. An extraordinary call rested on Abraham, Sarah, and their son Isaac.

Diamond Facet of Truth
God uses delay to prepare us for something unique.

Just like a lump of graphite, while waiting deep in the mantle of the earth to be turned to diamond, the longer it stays there, the larger it grows.[21] God used delay to prepare and develop Abraham and Sarah into the parents of His chosen people.

Perhaps the delay in your quest for a child is the time God needs to prepare you for something unique. What have you learned while you have been waiting? List what you have learned.

Diamond Facet of Truth

Remember, we find these words in the middle
of this story of infertility.
"Is anything too difficult for the LORD?"
Genesis 18:14

Isaac and Rebekah
The Birth of a Blue Diamond Family and More

Abraham sent his servant back to the land of Ur to find a wife for his son Isaac from among his relatives. Abraham did not want Isaac to marry a Canaanite, as Esau had. Through miraculous means, the Lord led the servant to Rebekah (Genesis 24:15–60).

Rebekah agreed to marry Isaac and arose with her maids and followed Abraham's servant back to Canaan. When they reached Isaac, he immediately took her as his wife and Scripture tells us Isaac loved her.

1. Read Genesis 25:20–21. Isaac and Rebekah waited twenty years before their twin sons were born. What did Isaac do for Rebekah?

Once again infertility hindered the family tree, and a long delay ensued.

2. Do you think Isaac's prayer moved the hand of God?

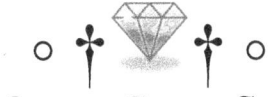

Diamond Facet of Truth
Husbands should pray for their wives.

Isaac and Rebekah had twin boys they named Esau and Jacob. In Genesis 25 the story tells how Esau held his birthright in light esteem and sold it to Jacob for bread and lentil stew. We pick up the story again in Genesis chapter 27. At the urging of Rebekah, Jacob deceives Isaac into giving him the firstborn blessing that belonged to Esau. This ensured that the promised line of descent would pass to Jacob.

In this story, we once again witness how God used infertility to announce to the parents that these two babies had special anointments. Two nations would come from them. The Lord continued the work He had begun in this family, and through infertility He confirmed His presence in their lives.

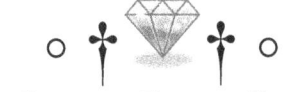

Diamond Facet of Truth
God uses infertility to announce
a special calling upon the child.

Jacob and Rachel
A Blue Diamond Family Blooms

Rebekah worried that Jacob would marry a Canaanite

woman since Esau had married a Hittite and had brought grief to Isaac and Rebekah. At Rebekah's urging, Isaac charged Jacob to go to his uncle Laban and to take one of his daughters as a wife.

Jacob traveled to the land where Laban lived, and the first person of Laban's household he met was Rachel. Rachel was Laban's daughter and a shepherdess of her father's sheep. She was beautiful of face and form, and Jacob immediately was smitten with her. In Genesis 29:13–20 Jacob made a deal with Laban to work for him for seven years to receive Rachel's hand in marriage.

Jacob completed his seven years of service and expected to receive Rachel for his labor, but he had met his match in his deceptive uncle. Rachel had an older sister, Leah, who was nearly blind. On the wedding night Laban gave a veiled Leah to Jacob as his bride. The next morning Jacob awoke horrified, when he realized he had married Leah instead.

Jacob possessed a wife he didn't want and now must work another seven years to get Rachel, the woman he loved. Just like a gem-quality diamond must wait in the mantle of the earth, Jacob waited seven years for Rachel and then faced another delay of seven more years to be free of his obligation to Laban (Genesis 29:21–30).

We can only imagine the turmoil, heat, and pressure that brewed in Jacob's household. Leah, painfully aware her husband had received her through deceit and didn't love her, found herself in a situation beyond her control.

1. Genesis 29:31 tells us the Lord saw that Leah was unloved. What did the Lord do for her?
2. What was Rachel's situation?
3. Read Genesis 29:32–35. How do you think Jacob and Rachel's relationship was affected when Leah bore four sons while Rachel was barren?
4. There was obvious sibling rivalry between Rachel and Leah. Jealous of her sister and desperate for a child, Rachel lashed out at Jacob in Genesis 30:1–2. What does she say to him?
5. What does Jacob say?

6. Have you ever blamed your spouse for circumstances beyond their control? What happened and how did it go?
7. How did Nancy feel about her coworker who was pregnant?
8. If you are dealing with infertility and friends or relatives get pregnant, how does that make you feel?

In Genesis 30:3–8, Rachel's drive to have a child was so strong she gave her maid Bilhah to Jacob just as Sarah had done with Hagar. Bilhah bore two sons to Jacob. Then Leah realized she had stopped bearing children, so she gave her maid Zilpah to Jacob, and Zilpah bore two sons also.

9. Do you think Rachel's desire for a child was really met when Bilhah gave birth to two sons? If so, why? If not, how come? Read Genesis 30:22–23.

Rachel experienced a delay of her desires for at t twelve years and probably more. She watched her sister Leah give birth seven times and the maids Bilhah and Zilpah give birth to two sons each.

10. After eleven children had been born to Jacob what happened? (Genesis 30:22–24)
11. What was Rachel's prayer when she named her son Joseph?

God answered Rachel's prayer. She gave birth to another son, Benjamin (Genesis 35:16–18). Despite all her disappointment, jealousy, turmoil, and untimely death in childbirth, God had great plans for her children of infertility. And although she only gave birth to two sons, she ultimately became the mother of three tribes of Israel. Jacob took Joseph's two sons as his own and made them fathers of Israeli tribes, thus giving Joseph two portions. (Gen 48:1-22)

The sibling rivalry between Leah and Rachel had poisoned not only Leah's heart, but also the hearts of her sons and the sons of Bilhah and Zilpah. This rift in Jacob's household laid the groundwork for Joseph's story, a son of infertility, who had a special call upon his life. You can read his miraculous story in Genesis 37–45.

What can we learn from these stories of infertility? God uses delay to shape people for His purposes. For three generations—from Abraham to Jacob—we see a pattern of infertility. God certainly planned something different for this family. Notice the hand of the enemy who tried his best to thwart God's plan, given the deception and jealousy present in these three stories. However, the molten rock the enemy caused to surround these first three generations of the nation of Israel was what God used to form and solidify a strong people.

Just like He did in the above stories, God uses delays to announce special callings upon the lives of children of infertility and to develop rare diamond hearts in their parents.

Diamond Facet of Truth
God uses infertility to announce
a special calling upon the child.

~ ♦♦♦ ~

Lesson Three
The Rob Red Diamond

*He makes the barren woman abide in the house
as a joyful mother of children.
Praise the LORD!*
Psalm 113:9

The Story of Diamonds
Mining

After the diamond has reached the earth's surface intact, it faces yet another long delay on its way to becoming a valuable gem of beauty. It must wait to be found or mined.

There are three types of places these diamonds must remain until their discovery—in the volcanic pipe that brought the diamond to the surface; in ancient riverbeds or ocean beaches where they were spewed out, displaced, and carried great distances by water and wind; or, much more rarely, left behind by glaciers. But these latter deposits are not good commercial sources of diamonds.[22] The process of extracting the diamonds left in the volcanic pipes is called pipe mining, while mining along water sources is called alluvial mining.

The largest lamproite pipe mine in the world is the Argyle Diamond Mine near Lake Argyle in northwestern Australia. This one pipe is the largest single producer of diamonds and produces the world's rarest and most valuable ones, ranging from delicate pastel rose to robust raspberry, full red and purple, white, champagne, pink-champagne, yellow, blue, and green.[23]

The Rob Red Diamond

The Rob Red is a natural red pear-shaped 0.59-carat diamond named after its owner, Mr. Robert Bogel. It was presumably found in Brazil at one of the alluvial or ancient river deposits.[24]

This special diamond is the purest and most saturated red diamond in the world to date, both visually and instrumentally. The Rob Red received the title of Fancy Intense Red because the purity and saturation of this diamond exceeds the saturation of red color in the famous Hancock Red Diamond. While other pure red diamonds have been found, they all have received color grades of simply Fancy, rather than the more saturated and prestigious grade of Fancy Intense.[25]

Brownish-red diamonds are more common than the ruby-like pure reds such as the Rob Red. Hence this diamond is the most saturated red diamond ever recorded with a modern instrument. What makes this diamond unique is its relative freedom from inclusions or impurities. It is noted as one of the "cleanest" red diamonds in existence. This expensive rock has the potential to be labeled the most important red diamond in the world.[26]

Red diamonds are among the rarest and most expensive jewels on earth, and it is thought that that their red shades are due to changes to the electron structure during the diamond's journey to the surface.[27]

In this lesson we will examine the stories of other people in Scripture who dealt with the social stigma of barrenness. While we can be certain these were not the only God-fearing people in Bible-times who faced infertility, these rare people merited a place in Scripture. What was it about them? They were not only diamonds, but also colored to be the rare brilliance of Fancy Intense Red. And what was God accomplishing in their lives by using the vehicle of infertility?

Let's seek the Lord for His insight.

Dear Lord, as we study the lives of women in Scripture who faced infertility, help us to see Your workings within our own lives. Give us hope and vision for what You may be doing in our families, and give us peace.

Manoah's Wife
Woman of Unbreakable Red Diamond Faith

Here is a woman whose name has been lost to history, but her story is important. She lived during a time when the children of Israel had been given into the hands of the Philistines as a judgment for their rebellion against the Lord. The Philistines dominated them for forty years.

1. Read Judges 13:2–5. What did the angel of the Lord announce to Manoah's wife, and what instructions did he give her?
2. Why were these instructions necessary? What did the angel prophesy that her son would do?
3. Read Judges 13:6–8. What was the first thing the woman did with the news?
4. How did Manoah respond to his wife's news?

It is important to communicate with your spouse what God has put on your heart. If your spouse does not have faith, maintain your confidence in God and pray for the faith of your spouse to increase. Why don't you do it now?

5. Continue to read Judges 13:9–14. How did God answer Manoah's prayer?

If you read Judges 13:15–23, you will find Manoah comes to realize the angel was a messenger sent by the Lord, and he is fearful God will kill them. His wife, however, had an unbreakable faith in God's good character and did not fear.

Through their faith, God blessed Manoah and his wife. Here again we see infertility as the announcement of a special calling upon the life of a child. The woman gave birth to a son and named him Samson.

Diamond Facet of Truth
Manoah's wife had an unshakable faith in God.

Although Samson had his moral failings, God used him as a judge over Israel for twenty years. His supernatural, God-given strength proved to the Philistines that his God stood mightier than all their idols. God allowed Samson one last act of great strength, in which he killed three thousand Philistines with one blow.

Scripture tells us Samson's brothers and his father's household buried him. This provides probable evidence that through Manoah and his wife's faith they were given more children (Judges 16:31).

Hannah
Woman of Red Diamond Prayer and Faith

Hannah was one of two wives to Elkanah. Peninnah was the name of Elkanah's other wife.

1. Read 1 Samuel 1:1–2. What did Peninnah have that Hannah did not have?
2. What reason does Scripture give for Hannah's barrenness?
3. In 1 Sam 1:6–7, who or what distressed Hannah, and why?

Elkanah tried to console Hannah in 1 Samuel 1:8. This is what the Scripture says: *Then Elkanah her husband said to her, "Hannah, why do you weep and why do you not eat and why is your heart sad? Am I not better to you than ten sons?*

4. What was Elkanah's perspective on Hannah's barrenness?
5. What did he want her to feel?

6. How did Hannah respond to Elkanah's questions? Read 1 Samuel 1:9–10.
7. Would Elkanah's words console you if you were in Hannah's situation? Why or why not?
8. Do you think Hannah felt like her feelings had been minimized?

In 1 Samuel 1:11, as Hannah prayed, she made two vows to the Lord. She promised that if the Lord would give her a son, she would give him to the Lord all the days of his life, and a razor would never cut his hair, which was a Nazarite vow (Numbers 6:1–8).

9. What did Eli the priest think of Hannah's open display of desperation as she prayed in 1 Samuel 1:12–17?
10. What did Hannah tell Eli?
11. What was Eli's response?
12. How did Hannah take Eli's response in 1 Samuel 1:18?
13. Read 1 Samuel 1:19-20. How did the Lord honor Hannah's faith?

Continue to read 1 Samuel 1:21–28. It would have been quite easy for Hannah to justify not relinquishing her only child to the Lord. Especially after loving and cherishing Samuel through every moment of his infancy.

14. Hannah prayed a prayer of thanksgiving and faith in 1 Samuel 2:1–10. In verse 5, she speaks something in faith. What was it?
15. What does the prayer tell us about Hannah's relationship with God?
16. How did Eli and the Lord bless Hannah for her faithfulness in 1 Samuel 2:18–21?

Once again we see God use infertility to announce a special calling upon a child's life. Hannah's son Samuel served as the last judge over Israel and also became Israel's first prophet. He succeeded Eli into the priestly office in place of Eli's wicked sons and was called upon to guide Israel through some of the greatest crises of her ancient history. Samuel's legacy stands just short of the stature of Moses.

Diamond Facet of Truth
Hannah was a praying woman who
stayed committed to fulfilling her vows.

The Shunammite Woman
A Red Diamond Heart of Hospitality and Faith

We come again to a woman whose name we have not been given. Scripture tells us she was a prominent woman in the town of Shunem. Elisha often traveled through the town, and in 2 Kings 4:8–10, we read that this woman would invite Elisha in and feed him each time he passed through the village. After time, it became his habit to stop in uninvited.

The woman perceived that Elisha was a man of God, and asked her elderly husband if they could build an upper room for Elisha when he passed through the area. The husband agreed, and the room was built.

One day as Elisha came and rested in the upper chamber, he wanted to do something special to show his gratitude for the woman's kindnesses.

1. In 2 Kings 4:11–13 Elisha comes up with a couple of ways to thank her. What were they?
2. Did you notice the Shunammite woman sought no favors from Elisha? Can you think of one or more people who need your acts of kindness? Write down their names.

3. In 2 Kings 4:14–16 Elisha asks his servant Gehazi for ideas of how to thank her. What was Gehazi's idea?
4. Why do you think the Shunammite woman asked Elisha not to lie to her?

In 2 Kings 4:16 we get a glimpse into the woman's heart. This is the first indication that one of her deepest desires was to have a child. So great was her desire that she implored Elisha not to tell her something that would deeply disappoint her if it did not come to pass. Up until this point, the Shunammite woman had learned to deal with her barrenness by focusing her energy on ministering to others. She turned her focus outward, and God honored her acts of kindness and service.

The next year, as Elisha had predicted, the woman gave birth to a son (2 Kings 4:17).

5. Read 2 Kings 4:18–37 and you will learn the child dies, but what answer does the woman give her husband to his questions in verse 23?
6. The mother goes to Elisha. He sees her coming and sends Gehazi to inquire about her husband and son. What did she say to Gehazi in verse 26?
7. What does the Shunammite woman ask Elisha that tells us she did not believe that God is one who takes back His gifts in verse 28?
8. How did the mother respond to Elisha sending Gehazi to her son in verse 30?

The Shunammite woman wasn't willing to compromise with Gehazi. She knew Elisha was the man of God and had the ear of the Lord. She would not take a chance on another. So Elisha goes to the boy's body lying on the guest-room bed and spreads his body over the child two times. Finally, the boy sneezes and is brought back to life.

The Shunammite's son did not receive a call to be a Joseph or a Samuel, but he had a calling on his life just the same. Through his presence on earth, a great miracle of God's power was manifested during a time when most of Israel had forgotten God.

Diamond Facet of Truth
The Shunammite woman dealt with her barrenness
by focusing her energy on ministering to others
and keeping her faith in God.

Zacharias and Elizabeth
A Couple with Blameless Red Diamond Hearts

Zacharias served as a Jewish priest, and his wife Elizabeth also came from the priestly line. Luke 1:6 tells us they were both righteous in the sight of God and walked blameless in all the commandments and requirements of the Lord.

1. What does Luke 1:7 tell us about them?

As Zacharias performed his priestly service before God, the priests drew lots, and it fell to Zacharias to enter the temple of the Lord and burn incense. As he went about his duty, an angel appeared to him.

2. What does the angel say in Luke 1:12–13 that indicates Zacharias had prayed for a son?

The angel Gabriel goes on to tell Zacharias the child's name was John. The child would drink no wine or liquor, and he would be filled with the Holy Spirit while still in the womb. He went on to speak these words in Luke 1:17: *"And it is he who will go as a forerunner before Him in the spirit and power of Elijah, to turn the hearts of the fathers back to the children, and the disobedient to the attitude of the righteous, so as to make ready a people prepared for the Lord."*

3. Zacharias doubted the angel's word. In Luke 1:18–20, what happens because of his disbelief?
4. What happens to Elizabeth according to Luke 1:24–25?
5. In Elizabeth's sixth month of pregnancy, her relative Mary receives a visit from the angel Gabriel. What does he tell Mary about Elizabeth in Luke 1:36–37?

Mary goes with haste to visit Elizabeth. At her arrival, Mary greets Elizabeth, and the baby leaps in Elizabeth's womb and she and her child are filled with the Holy Spirit.

Elizabeth gives birth to a son in Luke 1:57. All the friends and relatives of Zacharias and Elizabeth expected them to name the child after his father, but to everyone's amazement Zacharias writes down that the child's name is John. At that very moment, his tongue was released and he began speaking praises to God.

This story affected all those who lived around Zacharias and Elizabeth, saying, "What will this child turn out to be?" (Luke 1:66).

Once again, God used the tool of infertility to announce a special call on a baby's life. John became John the Baptist, who preached repentance and prepared those who were willing for the coming of Christ. In a unique way, this infertility story of Zacharias and Elizabeth not only announces the anointing upon John, but also announces the coming of the Messiah, Jesus Christ. Scripture bookmarks the story of the angel Gabriel's visit to Mary within Elizabeth's sixth month of pregnancy. As Gabriel tells Mary about her relative's pregnancy he says, "For nothing will be impossible with God" (Luke 1:37), a well-known statement about the character of God.

We are given a question and an answer, standing like bookends to the topic of infertility. In the first infertility story of Scripture—Abraham and Sarah—we are given the question: "Is anything too difficult for the Lord?" (Genesis 18:14). In our last infertility story of Scripture—Zacharias and Elizabeth—we are given the answer: "For nothing will be impossible with God" (Luke 1:37).

So what have we learned in these past three lessons on

infertility? If there is a struggle with infertility in your life, have confidence in God that He is doing something different in your family. It could be His way of leading you to adopt or to prepare you for a birth child of special calling.

Either way, we should spend time in prayer and Scripture to develop a deeper relationship with the Lord. This will give us unbreakable faith and trust in Him and a trustworthy character. If we have made vows to the Lord, we need to stay committed to them, and to the best of our ability, do what is right in the sight of God. And finally, as we wait for our breakthroughs, we should develop an outward focus and use our talents in the service of the Lord.

Diamond Facet of Truth

"Is anything too difficult for the LORD?"
Genesis 18:14
"For nothing will be impossible with God."
Luke 1:37

~ ♦♦♦ ~

Lesson Four
The Dresden Green Diamond

> *Blessed is a man who perseveres under trial;*
> *for once he has been approved,*
> *he will receive the crown of life,*
> *which the Lord has promised*
> *to those who love Him.*
> James 1:12

The Story of Diamonds
Sorting

After diamond-bearing rock has been mined, it is transported to a screening plant. There the diamonds are then removed from the host rock—called "rough diamonds" in this natural and uncut state. Each rough diamond is inspected and sorted into one of three categories.[28]

Gem-quality diamonds are put into the first class. Each stone in this category must display a high standard of excellence. The clarity of these diamonds range from flawless to visible inclusions. Only 20 percent of the diamonds mined meet the standards. These are the stones set in jewelry.[29]

The next grouping is for industrial use only. These diamonds are badly flawed and are only suitable for machinery used in cutting or drilling. These defective stones are used in instruments as small as dentist drills to as large as earthmoving equipment. The majority of the rough diamonds—about 80 percent—go into this category.(30)

The last category accounts for a very small percentage of the rough diamonds. is crushing-boart or boart. These very low-quality diamonds are called crushing-boart or boart. Crushed into diamond dust, they are a useful abrasive for diamond polishing.(31)

Just as man selects diamonds for different purposes, God chooses each one of us for His plans.

The Dresden Green Diamond

The Dresden Green gets its name from the capitol city of Saxony in Germany, where it has been on display for more than 200 years. The earliest known reference to its existence occurred in 1722. Weighing in at 40.70 carats, it has a pear-shaped cut. The Dresden Green is the largest and most perfect natural green diamond ever found.(32)

Greenish diamonds in the rough occur as one of three types: a crystal-shaped stone possessing a light tinge of color, a stone with a dark green skin, and a yellowish-green stone. After cutting and polishing the diamonds of the first and second category, they tend to lose their green color and become white gems, or they become light yellow stones called "silvery capes." The few truly green diamonds, like the Dresden Green, are extremely rare gems and originate from the third type.(33)

Natural green diamonds obtain their color by coming into contact with radioactive rocks at some point in their lifetime and remaining with them for a considerable amount of time. The most common form of irradiation diamonds come when the alpha particles present in uranium compounds or percolating groundwater bombard the rock containing diamonds. Beta and gamma rays along with neutrons color the diamond deep within the stone, instead of producing a green skin. In some cases the whole stone's interior has turned green.(34)

In this lesson we will look at what the Bible says about adoption. Just like rare natural green diamonds, many who seek to adopt, have been colored through the radiation of infertility.

Let's ask the Lord's insight on adoption.

Please, Lord, show us what is in Your heart concerning

adoption. Help us to see Your love and care, help us trust you in all we face.

What the Bible Says about Adoption

Let's study the greatest story of all as we sort things out. We may never read or say the words *Heavenly Father* in the same way again.

As Adam and Eve bit into fruit from the Tree of Knowledge of Good and Evil, the first piece of "knowledge" gained was their own nakedness. They became fleshly minded, fallen, and separated from God. That one choice severed their familial relationship with God and rendered them children of sin with no way to reestablish their relationship.

Immediately God set His divine plan into motion. After covering Adam and Eve with animal skins, He sent them away from the Garden of Eden as a protection. God set up a flaming sword and stationed cherubim to guard access to the Tree of Life. He did this to safeguard mankind from immortality and thus an eternal fallen state.

Did you know adoption is God's idea? It is. The plan of redeeming mankind from the father of evil, the devil, is God's plan. The redemption story is a plan of adoption.

1. Read 1 John 3:9–10. How do we know who the children of God are?
2. How do we know the children of the devil?
3. Look at Ephesians 1:4–5. What did God predestine us to?
4. John 1:12–13 says, "But as many as received Him, to them He gave . . ." What?
5. Read Galatians 4:4-7. In verse 5, what did we receive from God?
6. When we become adopted children of God, who does God send into our hearts that will cause us to call Him "Father" in verse 6?
7. In verse 7, it says we are no longer slaves. If we are adopted, what are we?
8. If we are adopted sons and daughters in verse 7, what else

do we become?

9. Take a look at John 3:16–17. What do you think the word *begotten* means?

In the Greek the word *begotten* means 'only born.' So Jesus is the only Child of God who possesses the essence of the Godhead or traits of God. Wow, what a concept! God the Father asked His only Son, who possessed His attributes, to lay down His life so we could not only be saved from our sinfulness, but also become adopted children with the Holy Spirit dwelling within us, causing us to cry out "Father." Not only that, we've become joint-heirs to Jesus' eternal inheritance. What love!

10. Read Matthew 28:9–10 and John 20:11–18. After Christ's resurrection, what does Christ begin to call his followers?

Jesus died a horrible death so that we could be adopted of God and become siblings to share in His inheritance. This is God's adoptive love for us. Take note, providing an inheritance for your adopted child, as well as any biological children, is a principle of Scripture. We can't go wrong following God's lead. For more study on our inheritance read Ephesians 1:13–14, Hebrews 9:15 and 1 Peter1:3–4.

In Genesis 17:5, 15 and Genesis 32:28 we see the two main attributes of adoption in the story of Abraham. God changes his earthly name Abram to Abraham and Jacob's name to Israel. Names always change with adoption. Abraham and his descendants were also given an earthly inheritance—the land of promise, Israel.

We see this in the New Testament also. Before Saul's conversion and ministry began, he was called Saul. After he begins his ministry, he is called Paul.

11. In Revelations 2:17 God will give those who overcome a white stone with something written on it. What is written?

As Christians, we are promised new names in heaven. On earth we are called Christians. We have Christ's name attached to us. Today, names change when adoption occurs. Nancy and her husband gave their adopted son a different name than Kelly had originally given him, although oddly enough we both gave him the same middle name of Aaron. Perhaps it's a God thing, maybe a sign of God's calling on his life.

As previously mentioned, another attribute of adoption is that an inheritance is given. As Christians, we are promised new names and a spiritual inheritance.

So what should we take from this lesson? First and foremost, God is the author of adoption. His plan for redemption is an adoption plan, and name changes and inheritances are true signs of adoption.

Diamond Facet of Truth
The redemption story is a plan of adoption.

Lesson Five
The Steinmetz Pink Diamond

And we know that God causes all things
to work together for good to those who love God,
to those who are called according to His purpose.
Romans 8:28

The Story of Diamonds
Cutting

A diamond in its natural uncut state appears much like a glass pebble.[35] Most people would pass over the stone without recognizing the gem for what it is. After the rough diamond has been sorted, the valuable rock must be cut. The skill of the master cutter is the one who unlocks the true brilliance within each jewel.

Because each diamond in the rough is different, the stone must be carefully examined and each impurity, inclusion, and flaw must be marked. Then the planning process begins. The master cutter analyzes the rough diamond and makes decisions on how the stone should be cut into a faceted gemstone.[36]

His first objective is to maximize the value of the stone, considering how to keep as much weight retention as possible since value increases with size. Even today with our modern techniques, the process of cutting and polishing a diamond crystal always results in a dramatic loss of weight of about 50 percent. He also takes into account how appealing the final shape will be, given the physical factors of the stone, the original shape of the rough diamond, and the location of the flaws or inclusions that need to be eliminated.[37]

Often the cutting process involves cleaving or sawing. Cleaving is the separation of a piece of rough diamond. This results in two or more separate pieces. These are then finished into separate gemstones.[38]

After a stone has undergone the cleaving process, a process known as bruiting or girdling rounds off the corners of the crystal. The master cutter uses the diamond's hardness as his tool. With two diamonds set onto spinning axles, each turning in opposite directions, the stones grind against each other to shape each diamond.[39]

It is important to distinguish between cut and shape. Some of the more popular shapes of diamonds include round brilliant, oval, marquise, pear, heart, and emerald. Within each of these shapes, it is the cut that determines the quality of the stone. Most diamonds are cut with fifty-eight facets, regardless of their shape.[40]

In colored diamonds, cutting is exceptionally important because the stone's cut can have a direct influence upon the color grade of the crystal, thereby raising its value. Certain cut shapes, such as the radiant cut, can intensify the color.

The Steinmetz Pink Diamond

The Steinmetz Pink is most likely the finest natural pink diamond in the world. The gem was discovered in South Africa and was unveiled as recently as 2003. The stone is the largest Fancy Vivid Pink diamond in the world, weighing in at 59.60 carats. The gemstone has been graded as Internally Flawless, which is an extremely rare and highly sought after clarity grade.[41]

It took a team of eight people and twenty months to cut this rare gem. One wrong move would have destroyed this priceless diamond. It was cut in an oval mixed cut with a step-cut crown and a brilliant cut pavilion, which made the gem's facet pattern very unusual.[42]

Changes in the electron structure, called "plastic deformation," during the stone's passage to the earth's surface create the various pink shades we see in these rare diamonds.[43]

In this lesson we are going to examine the lives of individuals in Scripture who were raised by at least one parent who was not their biological parent. These individuals were cleaved from their families, only to be shaped into extraordinary people.

We thank You, Lord, that we can go to Scripture and learn how You have used adoption in people's lives, and how You shaped them for Your purposes. Help us to see Your hand in the stories of the people we study, and give us a vision for how You are working in our own lives.

Joseph, the Ruler

Joseph is a unique individual. We've already mentioned him as a child of infertility since he was the son of Jacob and Rachel. Joseph would also qualify as someone who was raised, at least in part, by someone besides both his natural parents. We will take another look at him because his life so clearly demonstrates the cutting process of our diamond hearts.

In Genesis 35:16–20, we read that Rachel gave birth to a second son, Benjamin, as they traveled from Bethel to Bethlehem. While Joseph gained a brother, Rachel died, and Joseph's mother was cut away from his life.

In Genesis 37:5–22 we read about two dreams Joseph had. These dreams predicted his family would all bow down to him. In these dreams, God revealed His call upon Joseph's life as a ruler and deliverer. This created friction and envy among his brothers and was the root of more cutting in Joseph's life.

Jacob sent Joseph to check on the welfare of all his older brothers who were shepherding their father's flock and to assess how the flock was doing. Joseph finally located his brothers in Dothan. When they saw him from a distance wearing his multicolored garment, they despised him and plotted to kill him. Reuben, however, convinced his brothers not to kill him outright but to throw him in a pit, for he planned on rescuing Joseph at a later time.

When Joseph reached his brothers in Genesis 37:23–28, he experienced several things cut away from his life in one day. His brothers stripped him of his multicolored garment and threw him into a pit; then they sold him into slavery, and he lost his freedom. Not only that, he lost access to his father who loved him.

In Genesis 39:1–20 we learn Joseph was sold to Potiphar as a slave, but he soon became the overseer of his household. Potiphar's wife pursued Joseph, hoping he would have an affair with her. One day she grabbed hold of his cloak and tempted him. He fled, leaving his garment behind.

> 1. Potiphar's wife told a lie, claiming Joseph had attempted to rape her. What happened to Joseph because of the lie in Genesis 39:19–20?

Joseph's mother, his garment of colors, his family, his freedom, and his reputation were all cut away from him.

Genesis 40:1–23 tells us Joseph was incarcerated with the king of Egypt's cupbearer and baker. Both men had dreams while in jail, and Joseph interprets them, telling the cupbearer he would be restored to his post, but the baker would be hung from a tree. Joseph asked the cupbearer to keep him in mind when he returned to his post as cupbearer.

> 2. What happens in Genesis 40:23?

After Joseph's hope for release had been cut away, we read on in Genesis 41:1 that he spent two more years confined in prison. Finally, Joseph was released, and God raised him up to be the second in command of all Egypt.

> 3. In Genesis 45:4–8 Joseph gave us insight as to what his calling was from God. What was Joseph's calling?

God sent Joseph ahead of his brothers so that their lives and families would be saved from the famine.

> 4. Remember, in Lesson 2, we learned there was a special calling on the descendants of Abraham. So what was Joseph's family called to be? (Genesis 12:1–3)

Here we see that God used all the cutting away Joseph

experienced. He announced an extraordinary calling upon Joseph's life, and He formed his heart into a priceless diamond. God used Joseph to deliver the chosen family from starvation and annihilation and to save the preordained line of descent for the Savior, who would bring salvation to the world. Thank You, Lord!

    5. Have you ever had something or someone cut away from your life? If so, write about it.

Benjamin, to Be Loved

Benjamin is the earliest recorded infant in Scripture raised by someone other than both his natural parents. He was Joseph's younger brother.

    1. Read Genesis 35:18. What did Benjamin's mother do before she died?
    2. What did Jacob do immediately after Rachel died?

Since Benjamin is Joseph's younger brother, this puts him in the center of an extremely dysfunctional family that we have already discussed. Benjamin, most likely, experienced some of the same prejudices Joseph encountered, and the callings of these two young men were forever linked.

In Genesis chapters 42 through 45 Joseph tested his brothers' hearts by demanding they bring Benjamin to Egypt. Jacob, with great reluctance, finally allowed Benjamin to travel to Egypt. Once there, Benjamin was accused of thievery and sentenced to slavery. Judah, the brother who had suggested they sell Joseph into slavery, begged to take Benjamin's place as a slave. Convinced that years of guilt had chipped away his brothers' hard hearts, Joseph broke down in tears and revealed his true identity.

    3. What was Benjamin's calling in this story? Write down what you think it is.

Benjamin had a unique calling on his life. Yes, it's true. He isn't known for his greatness, at least not like his famous brother, but God did have a special purpose for him. Benjamin's calling was to BE. Yes, that's right, to BE. He was called to be who he was. He was Rachel and Jacob's son.

Benjamin's calling was to be the vehicle God used to place similar circumstances in front of his brothers—the same brothers who sold Joseph into slavery. God used Benjamin to change the hearts of his family. Would they treat him the same way they treated Joseph, or would they change their ways? Benjamin's existence also brought Joseph the opportunity to see what lay in the hearts of his brothers.

Benjamin was just *there* for his father, Jacob, to love. He was also *there* to appear before Joseph, which brought deliverance to Israel. God worked His purposes through Benjamin. In the end, Benjamin became the father of the Hebrew tribe of Benjamin. God blessed him with ten sons, more than all his brothers received.

Many children of adoption are called just to BE. To be present in the lives of others, so the Lord can work His purposes because they are *there*.

Moses, the Deliverer

About four hundred years after the days of Joseph and Benjamin, the children of Israel had turned from a small tribal family into a large nation of people. Because of their number, the Egyptians feared they would join their enemies and defeat them. As a result, the Egyptians enslaved the children of Israel, hoping to keep them weak.

The reigning pharaoh also enacted a law that would weaken the Jews further. He decreed that every infant Jewish son must be thrown into the Nile. It was into this environment that Moses was born.

The decision to relinquish a child must be one of the toughest decisions anyone must face. However, it's hard to comprehend what Jewish mothers of infant sons went through in Egypt at the time Moses was born.

1. Jochebed was one such Hebrew mother. What did she do in Exodus 2:3–4 to give her son a chance at

survival?

When Jochebed laid Moses into the Nile, she placed him into the hands of God. The Nile was a hostile and dangerous environment where crocodiles roamed.

2. How would you feel if you had to do something like that?
3. Read Exodus 2:5–10. How did God honor Jochebed's faith?

Moses, born a slave, was raised as royalty. We don't know for certain which Pharaoh's daughter became Moses' adoptive mother, but some scholars believe its plausible Hatshepsut adopted Moses. Hatshepsut ruled as a powerful regent of Egypt. If true, Moses might have been a contender for the throne.

In any case, the Lord provided him with the best education, training, and cultural understanding he would need to fulfill his calling. What better preparation could he have had than to be raised alongside the future Pharaoh?

After killing an Egyptian for his harsh treatment of a Hebrew, Moses was forced to flee to Midian, married Zipporah, and settled there. One day, while pasturing his father-in-law's flock, Moses came across a burning bush. But the bush was not consumed. God spoke to Moses and told him to remove his sandals because he was standing on holy ground.

4. God placed a calling on Moses' life in Exodus 3:10. What was it?

We can see the mighty calling God placed on the life of Moses, and we all have heard of the wondrous miracles God accomplished through this man. Moses became the long awaited deliverer of the Israelites. Through him, God gave us the Ten Commandments, which is why he is still revered even today by many peoples.

Esther, the Queen Willing to Die

A young girl by the Hebrew name of Hadassah became an

orphan. Scripture doesn't tell us how her parents died, but her older cousin Mordecai took her as his own daughter. She grew into a beautiful young woman. Today, the world knows her by her Chaldean name, Esther.

It seems Esther lived an uneventful life as Mordecai's daughter. Scripture shows us Mordecai cared deeply for Esther, as if she'd been born to him. They possessed a good relationship, and Esther listened to Mordecai's wise advice. This trait would serve her well in the days that followed.

They lived in the capital city of Susa where King Ahasuerus reigned. When the king's queen disrespected him publicly, he stripped her of her royal position and set out to find a woman to replace her as queen.

All the beautiful virgins throughout Ahasuerus's kingdom were brought into his harem. He would pick a new queen from them. When Esther was picked to be one of the young beauties, Mordecai warned her not to tell anyone she was a Hebrew, so she kept her ethnicity secret. Through Esther's wise choices and humility, she was chosen to be the new queen.

One day, Esther heard that Mordecai sat in the center of the city, wearing sackcloth and ashes, in great distress. She sent servants to find out the reason for his grief. They returned and relayed how Haman had tricked the king into signing an edict demanding the death of all Jews. All Israelites were to be killed on the thirteenth day of Adar.

> 1. Mordecai made a request of Esther, telling her what he thinks her calling was in Esther 4:13–14. What does he request of her, and what does he think her calling is?

Esther had a huge problem. No one, not even the queen, could approach the king without being summoned. Anyone brave enough to attempt entering his presence without his request would stand under the penalty of death, unless the king put out his scepter to them. Esther requested all the Jews in Susa to pray and fast for three days. Then she would risk her life for her people.

After the fast, Esther approached the King. He put out his scepter, and her life was spared. Esther requested the king's presence at a banquet she would prepare. She also asked him to invite Haman. When both men attended the meal, she asked them to return the following day for another feast.

Finally, Esther revealed her Jewish heritage and pleaded for her people. Stunned by Haman's wicked manipulation, the king ordered Haman hanged on the very gallows he had built for the execution of Esther's cousin, Mordecai. Haman considered Mordecai worthy of death because he would not bow to Haman.

The king established a new edict, which allowed the Israelites to defend themselves against anyone attempting to carry out the first edict. This resulted in saving the nation of Israel.

We see two callings on Esther's life. For the most part, she was just called to *BE*—to be her beautiful self and to enjoy the life of a royal queen. When the time of great need arose, her calling required her to speak out to the king. Although her life was on the line, she delivered her people, the Jews, from a massacre.

Josiah, the King, who Turned Israel Back to the Lord

Josiah was the son of King Amon of Judah. Although an Israelite, Amon worshiped idols, sacrificed to them, and did much evil in the sight of the Lord. One day servants of King Amon rose up and murdered him. This left little Josiah a king at eight years old.

Even though very young, King Josiah did not follow the evil ways of his father. At Eighteen years of age, he sent Shaphan, a scribe, to the house of the Lord, ordering the high priest to distribute the money in the house of the Lord to workmen to repair God's house.

The high priest told Shaphan he had found the book of the law and sent the book back to King Josiah. When Shaphan read the book to King Josiah, Josiah tore his clothes (2 Kings 22:1–13). In the book Josiah discovered that a man of God had prophesied about him by name approximately two hundred seventy years earlier. Within the prophecy King Josiah was given his calling and purpose—to eliminate all idol worship from the land (1 Kings 13:1–2).

In obedience, Josiah made a covenant before all the people to turn back to the Lord and destroyed all the idols and high places his father and grandfathers before him had erected. He also burned the bones of the false priests on the broken altars of the false gods (2 Kings 23:4–14).

Scripture doesn't tell us who mentored King Josiah as a child, but it must have been a God-fearing person. Someone held great influence in the young king's life.

King Josiah did his best to eliminate all idol worship throughout his kingdom and led his people in repentance before the Lord. He also reinstated the celebration of the Passover, since his people had forgotten the command to observe the feast.

1. What does 2 Kings 23:25 say about Josiah?

God had a special calling on King Josiah's life, even prophesying about him hundreds of years earlier. This gave Josiah direction for his life, since there was no one to lead him into such a strong commitment to the Lord. The Lord allowed King Amon to be murdered so Josiah would not grow up in the ungodly influence of his father's evil ways.

2. The cutting away process of losing one or more parents and being raised by others was used to form the lives we've just studied. How do you think the cutting away process shaped Kelly?
3. We have shown that God uses the cutting process to develop people for their callings. What do you think might be the call of God upon your life?
4. Is it possible the Lord may be calling you to adopt? Why or why not?

We have looked at Joseph, Benjamin, Moses, Esther, and King Josiah, all of whom lost at least one parent in their youth. So what are we to conclude? If you are a child of adoption or struggle with infertility or have plans to adopt, be encouraged. God is working something different in your life and family. With this body of evidence we can be certain. God uses these types of situations to develop, mold, and shape people for a special call. Look toward the future with hope. The things God has planned for you are awesome.

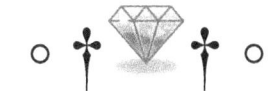

Diamond Facet of Truth

God uses difficult situations to develop, mold,
and shape people for a special call.

~ ♦♦♦ ~

Lesson Six
The Royal Purple Heart Diamond

*"Take heed to the ministry which you have received
in the Lord, that you may fulfill it."*
Colossians 4:17

The Story of Diamonds
Polishing

In the previous lessons we have studied how diamonds were formed in the center of the earth. They then made their journey to the surface where they were mined, sorted, cut, and finally they are polished into a gem of value and beauty.

The process of polishing a diamond is not at all like the gentle act of polishing a piece of fine furniture. No, each facet of a diamond is ground on a stone individually. So, if most diamonds are cut with 58 facets, a diamond must face the grinding stone the same number of times. The diamond is put into a holder that sets it against a turntable that revolves at a high speed.[44]

Today, with modern technology, polishing takes far less time than it did when each facet had to be done by hand. The technique requires polishing, checking, and polishing some more until all the facets are clean, sharp, and symmetrical.

Just like a diamond must go through the refining process of polishing, we who are considering adoption must face the refining process as well. This final lesson is designed to smooth out any rough patches in our thinking, to help us to enter this endeavor with wisdom, love, and confidence.

The Royal Purple Heart Diamond

The Royal Purple Heart is the largest natural fancy vivid purple diamond in existence. It weighs 7.34 carats and has the clarity of 11. The unique stone was mined in Russia and has been cut and polished into a perfect heart shape, which allows the brilliant purple color to be seen with maximum effect. Natural purple diamonds are one of the rarest and highly sought after colors in which diamonds occur. So rare that most jewelers have never seen one.[45]

Many scientists believe natural purple diamonds are formed by the post-growth plastic deformation during its journey from the earth's mantle to the surface. Natural purple diamonds make up only 1 percent of the diamonds mined at the Siberia's Mir kimberlite field.[46]

The Royal Purple Heart is a fitting gem for this lesson. The United States awards a medal of honor, called the Purple Heart, to those who have risked their lives in heroic acts during times of war. People who go beyond the call of duty and give their lives to raising children, who otherwise would not have families, most certainly can be counted among heroes. But just as a soldier must be prepared for battle, so too, must adoptive parents be trained for the task at hand. This lesson has been written with the hope it will be a tool for your use, in such a necessary preparation.

Are You Ready to Adopt?

In April 2010, a Tennessee adoptive mom stunned the world when she put her seven-year-old son on a flight back to Moscow without a chaperone. The boy carried a note in his pocket telling the Russian officials his adoptive mother didn't want him anymore. She claimed he threatened her family and friends with violent behavior, in spite of the fact the doctor at the orphanage told her, "He's healthy," when she asked if he had any physical or mental problems.

While no one condoned the woman's choice to send him back in such a heartless manner, many could sympathize. The voices who spoke out on her behalf, surprisingly enough, were other adoptive parents. They blamed the adoption agencies for not accurately describing a child's troubled past or providing adequate training and options. Yet, thousands of overseas adoptees have flourished in their American families. So what's up? What's one to do when considering adoption?

Preparation Is Key

*Prepare your work outside
and make it ready for yourself in the field;
afterwards, then, build your house.*
Proverbs 24:27

Let's ask for the Lord's help.

As we investigate all aspects of adoption, Lord, we ask for Your wisdom to prepare us for what may lie ahead. Give us strength to look at all issues honestly, and to be willing to change the things that may need to be changed. Help us to submit to Your will in our lives, whatever that may be.

We didn't write this book with the purpose of demeaning Kelly's adoptive parents. Anyone with children will tell you parenting is hard, and kids don't come with instruction manuals. Unfortunately, in Kelly's case, something fell through the cracks. We don't know if the adoption agency dropped the ball or whether things were hidden from them. In either case, she suffered many hardships growing up in an ill-prepared family.

Kelly's father struggled with alcoholism, and much of the heartache and downward spiral of the family could be laid at the feet of this problem. Perhaps adequate groundwork had not been laid to give her parents the tools they needed for adoption. It is our hope that this book will be a tool of preparation for those considering such an endeavor.

The Tennessee woman, and the many adoptive couples who came to her defense, obviously felt under-prepared and perhaps taken advantage of. While the adoption agencies in their cases may bear some blame, it's unfair to expect an agency to cover every possible scenario that may arise.

Adoptions come with unknowns. It's the nature of the

beast and it's an issue, we as adoptive parents, must accept. Often the information adoptive parents receive is second- or third-hand and may not be completely accurate. We've all played telephone as kids and found the game amusing when the final version of the original message was revealed. Agencies can only give the information provided to them. They do their best, but they have no control over information that is withheld or deemed unnecessary to pass on. This is especially true in foreign adoption where cultural perceptions of a healthy child may be different from ours.

Orphans from foreign countries are in desperate need of forever homes and what I have to say is in no way intended to discourage people from pursuing these adoptions. However, even though I have not participated in foreign adoption, the subject needs to be addressed. I am obligated to point out that there seems to be a black hole for some families after the adoption takes place. Some families are left reeling with their child's emotional baggage with no support from the adoption agency or social programs.

Children are not cats or dogs that can be rehomed. Unfortunately, there have been families that have gotten in over their heads, and out of desperation, have done just that. Through the Internet they have opted for the "easy" way out and placed their child with strangers that have not been vetted in anyway, with no home study, background check, etc. This has opened the door for child molesters, parents deemed unfit, and criminals to possess a child for their own purposes.

"Rehoming" is not an option and should never be considered. How sad for a child that has been rescued from one hell only to wind up in a hotter one.

In many cases, God may be the only person in the universe who knows what your child has experienced or been through. Orphanages in foreign countries may mean well, but have scant financial resources or be understaffed. Depending on the country's culture there may be a negative stigma toward orphans that might consider them as throw away kids.

Prepare yourself. Study up on attachment disorders. Look for an adoption agency that provides "after adoption help" for families who need it. What kind of social services are provided in your area that might provide counseling, etc. Look for a Christian orphanage that understands the need for love and attention, and most of all, pray, pray, pray. Don't go into this on your own. Follow the Lord's leading. He will either open the right doors or He will close them.

Our adoption of Bryan was an open one and considered cutting edge at the time. We met both birth parents and had good communication with Kelly's stepmom and dad, yet information that should have been passed on, was not. Not until Kelly and I sat down to write this book, did I find out that Bryan had been born a month premature or that he came out black and not breathing. Molly thought Kelly had given birth to a stillborn child. Although this information was relayed to the adoption agency, yet, someone failed to pass on the information to us.

Bryan turned out to have ADHD. We found out, when he was about seven years old, that his birth dad also had the disorder, but he simply failed to pass on that information. The truth is this: how many ADHD teenage boys would even think about it?

This information is not to scare one off from adopting but to give realistic expectations. Don't depend on the adoption agency to prepare you, even though many of them do a good job. Take it upon yourself to do the research. Reading this book is a great start. Keep reading. Go through the questions in this lesson and answer them as honestly as you can. It is our hope you will have a greater understanding of yourself, spouse, and the realities of the adoption process.

1. Do you want to adopt? List the reasons.
2. What do you think adoption will be like?
3. What are your greatest fears concerning adoption?
4. It is normal to have concerns. All couples do.
5. How would you handle things in the event that one of your fears was realized?

The best way to deal with fear is to face it head-on. Research how people who have encountered your concern handled the situation.

6. Do you feel adopting will fulfill your desire to be a

parent? How?
7. How does your spouse feel about adopting?
8. Do you and your spouse have similar expectations concerning adoption? If not, why not?

If not, you need to come to some agreement. Good communication is key. Adoption is a big decision. Be careful not to manipulate your spouse to give in. You will be setting yourselves up for problems down the road.

9. Do you or your spouse battle alcoholism, drug addiction, or mental illness?

Don't complicate your life anymore if you answered "yes" to any of the above questions. Children of alcoholics and drug addicts rarely come out unscathed. Is it fair to bring a child into such volatile circumstances? With the help of our good Lord, these issues can be overcome. Pursue help in those areas first, then, if the problem is dealt with and you develop a track record of a good number of years, seek to adopt.

10. Are you or your spouse hooked on video games or other time-consuming pastimes?
11. Are both of you prepared to give the time and emotional energy a new child requires?

A child will disrupt your game playing for sure. In today's world we see a growing number of video gamer widows. The raising of children has been left to mothers who receive little or no support from their husbands. The children are the big losers in a situation of this kind, and adopted children will read it as rejection.

Kids need both Mom and Dad!

12. Do you fear that you might not be a good parent or that you won't love the child? Why do you feel that way?

These are normal feelings. If you are concerned about being a good parent, you will most likely do just fine. There is no such thing as a "perfect parent." We all make mistakes. If you care about doing well, with God's help, you will.

Real love is choosing what is best for someone. If you take good care of the child and express affection, the child will feel loved. How can you not become attached to an innocent child who needs you? This concern usually vanishes for most people as soon as they see the child.

Do you fear that something may be wrong with the child?

The reality is this: bringing a baby into your home carries a risk, whether by birth or adoption. There are no guarantees. This risk is part of parenthood. Fear that a child might not be perfect should not prevent us from adopting. None of us are perfect. Just as our heavenly Father adopted us with our weaknesses, we should be willing to take the risk to open our homes to a child who needs one. Jesus saw us as redeemable. Can we think any less of an unfortunate child?

Recent research shows that traumatic events, like the death of a family member or depression impacts not only the mother carrying a child, but also impacts the child's later behavior.[47] This is true for all children whether biological or adopted. Adoption agencies cannot know all a birth mother experiences during her pregnancy. Human beings are complex, and you cannot have a guarantee your child will not come with issues.

The best thing you can do is be proactive. Check into what your insurance will cover. Find out what services are available in your area if your child turns out to have health risks, such as fetal alcohol spectrum disorders, attachment disorders, mental health issues, and other disabilities. Educate yourself on these issues so you will recognize symptoms and be able to get early intervention help if needed.

Most adoptions do well. The disruption rate falls between 10 and 15 percent. Just like divorce, no one wins if a disruption occurs but the child has the most to lose. Adequate preparation may help eliminate this unfortunate outcome. With 85 to 90 percent resulting in successful placements, be encouraged. Pray, pray, pray. As Kelly's and my story attests, the Lord wants to be involved. He will bring the child He desires to your family.

When Bryan was still a preschooler, I had a nagging suspicion he struggled with ADHD. At the time I believed ADHD to be an excuse for parents not bothering to discipline their child. I lived in denial not wanting to recognize my thinking to be wrong. Nor did I want to label my child.

At the end of his kindergarten year, his schoolteacher strongly suggested that I medicate him before he entered the first grade. She feared none of the first grade teachers would have the ability to handle him. I dismissed it. Then one day I took Bryan, now a six-year-old, to the pediatrician's office. As the doctor and I discussed Bryan's health, she calmly asked me when I planned on addressing my son's ADHD issues. She told me to look at him. Bryan lay belly down across the doctor's rolling stool. As he zoomed across the room, I had to recognize he literally bounced from wall to wall. I no longer could deny it.

The first day I medicated him I couldn't help but be stunned. Legos had been nothing more to him than missiles to be thrown throughout the house, but on medication he actually built something for the first time. I realized the turmoil our family had been in, due in part, to our not wanting to admit he had a problem.

If you adopt a child with challenges, don't be trapped in the denial syndrome. Get help. Your entire family will benefit, and you will avoid feeling like a failing parent. A common misconception of outsiders is to blame your parenting. This goes across the board, whether the child is biological or adopted. Get professional help, and do what you can to help your child. Be gracious to friends and family who misunderstand. They have not walked in your shoes.

13. How would you feel about your adopted child if a month after the adoption you discovered you were pregnant?
14. What plan could you implement that would ensure the adopted child would be treated equally to the biological sibling?

We originally celebrated "Gotcha Days" each year on the day we brought Bryan home. This gave way to the extra birthday parties we would have with Kelly's family. Bryan got the message of love and felt special. Life is full of unforeseen curve balls. We can't always predict what life is going to throw at us. But we always must come up with a strategy to keep the adopted child from feeling marginalized. This helps us accomplish the goal.

Brianna, our biological daughter, went through a number of years where she endured a seizure every twenty seconds. This will throw the best of families into turmoil. Our focus had to be helping her achieve a better quality of life. I worried Bryan would feel marginalized. It might not have been the best solution, but when John was home, he took over Bryan's care and I tended to Brianna. Bryan does remember his dad spent more time with him than I did, but as he grew older he understood why.

15. How strong is your marriage?
16. Has your marriage struggled with major issues before you began a quest for a child?
17. If there are problems in your marriage, do you think having a child will heal your relationship with your spouse?
18. In what way would a child help?

Children tend to poke holes in marital relationships because they are needy members of the family. To hope a child will bring the two of you closer together is unrealistic.

19. Has infertility treatment strained out your marriage?
20. Has the spontaneity of your love life taken a hit?

If you said yes to the above questions, focus on restoring that part of the marriage as you pursue adoption. You will be glad you did.

21. How open is the communication between you and your spouse?

You will be taking on a great responsibility when you adopt. It's important that you are both on the same page.

22. How do you feel about adopting a child of a different race?
23. How does your spouse feel about adopting a child of a different race?
24. How does your extended family feel about you adopting?
25. How would your extended family feel about your adopting a child of a different race?

You may choose to adopt, even if you have family members who don't want you to. By answering the above questions, you will know where they stand. This will help you to plan strategies to protect your child from any bias. This is especially important if you intend to adopt a child of a different race.

My mother worked as a principal and schoolteacher. Growing up I heard her say negative things about problems adoptive children seemed to have. This attitude came from a few bad experiences she encountered at work. When we considered adoption, I knew my mother might not be thrilled with the idea. However, I knew she loved children and that she'd fall in love with our child. This turned out to be the case. She became hooked the minute she held Bryan as a baby.

26. Do you feel that the Lord may be calling you to the ministry of adoption? Why or why not?

When a child is brought into your home, you take on the unglamorous task of being the child's servant. All babies come with needs and frailties. This is true whether the child is biological or adopted. Adopting a child is a ministry, just as any other call of God, and it should be approached as such. What you have experienced in bringing you to consider adoption may be God's direction and preparation. He will bring good out of your pain if you trust Him.

There are thousands of innocent children who need forever families. Is it possible the Lord is asking you and your spouse to rise to the challenge to love, nurture, and care for one or more of these little ones? Every child deserves a loving family, don't you think?

The Needs of the Adopted Child

Adoption is like a marriage. It takes love, commitment, and hard work. One should enter marriage with the idea that divorce is only a last option under specific circumstances. The same is true of adoption. When going into an adoption, the idea of disruption should only be considered as a last resort. Just as the wedding altar is a promise of love and commitment, so too is adoption. However, there is a difference. The commitment is one-sided. It comes from the parents. The child promises nothing. A child doesn't yet understand love and commitment. It is up to you to teach him or her by your example.

Hundreds of thousands of children worldwide need loving families. What is love? Love is a choice. It's the choice to do what's best for the child even if it's not to your benefit. Let me take it a bit further. Adopted children not only need love and commitment, but they need *acceptance* as well. They need to know they belong in your world and not be left standing outside looking in.

1. Do you believe that by your influence alone your adopted child will excel at the same things you and your spouse do well at?
2. Would there be disappointment if your adopted child takes no interest in the things you and your spouse love to do?
3. If your adopted child enjoys something you have no interest in, how do you plan to handle the situation?

Many adoptive parents encounter something different in the child's makeup quite unlike their own. This uniqueness should be accepted and celebrated. Unfortunately, this is the rock many adoptive parents stumble over. Give the child the freedom to be who God created them to be.

Perhaps your adoptive child loves sports but everyone else in the family is musical. Don't try to force your child into the musical box. Along with ADHD, Bryan struggles to keep organized. This translated into a messy house that I wanted to keep perfect. Neighbors in our previous neighborhood would call our house the *Better Homes and Gardens* house. His messiness irritated me. Then the Lord reminded me that on judgment day He wouldn't ask me how clean I kept my house. He would be concerned about how I treated my son. I needed to change and accept that Bryan struggled with something I did not.

We live in a cold climate. For years we would discover our son's window open in the middle of the winter, causing the rest of the family to freeze. This always served as a bone of contention. It wasn't until Kelly and I shared a travel trailer at a writer's conference during a snowstorm that it dawned on me—we dealt with a genetic predisposition. If Kelly was comfortable, I froze. If I was comfortable, she boiled. God has created us as unique individuals. And we should accept our differentnesses and celebrate them.

4. If you end up having both adopted and biological children, what strategies will you use to keep favoritism from creeping into your family?

The parents hold the responsibility to be the great equalizers. Adoptive children are sensitive to any discrepancy in treatment. It all boils down to acceptance, and this is especially true if there are biological children in the family. If you have biological children and only one adopted, take great care to make sure the child is not treated any differently. We always counted and recounted the Christmas gifts we bought for each of our children to make sure they each received an equal number. We did this to give them a sense of equality.

5. Be honest. Is adoption a way to meet your own needs? Why or why not?

6. Have you lost anything through infertility? If so, what?
7. What has an adopted child lost?

Adoption is born out of loss. You may have lost the dream of being pregnant or giving birth to a biological child, but the adopted child has lost his or her biological parents, too. It's natural to want to heal the pain in your own life, but I suggest you shift your focus to the child's needs. Let the Lord tend to yours. He's far better at meeting your needs than you are.

8. Do you plan on telling your adopted child he or she is adopted at an early age? Why or why not?

A word of caution—don't fall into the temptation of pretending your adopted child is biological. It's dishonest and unfair to the child. They will sense something's up, and in the end they will be devastated when they find out. We never sat Bryan down in a face-to-face conversation to break the news that he was adopted, but we talked about the matter openly in natural conversation. He grew up hearing the word. When he reached the age to understand its meaning, he didn't feel his adoption to be unnatural or something to be ashamed of.

The End of the Diamond Story

The final destination of the diamond's journey is to be set into a piece of jewelry. It may be placed into a ring, necklace, earring, brooch, bracelet, or perhaps even a crown. Just like a diamond must be set into something so that its glory can be seen and admired, an adopted child must be set into a family so that the child will become what God has intended for him or her to be.

People are like flowers, with thousands of varieties, shapes, colors, and perfumes. God is creating your family bouquet. Some families are made up of all red roses, and while the bouquet is still pretty, it's not as unique as a bouquet with several different flowers and colors.

Be encouraged. The Lord is doing something different in your family, and He has a beautiful plan for you and your future. He will take an ordinary couple, turn them into an extraordinary and dynamic family, and fill their house with blessings and diamonds.

Diamond Facet of Truth

*" 'For I know the plans that I have for you,'
declares the LORD, 'plans for welfare and not calamity
to give you a future and a hope.' "*
Jeremiah 29:11

PART THREE
Black Diamonds

Study Journal

For Teen Moms and their Families

Black Diamonds

Introduction

Years ago while on a trip to Cozumel, Mexico, my husband Scott and I ventured into an upscale jewelry store. Surrounded by expensive jewels of every size and color and in a multitude of arrangements, I was struck by all the variations. One necklace in particular caught my attention. It had a dark gray almost black gem, not much bigger than a pea, surrounded by a cluster of white diamonds. The contrast with the gray/black and white was astounding. So too, was the price tag. Watching me eye the necklace, the jeweler brought the necklace out of the case for me to get a closer inspection. I asked about the gray/black stone since I had never seen one quite like it. The jeweler told me the jewel was a black diamond or "carbonado."

Though the black diamond has some of the same qualities of a white diamond, it is softer, and really is just a step up from graphite. The black diamond is very common. The stone fractures more easily than gem quality diamonds, but it is rare to find one uniform in color.

I didn't buy the necklace that day, though my interest in the black diamond was piqued. I thought about how all of us are like black diamonds, scarred by sin and imperfect. As pressure and heat are turned up in our lives, God gives us opportunities to reflect His love. As we choose to give our hearts and minds to God, we reveal His love and we begin to leave the graphite behind.

In this study, we are going to use the analogy of diamonds as we explore what God has for us concerning teen pregnancy and the trials of being a parent of a teenage mother. So let's go mine some diamonds.

Lesson 1
Graphite

"Do not let your heart be troubled;
believe in God; believe also in me."
John 14:1

The Story of Diamonds

Did you know diamonds can be found in every color of the rainbow? The word diamond comes from the ancient Greek word *adamas,* which means unbreakable. [48]

When you think of a diamond, the hardest natural substance on earth, it may come as a surprise to you that it's made out of the same stuff—carbon—as graphite. Yes, that's right graphite. How? Through great hardship, the carbon atoms of the diamond are rearranged in such a way that they take on the opposite characteristics of graphite.[49]

In fact, every natural diamond was once an ordinary lump of graphite. As the Earth was formed, deposits of graphite were laid deep beneath the Earth's crust, down in the mantle, eighty-seven to one hundred twenty miles below the surface. The weight of all that rock and earth caused an enormous amount of pressure. Down that deep, the heat was massive as well. When graphite was exposed to that amount of pressure and heat, the stone transformed into diamonds.

All diamonds endure immense amounts of pressure and heat.[50] So do teens. If you are pregnant, pressure and heat are amplified. In this lesson we will look at what the Bible has to say about trials and pressure.

I've been in your shoes, and as bad as it seems right now, life will get better if you turn to the Lord. You've read my story, and you know how I dealt with being a pregnant teen. My hope is that this study will be an encouragement and a place for you to journal your thoughts and feelings while you go through this phase in your life.

I thank You, Father, for the young mothers now reading this. I ask that You encourage them during this difficult time and that You open each of our hearts to Your words, Lord. Thank You for loving us so much, Father, and for showing us that nothing is impossible with You.

If you have a pencil handy go and get it. Now, look at the lead in the pencil. Is the lead soft and easily broken if too much pressure is applied? Yes, why? The pencil is composed of graphite, that's why. So, now, you may be asking, what's up? I'll reveal more in a minute. Remember the graphite in that pencil as you embark on this study.

You now know how diamonds are formed, but how does that relate to you? Good question. Because of Adam and Eve's sin, each of us are born with a graphite heart that is broken by sin, but the Lord wants to save us from our vulnerable condition and to develop in us hearts like diamonds. Hearts that are unbreakable toward disobedience. Because we are born with hearts that are soft and pliable toward sin, the Lord must rearrange our perspectives, priorities, and values to make our hearts like diamonds. There are many difficulties cutting and polishing a black diamond, because many times the stone will fracture from the pressure.

Look at the pencil and think of yourself as a lump of graphite. You will need to have a notebook handy to write down your answers as you go through this study.

1. What situations have you gone through or are going through, where you feel like the pressure and heat had been turned up? Write about them.

In Mathew 11:28–30 the Lord tells us to come to Him if we are weary and burdened. He gives us rest. When we take up His yoke and humble ourselves and learn from Him, we find rest.

Mathew 11:30: "For my yoke is easy and my burden is light."

2. What does He mean by yoke?

The dictionary definition of *yoke* is: a wooden crosspiece that is fastened over the necks of two animals and attached to a plow or cart that they are to pull.

What Jesus is saying in this passage is that because of man's sinful nature, keeping the law of God is impossible. We cannot bridge the gap between our sinfulness and God's holiness. We cannot earn our way into heaven. When we take up His yoke, we find rest because it is the yoke of repentance and faith followed by a commitment to follow Him.

In 1 John 5:3 John says, "This is love for God: to obey his commands. And his commands are not burdensome."

3. Are you looking for rest? Can you rely only on God in your pregnancy? What worries do you have? Write about them.
4. Do you feel that because you are pregnant your life is over?
5. If you answered "yes" to the above question, what things make you feel that way? Write them down.
6. Be honest. Are those things temporary, most likely to change with time?
7. Picture life in a few years. Does it look brighter?
8. Now read Mathew 11: 28–30. Are you willing to take up His yoke by repenting with a commitment to follow His ways and find rest?
9. If you answered "yes," what does it mean to repent?

Repentance is a change of heart and mind that brings us closer to God. Repentance means to turn around from the direction you are going and go in the opposite way. We must turn away from sin and turn to God for forgiveness. Repentance is a love for God and a sincere desire to obey His laws.

I remember my peers pressuring me to conform to what they thought I should do and be. Many teens are caught in the traps of drugs, alcohol, and sex because of peer pressure, often digging pits for themselves that they will spend the rest of their lives trying to dig out of. Beware of peer pressure traps, and determine to make the right choices with God's help.

As much as I desired to be my own person, I did want to fit in. The thought of losing my boyfriend if I didn't have sex was huge. Others were doing it. I really thought I wouldn't go that far, but as the heat turned up in our relationship, I gave in. To this day, I feel guilty about my choice. I failed God, my parents, and myself. I found that giving my life to Jesus was the only true way to dig myself out of the pit I had dug for myself. Do you feel guilty? Write about what you're feeling.

10. What has this pregnancy taught you so far?

Through my failure, I learned a lot and found I was stronger than I thought I was. People whispered and said hurtful things behind my back. The words *whore* and *slut* stung the most. I didn't go to my Junior Prom because I worried about what people would say. Eventually, I stopped talking to friends, and I found out later, some of them were really hurt by that. I grouped them in with the ones who laughed at me and spread rumors. My advice is, learn from your mistakes and change your ways. Not all of your friends will turn on you. Friends are important, and the ones who are really your friends will be there to support you.

11. Make a list of people who you think are real friends. It's important to remember them. They may not know what to say, but knowing they are there for you will go a long way.

Now, think of Mary, the mother of Jesus. She didn't get pregnant the way we did, but can you imagine the horrible things people said about her? She trusted God enough to know He had a plan for her and her baby.

I encourage you to put that same faith in God now. He has

a plan for you and for your baby. Just as a diamond must face heat and pressure, life is full of both, but as we grow and submit to God, we can leave the graphite behind. Remember, the Lord's yoke is easy and His burden is light.

Diamond Facet of Truth

There will always be heat and pressure in life,
but if we turn to the Lord, He will give us rest and
turn graphite to diamonds.

~♦♦♦~

Lesson 2
Yellow Diamonds

*Now flee from youthful lusts
and pursue righteousness, faith, love and peace,
with those who call on the Lord from a pure heart.*
2 Timothy 2:22

The Story of Diamonds
Graphite, the Stuff of Diamonds

During the formation of a diamond, it is possible for minute particles to get caught within the diamond itself. These imperfections are called inclusions and make each diamond unique. These imperfections may not always be seen by the naked eye, making the diamond much like humans, imperfect beings.[51]

It's interesting to note that as a diamond is formed these imperfections occur. When we look at the yellow diamond, its shades vary, but it is often passed over for the pure white diamond. The presence of nitrogen during the formation stage makes the stone yellow.

It's amazing that when you introduce one gas, what would have been a white diamond becomes yellow. Just like one act of sex can totally change a person too.

I ask, Father, that You open our hearts and minds to Your words. I ask that You fill us with the Holy Spirit and guide us in this study. Thank You for all that You have done and continue to do in our lives.

    1. Did you know that when a diamond takes too long to reach the surface it reverts back to graphite? Have you

ever felt like you missed the lesson God was trying to teach you, and you had to go around the mountain again? Write about it.

I've felt like that many times. The great thing about God is that He is a patient teacher, and He does forgive us. It does not, however, give us license to go on repeating the same sin over and over again.

Now you may think, *I'm a pregnant teen. I've really gone and done it this time. There's no way God is going to forgive me now.* If you are a parent of a pregnant teen, you may feel failure as a parent, but Scripture brings hope.

In John 8:1–11, we read about a woman brought to Jesus by the Pharisees. The woman had been caught in the act of adultery, and the Pharisees hoped to trap Jesus in order to have a basis for accusing him. Instead of falling into their trap, Jesus made this statement: "He who is without sin, let him cast the first stone."

The Pharisees knew, we all have sinned, and no one could throw a stone. Once everyone left, and only Jesus and the woman remained, He asked her, "Where are your accusers, did no one condemn you?"

She replied. "No one, Lord."

Jesus then said, "Then neither do I condemn you, go and leave your life of sin."

Jesus didn't tell her to go and continue her life of sin and adultery, He told her to leave that type of life behind.

We see another example of God's forgiveness of our sin in Luke 7:36–50. Jesus is visiting the house of a Pharisee named Simon, when a woman who had lived a sinful life starts washing His feet. As she wet His feet with her tears, she wiped them with her hair and then kissed them. Simon is shocked and thinks to himself, "If this man is a prophet, he would know that this woman is a sinner." Jesus allows the sinful woman to continue, then confronts the Pharisee with a story.

Jesus tells about two men owing a debt to a moneylender, one larger than the other, but both of the men's debts were canceled. Then He asks Simon which man would love the moneylender more? Simon replies, "The one with the larger debt."

The passage goes on to show how Jesus saw the woman at his feet. He was blessed to have her anoint them with her tears, dry them with her hair, kiss them, and then pour perfume on them, because she did it with a repentant heart. He turned to Simon and tells him that he did not do half of what the woman weeping at His feet had done. Jesus then tells the woman, "Your sins have been forgiven. Your faith has saved you, go in peace."

Clearly this was a woman who was so distraught by her many sins that she weeps at Jesus' feet. But Jesus saw her heart, forgave her, and told her to go in peace. He didn't say go and keep on sinning. If we want to leave the graphite behind and become a beautiful diamond, we must leave the sin behind. Are you willing to follow Jesus?

If so, ask Jesus to forgive your sins right now. It doesn't need to be a flowery prayer, just sincere words from your heart to His and He will hear you, forgive, and make you His child.

I encourage you to take the step of leaving the graphite behind. Life is not easy, and there are times when it seems the pressure will destroy you, but keep your eyes on Jesus, He will carry you through. We don't have to remain as black diamonds.

If you prayed a prayer of forgiveness and repentance, write a thank-you note to Jesus, because He has done what you've asked. Write down the date and time. This is the moment your new life begins.

Diamond Facet of Truth

Keep your eyes on Jesus. He will carry you through.

Lesson 3
Green Diamonds

*Trust in the LORD with all your heart
and do not lean on your own understanding.
In all your ways acknowledge Him,
and He will make your paths straight.*
Proverbs 3:5–6

The Story of Diamonds
Journey to the Surface

As we have learned, the longer a diamond stays in an environment of pressure and heat, the larger the diamond crystals grow. This, however, is only the beginning of their difficult journey to becoming a gem of great value and beauty.

If diamonds are formed beneath the earth's crust, how do we find them at the surface? It is believed there are three ways diamonds were deposited on the earth. The most common was by a rare type of volcano. We no longer see this type today.[51]

This special volcano eruption must occur to bring the valuable gems to the surface. It happens so infrequently that man has not experienced such an eruption. These deep-seated volcanoes must originate from three times the depth of the source magma for most volcanoes.

Diamonds must then be transported violently and with extreme speed to the earth's surface. This must happen in a matter of a few short hours to ensure the diamonds are not converted back to graphite, which can happen under conditions of high heat and low pressure.

Think about what happens when you shake a bottle of pop. The pressure builds and if you try opening the container before you let the pressure settle, what happens? We end up with sticky soda all over us.

Diamond-bearing rocks need a lot of pressure to shoot up with force. This speedy delivery, along with the gases, ensures the diamond's survival so that it does not revert back to graphite.

When we think of a green gem, most of us automatically think of emeralds. What's interesting though, is that diamonds also come in green. An emerald is very soft and is scratched easily. However, a green diamond is very hard, just like white diamonds. Scientists believe that the diamond turns green because of vacancies in the atoms themselves. They believe this happens when the diamond comes into contact with a radioactive source that knocks the atoms out of position. When the stone is exposed to pressure the carbon atoms are knocked out of position, resulting in the green color.[52]

I thank You, Father, for all the teens and parents out there who are reading this. I pray that You send supportive people to surround them. May You give them peace that passes all understanding, and that You wrap them in Your arms, so that they know how much You love them.

1. How do you think this part of the diamond story relates to us?

I believe God uses pressure to shape and mold us.

2. In the last lesson I asked you to write down what pressures you are facing. Are you still facing those same pressures? Write about it.

Just as when a diamond comes into contact with radioactivity and its atoms are knocked out of proportion, following a path into sin knocks us off the course that God intended for us. Life is always full of choices. Those choices come with consequences, both good and bad. God can take any bad situation and have good come from it. When we have made wrong choices, we can continue to go down that direction and revert back to graphite. Or we can repent and have God transform us into green diamonds.

In Luke 15:11-32 we read the parable of the prodigal son. A man has two sons. One day his younger son comes to him and asks for his inheritance. The Father gives it to the son, and the son takes off. The passage goes on to show that the son spent the money unwisely with loose living. When the money ran out, the son needed food and hired himself out, only to find that the pigs he fed had more to eat than he did.

The son thinks about his father and how even his father's servants have more to eat than he does. He decides to go home and offer himself as a servant to his father. While the son is still a ways off from home, his father spots him in the distance. The father is filled with compassion and runs to him. He tells his father that he is not worthy to be called his son.

3. What do you think the father's reaction will be? Read Luke 15:20.

When the older brother comes home, he hears that his younger brother has returned and finds everyone celebrating. Angered by this, he goes to his father and complains. His father listens to his complaints but then explains that all he owns is his. However, they need to celebrate because his brother had been dead and now was alive again, he was lost and had been found.

What is the point of this story?

God will not take away our free will. He wants us to choose to belong to Him whole-heartedly. The father gave his son what he asked for, probably knowing what would likely happen. He let his son make his own choices, as difficult as the decision was. God, is the father in this story, He lets us make our own choices, good or bad, but is always happy when we come back. For me, my choice to have sex at sixteen did not go without consequences. I had the choice and I knew it was wrong, but I gave in to the pressure.

My advice to teen mothers struggling with what to do is this: Picture yourself five years down the road, then ten. Do you have dreams you want to accomplish? Perhaps college? Now think of your unborn child. Is it important for your child to have everything? Maybe you can provide for your child and maybe you can't. Remember adoption does not mean you do not love your child. A wise woman once told me that many of the great men in the Bible were raised by different people other than their birth mothers.

If you choose adoption, I hope and pray you will find the peace I have. I also pray God will bless your sacrifice and that you will have a happy and enriched life.

When one is pregnant out of wedlock, consequences must be dealt with. The choice must be made to keep your baby or give the child up. For those of you considering adoption, there are a few important points I'd like to make. As I've stated from my own experience, I was allowed visits with Bryan once a year. This is in no way a right. Each open adoption has stipulations and some open adoptions only allow contact the first two years. Closed adoptions offer no contact at all. It is, and always will be at the discretion of the adoptive parents. Being a part of your birth child's life is a privilege, and one that can be taken away should you overstep the boundaries set in place by the adoptive parents.

This brings me to my second point. When you as the birth parent sign the form releasing the child, you are also releasing yourself as their parent. This does not mean you don't love the child, but only that you are relinquishing all parental rights to that child. In the eyes of the law, the adoptive parents are now the child's parents.

To have a positive outcome in the open adoption experience, respect them in their role as the parents to your child. You may not always agree with them, but recognize it is no longer your place to interfere. Please do not let this scare you from choosing adoption. Know this, as with anything in life, boundaries are important on both sides to achieve a good and sustaining relationship.

Now I'm writing to the parents of a pregnant teen. If your teen is pregnant and you are having a difficult time with your daughter's pregnancy, be at peace. You are not alone. Since I've not been the parent of a pregnant teen, I interviewed Molly to get her perspective from the parent's view of a pregnant teen. Here is what she had to say:

My stepdaughter was sixteen when she found out she was pregnant. Shock was my first reaction, then disbelief. I couldn't come to terms with the fact she had sex at sixteen. I blamed myself. I cried when she told me. I didn't think she had any idea of what she had gotten herself into. In my mindset, she was still my little girl. It broke my heart.

Anger came next. How could she have gotten into this position? Hadn't I drilled into her head often enough the importance of waiting till marriage? We were a Christian family. What were people going to think?

After anger came guilt. I've failed as a mother. It's my fault. I should have been there for her more. I should have seen how serious things were getting with her boyfriend. The 'should haves', the 'would haves', and the 'could haves' plagued my mind.

Next came fear. I feared how her body would handle being pregnant. My own pregnancies had been traumatic, and I worried my daughter's would be, too. I feared for her concerning teasing at school. I worried the situation would be too much for her. I feared for the choices she now must make on her own, and I feared I would try to rescue her. Some things you can't take away from your children, no matter how much you want to.

Over the entire pregnancy, I prayed every day God would guide my daughter into whatever choice she needed to make. I vowed to support her in whatever she decided. I prayed for strength to remain strong.

In order to prepare her, my husband and I felt she needed to hold down a job twenty hours a week or less. She was lucky to find one that allowed her to sit and answer phones. Although she didn't want to work, we believe the experience taught her the value of an education.

We set limitations in place concerning her boyfriend. He, too, had to get a job and help support her if he wanted to see her. We were proud that the two of them really did try, and together they covered the cost of all of our daughter's maternity clothes. Since our medical insurance covered our daughter, they didn't need to worry about those expenses, but we wanted them to save up for diapers, formula, baby furniture, etc. We even had them go and find out how much everything cost. Then they would have an idea of what they would be dealing with. The money they earned went into a baby fund.

We insisted they go to counseling during most of my daughter's pregnancy. If they were going to be parents, they needed to understand what that meant. They needed to comprehend the sacrifices they would be making and to realize a baby isn't a toy that can be put on a shelf. If after all this, they still chose to keep the baby, at least we, as our daughter's parents, would make sure they were prepared.

In some ways we were lucky because our daughter didn't fight us. She accepted our terms and expectations gracefully, and though the ordeal was difficult on her, she rose to the occasion. She ended up choosing adoption for her baby, and we were proud of her. Had she kept her baby we would have been supportive, too. But I think part of her decision for adoption had to do with what she learned during those nine months.

I can't say we did everything right, but we tried to show her what life would be like raising a child, while still being a child herself. All kids make mistakes. Some are bigger than others, but we learned you can love your child and still set expectations that prepare them.

The only advice I can give to other parents dealing with a pregnant daughter would be to love your child and be there to support them in their decision. Set ground rules and be prepared to be flexible as you chart your way through unknown waters. Pray often and pray over your children daily. God is gracious and a loving Father even in our mistakes.

Diamond Facet of Truth

God doesn't use consequences
of our bad choices to punish us.
He uses them as tools to teach us.

Lesson 4
Purple Diamonds

*"Greater love has no one than this,
that one lay down his life for his friends."*
John 15:13

The Story of Diamonds
Mining

In the story of diamonds, we have now learned how the diamond forms and how it makes its journey to the surface. Does that mean we can all grab a shovel and venture out into our back yards and start digging up diamonds? No, diamonds like other precious metals are only found in certain locations.

Pipe and alluvial are two types of mining for diamonds. Pipe mining refers to the extraction of diamonds from volcanic pipes. Alluvial mining refers to the extraction of diamonds from riverbeds or ocean beaches.[52]

Of all the mined diamonds in the world each year, less than half are gem quality. That means that most of them are discarded, only used in industrial work such as cutting and grinding tools. A gem quality diamond is really special, when you think about it, just like God's love for us.

Diamonds have fascinated people since before the Dark Ages and continue to do so today. It wasn't until the Middle Ages that the popularity of diamonds surged. The discovery of large diamonds like the Kho-i-Noor and the blue Hope diamonds fueled this intrigue. What is it about the diamond that captures attention? Maybe it's their dazzling beauty and endurance. Unlike other commodities, the diamond has lasting value.

The purple diamond is one of the rarest diamonds on earth, and it's only fitting that we put it in this chapter. In fact, a natural purple diamond is so rare that most jewelers have never seen one and will never own one. It is thought to be the most valuable natural object in existence on a weight for weight basis.[53] When you hear people describing the purple diamond, words like *rare*, *expensive*, and *never seen* are thrown around. I think it's fitting that in this lesson we are going to talk about a very rare thing—the ultimate sacrifice.

Please guide us, heavenly Father, in this study as we begin to uncover the differences between love and lust. I ask that You fill us with Your Holy Spirit and give us wisdom as we venture into this subject.

Love versus Lust or Real versus Synthetic

God's love is like a diamond that is not synthetically altered. Its value never wavers. *Love* is a simple four-letter word, but what does it mean?

Webster's Dictionary states that the word *love* can be both a noun and a verb. It is defined as "a feeling of deep affection, passion, or strong liking." Or the word means "to show or have deep attraction, affection or emotional attachment to a person, people, or thing."

In Exodus 1:22 we read that Pharaoh gave the order to kill every baby boy born to a Hebrew family. The child was to be thrown into the Nile. But in Exodus 2:1–10, we learn of a woman who gave birth to a son and hid him for three months. When she could no longer hide him, she got a basket and coated it with pitch and tar to ensure that it would float. Then she placed her child inside and set the little ark to float on the Nile.

Do you think she didn't love him? Or did she love him so much she placed him in God's hands as she placed the basket on the water?

The Bible doesn't tell us she hated him. I think her actions show us her love. She ensured the basket would float, and she hid him as long as possible.

The Nile is full of crocodiles, hippopotamuses, and other

large carnivorous animals, all of which would happily consume a small child. This mother risked a great deal. She loved her child so much that she did all she could to give him a chance at life.

Out of all the places the basket could have floated to, Pharaoh's daughter found the ark among the reeds. Yes, Pharaoh's daughter, the daughter of the same Pharaoh who gave the order to kill all Hebrew boys. Did she reject the child? No, she took him and he became her son. She named him Moses, because she drew him from the water.

We see another example of love in John 3:16: "For God so loved the world that he gave his one and only Son, that whoever believes in him shall not perish but have eternal life."

God loved the world enough to send His Son. In Mathew 3:17 and Mark 1:11 John the Baptist baptized Jesus. And then a voice came from heaven saying, "You are my Son, whom I love; with you I am well pleased."

God, the creator of love, understands what giving a child up feels like. Not only did He give up His Son. He sent His Son to die on the cross in our place so that we might have eternal life.

I loved my child enough to realize I couldn't give him the stable environment he deserved. By giving him to a family who could provide stability, I knew his life would be better. True love is putting the needs of another before myself.

Diamond Facet of Truth
"For God so loved the world,
that He gave his only begotten Son."
John 3:16

I can't tell you how often I've heard, "You must not have loved your baby very much if you gave him up for adoption." Ironically, after I delivered someone said this. The fact that anyone would actually utter such nonsense astounds me. Giving up my child was the most gut-wrenching, emotional experience I've ever had. Nothing about giving a child up is easy. To think someone doesn't love their child if they choose adoption, in most cases, is so far from the truth.

At seventeen years old I had barely experienced life. I wasn't emotionally ready to be a mom and raise a child while still attending high school. Looking back, I recognize teenagers often confuse lust with love. It has been said that true love waits. Hormones rage at this age, and it is easy to get caught up in the fantasy of love.

Statistically, as an unmarried teenager, the odds of me and the father of our child staying together were stacked against us from the beginning. Going life alone would have been hard—not impossible but extremely difficult.

Counterfeit Love

Just as God is the creator of love, the enemy uses lust disguised as love to lure us into temptation. The definition of *lust* is "having a self-absorbed desire of an object, person, or experience. When we are in lust, we place the object of our desire above all things in our lives."

Another way to look at lust is worshiping anything above God. First Timothy 6:10 says, "The love [lust] of money is the root of all kinds of evil."

I compare lust to cubic zirconia, a counterfeit diamond. The stone is a synthetic attempt to look like a diamond but really is only a silicon carbide that has no value. As I stated above, a real diamond will hold its value, but something that has no value doesn't last. We see this also in synthetic diamonds that are colored by man. The color fades over time because it's not the genuine article.

An example of lust in the Bible is the story of David and Bathsheba. In 2 Samuel 11:1–17 we read about King David getting up one evening and seeing Bathsheba bathing. He thought her beautiful and inquired about her. He found out she was married, but he summoned her to him and slept with her. Now you may think to yourself, why didn't she refuse the summons? In that time period, the king was the absolute authority. To defy a summons risked death.

Bathsheba became pregnant and sent word to David. In a nutshell, David freaks out and tries to bring her husband back from war to sleep with her. The plan backfires on David when Bathsheba's husband refused to sleep with her due to his military obligation. The heat turned up for David as he realized this could go very bad. In that day a person was stoned for adultery.

David sends Bathsheba's husband back to war with orders to put him where the fighting was the fiercest. The troops were then ordered to draw back so that Bathsheba's husband would be killed. Pretty elaborate cover-up. Right? Imagine what his troops were thinking. This one act of lust caused an innocent man's death.

I don't believe King David set out to sin, but once the deed was done he had to face the consequences. Instead of repenting and owning up to his misdeed right away, he goes on to commit another sin, then another.

Lust became a web that entangled him so entirely he couldn't see beyond it. It made him continue to lie, to cover his tracks. King David had Bathsheba's husband killed to prevent his secret from coming out. But nothing is hidden from God.

We go on to read that the child conceived by David's lust dies. When David repented, God forgave him. David and Bathsheba married and were blessed with another son. This is a great example of what happens when we let lust rule our minds: we end up doing things we know are wrong.

As teenagers we fall in love with the idea of love. It was wrong to have sex at sixteen, but I was so afraid of losing what I thought was love that I gave in. It wasn't real love at all, only lust.

1. Can you think of a time where you thought you were in love and soon realized it wasn't real? Write about it.

When we try to compromise and have one foot in the world and one foot on God's path, it never works. God wants us to belong completely to Him. He doesn't want to share us.

2. I don't want to be cubic zirconium. I want to be a real

diamond in God's kingdom. What about you?

Diamond Facet of Truth
"Real love waits."

Lesson 5
Brown Diamonds

*The stone which the builders rejected
has become the chief cornerstone.
This is the LORD'S doing; It is marvelous in our eyes.*
Psalm 118:22–23

The Story of Diamonds
Sorting

After a diamond-bearing rock is mined, it is transported to a screening plant. The diamonds are then separated from the host rock and put into three categories. A diamond in its natural, uncut state is described as a "rough diamond." Each one must be inspected and then sorted into the categories.[54]

The first category is gem quality. To be in this group the stone must display a high standard of excellence. The clarity of these diamonds range from flawless to visible imperfections. These are diamonds used in jewelry.

The next category is near-gem quality. These are stones that can be used as either a gem for jewelry or for industrial uses. Their clarity ranges from visible imperfection to industrial grade. Each stone is evaluated and, depending on the stone's quality, transferred to the first or last group.

The last category is industrial. These diamonds are of low quality or are badly marked and are only suitable for industrial use. They are used in instruments as small as dentist's drills to as large as earthmoving equipment.

Most diamonds are actually rejected. Only 20 percent are

placed in jewelry.(55)

As we have mentioned in the last few chapters, for a diamond to form it needs a lot of pressure and a lot of heat. Brown diamonds were considered the most unloved of all the diamonds next to the black. This diamond gets its brown-like color from the presence of nitrogen or from a defect in the structure of the diamond.

For many years the brown diamond was strictly used for industrial purposes, as jewelers discarded it for its unappealing color. However, due in part to better marketing and more research, the brown diamond is now recognized as a gem and considered valuable. Notable jewelers like Harry Winston have created beautiful settings for these once rejected diamonds. Royalty from around the world now have brown diamonds in their collections.

1. Have you ever felt rejected? Write down an experience you have had.

I understand feelings of rejection and not being wanted. The more I thought about it and prayed about it, I realized God understands rejection, too.

In John 15:18 we read the world hated him first. What? How can that be?

In Isaiah 53:3 we see what the Son of God had to endure. "He was despised and forsaken (rejected) of men, a man of sorrows, acquainted with grief; And like one from whom men hide their face He was despised, and we did not esteem Him."

In John 1:11: "He came to His own, and those who were His own did not receive (accept) Him."

2. Now read I Peter 2:4. Imagine the Son of the Most High God being rejected by the very people He was sent to save. A man who came to heal the hurting, to give sight to the blind, to make the lame walk was despised by men then beaten and hung on a cross. Why do you think?

Mankind resented being told what we were doing was

wrong.

3. As humans we love having choices, but we hate accountability. Why do you think that is? Write about it.
4. What areas in your life are you trying not to own up to or accept responsibility?

Diamond Facet of Truth
We are chosen and precious to God.

5. What lie does Satan want you to believe about yourself?
6. How does this lie affect your day-to-day life?
7. Why do we fear being rejected?
8. Does that fear make us do things we normally would not? Write about it.

I don't know about you but, as you read my story, I always felt rejected. In high school, I was unsure of myself and self-conscious about my body. Society says if you're not a size zero you are worth nothing, and I was not a size zero. How could anyone want me? But then I meet this great guy and he likes me, but I'm so afraid of losing his "love" and having him reject me, I'm willing to do anything to prevent that from happening.

I believed the lie that I was not worthy of love. But you see I didn't love myself enough to override those feelings and see my own beauty. I didn't ask God what He saw when He looked at me. Instead, I hoped others would see me as beautiful. When they did not, I felt rejected and unloved.

It wasn't until I read Psalm 139:13–18 did I realize how much God loved me: "For you formed my inward parts; you wove me in my mother's womb. I will give thanks to You, for I am fearfully and wonderfully made; wonderful are Your works, and my soul knows it very well. My frame was not hidden from You, when I was made in secret, and skillfully wrought in the depths of the earth; Your eyes have seen my unformed substance; And in Your book were all written the days that were ordained for me, when as yet there was not one of them. How precious also are Your thoughts to me, O God! How vast is the sum of them! If I should count them, they would outnumber the sand. When I awake, I am still with You."

God knew us before we even took our first breath. He knows the number of hairs on our heads, because He made us. God doesn't make junk. Just like the brown diamond, we are all beautiful to God. Others may not see the beauty in us, but our Father in heaven does, and to Him you are precious and loved. If you surrender your life to the Lord, this scripture will apply to you.

Romans 8:1 "Therefore, there is now no condemnation for those who are in Christ Jesus."

I ask You, heavenly Father, to reveal how You see each one of us. I ask You to help us find the beauty within ourselves. For those who are feeling rejected, renew their hope in You. Please show them how much You love them. Thank You, Lord, for loving us enough to send Your Son to die for us, even when we rejected Him. Show us that You will not reject us if we don't look a certain way. You created us. Help us to accept our mistakes and take responsibility and move forward. Thank You for not rejecting us.

Diamond Facet of Truth

How precious also are Your thoughts to me,
O God! How vast is the sum of them!

~ ♦◆♦ ~

Lesson 6
Red Diamonds

With all my heart I have sought You;
Do not let me wander from Your commandments.
Psalm 119:10

The Story of Diamonds
Cutting and Polishing

The appearance of a natural, uncut diamond resembles a glass pebble. Most people would pass over the gem without knowing it's a diamond. It's the skill of the master cutter who unlocks the brilliance within each stone

Because each diamond in the rough is different, the rock must be carefully examined and each imperfection must be marked. Then the planning process begins. The master cutter studies the rough diamond and makes decisions on how the stone should be cut into the gemstone.

His first objective is to maximize its worth, considering how to keep as much weight retention as possible, since the value increases with size. Even today, with our modern techniques, the process of cutting and polishing a diamond always results in a dramatic loss of weight, about 50 percent. The master also takes into account how appealing the final shape will be, given the physical factors of the stone—the original shape of the rough diamond and the location of the imperfections.

The diamond then goes through a sawing or cleaving process. Cleaving is the separation of a piece of rough diamond. This results in two or more separate pieces. These are then finished into separate gemstones. Most diamonds are sawed across the grain, by a paper-thin metal disc coated with diamond dust. The master cutter uses the diamond's hardness as his tool.[56]

When it comes to cutting in our own lives, most of us think of people who purposely cut themselves with sharp objects. In regards to this study, however, I use the word *cutting* to reference the focus of removing ourselves from certain situations or people.

The red diamond is perhaps the rarest gemstone in existence today. Most people have never laid eyes on one, which makes its uniqueness far greater. Scientists believe that the red color comes from changes in the electrons during their journey to the surface. Colored diamonds in general are highly sought after, due to their rareness, but the red diamond tops the chart. In fact, a natural red diamond is so rare, that some claim less than twenty actually exist. Man has been able to color diamonds in a red hue, but the color fades over time. A natural red diamond is worth a great deal because its color never changes.[57]

I ask, heavenly Father, that You come and guide us in this study. I pray Your words will come through and sink deep into our hearts and minds. Thank You for all the diamond facets of truth you have shown us along the way, and I pray You will continue to encourage those reading this and embrace them in Your arms as our Father. Thank You.

We find a good example of how God cuts away things in our lives and brings change in Genesis 37:1–28. Here we find the beginning of the intriguing life of Joseph. He was the favored son of his father and given a beautiful coat. His brothers hated him and sold him into slavery. So he is cut from his coat, cut from his family, and cut from the only home he knew. Talk about change! But God was with Joseph and blessed him wherever he went.

In Genesis 39, Joseph is taken to Egypt. He becomes the head over the household for one of Pharaoh's officials, a man by the name of Potiphar. The Lord gives him success in this household. People start to take notice of Joseph. He is well liked and respected. As the story continues, we find that Potiphar's wife also takes a liking to him. She wants to sleep with him.

Time and time again he turns her down. One day he finds her waiting for him, and she entices him. When he tries to leave, she grabs his cloak, and he flees leaving the garment behind. Now this woman did not take rejection well. She lied to her husband claiming Joseph raped her. Joseph was thrown in prison, and once again something is cut from him and things changed.

God blessed him even in prison. Joseph would not bend to Potiphar's wife, and at one point he had to run from her. Now, you may be thinking, wouldn't it have been far easier for him to just sleep with the wife and avoid prison?

Joseph knew the act would be wrong in God's sight, and he would not disrespect his master by sleeping with his wife, no matter what the consequences would be.

1. Do you have people in your life pressuring you to do something you know is wrong?
2. Who?
3. What are they pressuring you to do?
4. Do you fear if you say no, you won't be wanted anymore?
5. Is it easier to say yes than no?
6. What could the consequences be if you gave into the pressure?

Sometimes we need to cut ourselves off from them negative influences around us. It's not easy, but as we saw with Joseph, when we make the right choices, it does not mean that something won't be cut from us. But we see God continued to bless Joseph even while things were being cut from him. God blesses him so much that Joseph goes on to become the second in command over all of Egypt.

If you are pregnant and reading this, please know that I in no way judge you. I've been there, and the choices I made may not be the ones you will make. However, I cannot stress enough that you should not allow anyone to pressure you into doing something you know is wrong.

Adoption turned a negative into a positive and left me with the assurance that my child would have a chance at a happy life. I have friends who have chosen abortion and to this day, they still regret making that choice.

I'm sharing my experience in the hope that my story is

helpful in some way. Being a pregnant teenager is hard and others can be cruel to you. Take heart, it won't last forever. God will give you the strength to overcome any situation. All you need to do is ask for His help.

Philippians 4:13, "I can do all things through Him who strengthens me."

God uses the experiences we face in this life to polish us. Some diamonds can stay in the polishing phase for a long time before finally being ready to be set in jewelry. Diamond polishing is a lengthy process of checking the diamond and polishing the stone, then checking it again, over and over, until all the facets are clean, sharp, and symmetrical.

I don't believe we will know what our true diamond color is until we are in heaven and God reveals it to us. The more we learn to trust in Him and follow His guidelines, the more we grow and the more diamond-like we become. The final journey of a diamond is to be set into a piece of jewelry when the Master feels it's ready.

I pray God will bless you on whatever path you choose with Him and that these lessons have been helpful. God will reveal Himself to you. Hold on to your faith, even when it seems there is nothing left to hold on to. He will carry you through.

7. Please take a moment to journal any lasting thoughts you may have.

Diamond Facet of Truth

"For I know the plans that I have for you,'
declares the LORD,
'plans for welfare and not calamity
to give you a future and a hope."
Jeremiah 29:11

Endnotes

1. Anne Marie Helmenstine, Ph.D., *10 Carbon Facts*, 7/31/2015
   http://chemistry.about.com/od/elemntfacts/a/carbonfacts.htm?utm_term=diamonds%20hi story%20facts&utm_content=p1-main-3-title&utm_medium=sem&ut...
   Author Unknown, *Diamonds and Diamond Simulants*, 6/28/2012
   http://nature.berkeley.edu/classes/eps2//wisc/Lect6.html
   Kevin Bonsor and Candace Keener, *How Diamonds Work – Carbon and Kimberlite*, 6/28/2012
   http://science.howstuffworks.com/environmental/earth/geology/diamond1.htm
   Anne Marie Helmenstine, Ph.D., *Chemistry of Diamond*, 7/31/2015
   http://chemistry.about.com/cs/geochemistry/a/aa071601a.htm?utm_term=5%20Types%2 0of%20Diamond&utm_content=p1-main-3-title&utm_medium=sem-r...
   Kanika Khara, *How Are Diamonds Formed*, 6/28/2012
   http://www.buzzle.com/articles/how-are-diamonds-formed.html
2. Author Unknown, *Diamond*, 6/28/2012
   http://en.wikipedia.org/wiki/Diamond
   Kanika Khara, *How Are Diamonds Formed*, 6/28/2012
   http://www.buzzle.com/articles/how-are-diamonds-formed.html
3. Kanika Khara, *How Are Diamonds Formed*, 6/28/2012
   http://www.buzzle.com/articles/how-are-diamonds-formed.html
   Author Unknown, *Diamond*, 6/28/2012
   http://en.wikipedia.org/wiki/Diamond
   Susan Ward Aber, *Everything You Always Wanted to Know about Diamonds*, 1/21/2014
   http://academic.emporia.edu/abersusa/go340/diamond.htm
4. Author Unknown, *Diamonds and Diamond Simulants*, 6/28/2012
   http://nature.berkeley.edu/classes/eps2//wisc/Lect6.html
   Author Unknown, *Diamond*, 6/28/2012
   http://en.wikipedia.org/wiki/Diamond
5. Kevin Bonsor and Candace Keener, *How Diamonds Work – Carbon and Kimberlite*, 6/28/2012
   http://science.howstuffworks.com/environmental/earth/geology/diamond1.htm
6. Author Unknown, *Diamonds and Diamond Simulants*, 6/28/2012
   http://nature.berkeley.edu/classes/eps2//wisc/Lect6.html
   Author Unknown, *Diamond*, 6/28/2012
   http://en.wikipedia.org/wiki/Diamond
   Kanika Khara, *How Are Diamonds Formed*, 6/28/2012
   http://www.buzzle.com/articles/how-are-diamonds-formed.html
   Photius Coutsoukis, *Natural History of Diamond – How Diamond Is Formed*, 2007
   http://www.photius.com/diamonds/diamond_natural_history.html
7. Author Unknown, www.theunitconverter.com, 8/6/2015
8. Cate Lineberry, *Diamonds Unearthed*, December 2006,
   http://www.smithsonianmag.com/science-nature/diamond.html
   Kevin Bonsor and Candace Keener, *How Diamonds Work – Carbon and Kimberlite*, 6/28/2012
   http://science.howstuffworks.com/environmental/earth/geology/diamond1.htm
   Author Unknown, *Diamond*, 6/28/2012
   http://en.wikipedia.org/wiki/Diamond
9. Hobart King, *How Do Diamonds Form?*, 6/28/2012
   http://geology.com/articles/diamonds-from-coal/

10. Author Unknown, *Diamond*, 6/28/2012
    http://en.wikipedia.org/wiki/Diamond
    Photius Coutsoukis, *Natural History of Diamond – How Diamond Is Formed*, 2007
    http://www.photius.com/diamonds/diamond_natural_history.html
11. Photius Coutsoukis, *Natural History of Diamond – How Diamond Is Formed*, 2007
    http://www.photius.com/diamonds/diamond_natural_history.html
    Author Unknown, *Diamond*, 6/28/2012
    http://en.wikipedia.org/wiki/Diamond
    Author Unknown, *How Are Diamonds formed?*, 6/28/2012
    http://wiki.answers.com/Q/How_are_diamonds_formed
12. Photius Coutsoukis, *Natural History of Diamond – How Diamond Is Formed*, 2007
    http://www.photius.com/diamonds/diamond_natural_history.html
    Author Unknown, *Diamond*, 6/28/2012
    http://en.wikipedia.org/wiki/Diamond
    Anne Marie Helmenstine, Ph.D., *Chemistry of Diamond*, 7/31/2015
    http://chemistry.about.com/cs/geochemistry/a/aa071601a.htm?utm_term=5%20Types%20of%20Diamond&utm_content=p1-main-3-title&utm_medium=sem-r...
    Kanika Khara, *How Are Diamonds Formed*, 6/28/2012
    http://www.buzzle.com/articles/how-are-diamonds-formed.html
13. Cate Lineberry, *Diamonds Unearthed*, December 2006,
    http://www.smithsonianmag.com/science-nature/diamond.html
    Kevin Bonsor and Candace Keener, *How Diamonds Work – Carbon and Kimberlite*, 6/28/2012
    http://science.howstuffworks.com/environmental/earth/geology/diamond1.htm
    Hobart King, *How Do Diamonds Form?*, 6/28/2012
    http://geology.com/articles/diamonds-from-coal/
    Author Unknown, *Diamond*, 6/28/2012
    http://en.wikipedia.org/wiki/Diamond
14. Kevin Bonsor and Candace Keener, *How Diamonds Work – Carbon and Kimberlite*, 6/28/2012
    http://science.howstuffworks.com/environmental/earth/geology/diamond1.htm
    Cate Lineberry, *Diamonds Unearthed*, December 2006,
    http://www.smithsonianmag.com/science-nature/diamond.html
    Author Unknown, *How Are Diamonds Formed?*, 6/28/2012
    http://wiki.answers.com/Q/How_are_diamonds_formed
    Author Unknown, *Diamonds and Diamond Simulants*, 6/28/2012
    http://nature.berkeley.edu/classes/eps2//wisc/Lect6.html
15. Cate Lineberry, *Diamonds Unearthed*, December 2006,
    http://www.smithsonianmag.com/science-nature/diamond.html
    Author Unknown, *How Are Diamonds Formed?*, 6/28/2012
    http://wiki.answers.com/Q/How_are_diamonds_formed
16. Author Unknown, *How Are Colored Diamonds Formed?*, 2009
    http://guide.diamondpriceguru.com/diamond-and-ring-basics/4cs/how-are-colored-diamon..
    Author Unknown, *Diamond*, 6/28/2012
    http://en.wikipedia.org/wiki/Diamond
17. John King, James E. Shigley, and Claudia Jannucci, *Exceptional Pink to Red Diamonds: A Celebration of the 30th Argyle Diamond Tender*, Gems & Gemology, Winter 2014, Vol. 50, No.4, http://www.gia.edu/gems-gemology/winter-2014-pink-to-red-diamonds-30th-argyle-diamond-tender

    Author Unknown, *The Famed Argyle Diamond Mine – A Source of Sparkle*, 8/8/2015

http://www.naturallycolored.com/diamond-education/argyle-diamond-mine
David Cowley, *The Facts about Blue Diamonds*, 8/8/2015
http://www.streetdirectory.com/travel_guide/61194/jewelry/the_facts_about_blue_diamond...

18. Kevin Bonsor and Candace Keener, *How Diamonds Work – Cutting Diamonds*, 8/31/2012 http://science.howstuffworks.com/environmental/earth/geology/diamond3.htm
    Author Unknown, *Blue Diamonds*, 8/8/2015
    http://www.webexhibits.org/causesofcolor/11.html
    Author Unknown, *Bombarded with Ultraviolet Light, the Blue Hope Diamond Glows Red*, August 2009, http://smithsonianscience.si.edu/2009/08/blue-hope-diamond-glows-an-erie-red-after-expos...
    Amanda Thornburg, *UV Rays Shed New Light on the Hope Diamond's Mysterious Red Glow*, 8/8/2015
    http://mineralsciences.si.edu/research/gems/hope_diamond/blue_diamond_research.htm

19. Author Unknown, *Blue Diamond*, 8/8/2015
    http://www.webexhibits.org/causesofcolor/11.html
    Author Unknown, *Diamonds and Diamond Simulants*, 6/28/2012
    http://nature.berkeley.edu/classes/eps2//wisc/Lect6.html
    Author Unknown, *Diamond*, 6/28/2012
    http://en.wikipedia.org/wiki/Diamond

20. Amanda Thornburg, *UV Rays Shed New Light on the Hope Diamond's Mysterious Red Glow*, 8/8/2015
    http://mineralsciences.si.edu/research/gems/hope_diamond/blue_diamond_research.htm
    Author Unknown, *Bombarded with Ultraviolet Light, the Blue Hope Diamond Glows Red*, August 2009, http://smithsonianscience.si.edu/2009/08/blue-hope-diamond-glows-an-erie-red-after-expos...

21. Author Unknown, *Diamond*, 6/28/2012
    http://en.wikipedia.org/wiki/Diamond
    Anne Marie Helmenstine, Ph.D., *Chemistry of Diamond*, 7/31/2015
    http://chemistry.about.com/cs/geochemistry/a/aa071601a.htm?utm_term=5%20Types%20of%20Diamond&utm_content=p1-main-3-title&utm_medium=sem-r...

22. Kanika Khara, *How Are Diamonds Formed?*, 6/28/2012
    http://www.buzzle.com/articles/how-are-diamonds-formed.html
    Kevin Bonsor and Candace Keener, *How Diamonds Work – Carbon and Kimberlite*, 6/28/2012
    http://science.howstuffworks.com/environmental/earth/geology/diamond1.htm
    Photius Coutsoukis, *Natural History of Diamond – How Diamond Is Formed*, 2007
    http://www.photius.com/diamonds/diamond_natural_history.html
    Author Unknown, *Diamond*, 6/28/2012
    http://en.wikipedia.org/wiki/Diamond

23. Author Unknown, *Argyle Diamond Mine*, 4/29/2015
    https://en.wikipedia.org/wiki/Argyle_diamond_mine
    Author Unknown, *Ores and Minerals – Kimberley, Australia*, 8/8/2015
    http://www.mining-technology.com/projects/argyle/
    Author Unknown, *The Famed Argyle Diamond Mine – A Source of Sparkle*, 8/8/2015
    http://www.naturallycolored.com/diamond-education/argyle-diamond-mine

John King, James E. Shigley, and Claudia Jannucci, *Exceptional Pink to Red Diamonds: A Celebration of the 30th Argyle Diamond Tender*, Gems & Gemology, Winter 2014, Vol. 50, No.4, http://www.gia.edu/gems-gemology/winter-2014-pink-to-red-diamonds-30th-argyle-diamond-tender

Author Unknown, *About Natural Fancy Argyle Diamonds*, 8/82015 http://www.leibish.com/argyle-diamonds-article-160
24. Author Unknown, *The Rob Red*, 7/12/2012 http://famousdiamonds.tripod.com/robreddiamond.html
25. *Ibid.*
26. *Ibid.*
27. Author Unknown, *How Are Colored Diamonds Formed?*, 2009 http://guide.diamondpriceguru.com/diamond-and-ring-basics/4cs/how-are-colored-diamon...
28. Author Unknown, *Rough Diamond Sorting*, 8/82015 http://www.info-diamond.com/rough/rough-diamond-sorting.html
Brian McHardy, *History of Diamonds*, 8/8/2015 http://www.heartsonfire.com/history-of-diamonds/from-a-mine-to-you.aspx
Author Unknown, *The Diamond Industry Fact Sheet*, 8/8/2015, http://www.diamondfacts.org
29. *Ibid.*
30. *Ibid.*
31. Author Unknown, *Rough Diamond Sorting*, 8/82015 http://www.info-diamond.com/rough/rough-diamond-sorting.html
Brian McHardy, *History of Diamonds*, 8/8/2015 http://www.heartsonfire.com/history-of-diamonds/from-a-mine-to-you.aspx
32. Author Unknown, *The Dresden Green*, 8/28/2012 http://famousdiamonds.tripod.com/dresdengreendiamond.html
Author Unknown, *Dresden Green Diamond*, 8/28/2012 http://www.internetstones.com/dresden-green-diamond-famous-jewelry.html
Author Unknown, *Dresden Green Diamond*, 8/28/2012 http://en.wikipedia.org/wiki/Dresden-Green-Diamond
33. Author Unknown, *Dresden Green Diamond*, 8/28/2012 http://en.wikipedia.org/wiki/Dresden-Green-Diamond
Author Unknown, *The Dresden Green*, 8/28/2012 http://famousdiamonds.tripod.com/dresdengreendiamond.html
Author Unknown, *Dresden Green Diamond*, 8/28/2012 http://www.internetstones.com/dresden-green-diamond-famous-jewelry.html
Author Unknown, *How Are Colored Diamonds Formed?*, 2009 http://guide.diamondpriceguru.com/diamond-and-ring-basics/4cs/how-are-colored-diamon..
34. Author Unknown, *The Dresden Green*, 8/28/2012 http://famousdiamonds.tripod.com/dresdengreendiamond.html
Author Unknown, *Dresden Green Diamond*, 8/28/2012 http://en.wikipedia.org/wiki/Dresden-Green-Diamond
Author Unknown, *How Are Colored Diamonds Formed?*, 2009 http://guide.diamondpriceguru.com/diamond-and-ring-basics/4cs/how-are-colored-diamon...
Author Unknown, *Diamond*, 6/28/2012 http://en.wikipedia.org/wiki/Diamond
Author Unknown, *Dresden Green Diamond*, 8/28/2012 http://www.internetstones.com/dresden-green-diamond-famous-jewelry.html
35. www.greport.com.au/the-beauty-of-rough-diamonds-image-gallery/
36. Jack Reiss, *The Journey of The Diamond from Rough to Polished*, 2015 http://www.jackreiss.com/cutting/
Author Unknown, *Diamond*, 6/28/2012, http://en.wikipedia.org/wiki/Diamond
Author Unknown, *Diamond Cutting*, 7/30/2012, http://en.wikipedia.org/wiki/Diamond_cutting
37. Author Unknown, *Diamond Cutting*, 7/30/2012, http://en.wikipedia.org/wiki/Diamond_cutting
Author Unknown, *Diamond*, 6/28/2012,

http://en.wikipedia.org/wiki/Diamond
38. Author Unknown, *Diamond Cutting*, 7/30/2012, http://en.wikipedia.org/wiki/Diamond_cutting
Author Unknown, *Cutting Process*, 8/9/2015, http://www.heartsonfire.com/the-diamond-cutting-process.aspx
Kevin Bonsor and Candace Keener, *How Diamonds Work – Cutting Diamonds*, 8/31/2012, http://science.howstuffworks.com/environmental/earth/geology/diamond3.htm
39. *Ibid.*
40. Author Unknown, *Diamond Shape*, 8/9/2015, http://www.lumeradiamonds.com/diamond-education/diamond-shape
Duncan Pay, *Describing 58-Facet Round Brilliant-Cut Diamonds at GIA*, 8/9/2015, http://www.gia-news-reasearch-round-brilliant-cut-diamond-pay
Jack Reiss, *The Journey of the Diamond from Rough to Polished*, 2015, http://www.jackreiss.com/cutting/
41. Author Unknown, *The Steinmetz Pink*, 8/31/2012, http://famousdiamonds.tripod.com/steinmetzpinkdiamond.html
42. *Ibid.*
43. Author Unknown, *How Are Colored Diamonds Formed?*, 2009, http://guide.diamondpriceguru.com/diamond-and-ring-basics/4cs/how-are-colored-diamon...
Author Unknown, *Diamond*, 6/28/2012, http://en.wikipedia.org/wiki/Diamond
44. H. P. Whitlock, *How Diamonds Are Polished*, June 1921, http://www.naturalhistorymag.com/picks-from-the-past/271575/how-diamonds-are-polished
Author Unknown, *Diamond*, 6/28/2012, http://en.wikipedia.org/wiki/Diamond
Author Unknown, *Diamond*, 6/28/2012, http://en.wikipedia.org/wiki/Diamond
Kevin Bonsor and Candace Keener, *How Diamonds Work – Cutting Diamonds*, 8/31/2012, http://science.howstuffworks.com/environmental/earth/geology/diamond3.htm
Author Unknown, *The Diamond Industry Fact Sheet*, 8/8/2015, http://www.diamondfacts.org
Jack Reiss, *The Journey of the Diamond from Rough to Polished*, 2015, http://www.jackreiss.com/cutting/
45. Author Unknown, *The Royal Purple Heart*, 7/12/2012, http://famousdiamonds.tripod.com/royalpurpleheartdiamond.html
Ned Haluzan, *Natural Purple Diamonds – Which Colored Diamonds Are the Rarest?*, 9/11/2011, http://interestingdiamondfacts.blogspot.com/2011/09/which-colored-diamonds-are-the-rarest.html
46. Author Unknown, *How Are Colored Diamonds Formed?*, 2009, http://guide.diamondpriceguru.com/diamond-and-ring-basics/4cs/how-are-colored-diamon...
47. Samuel Lopez De Victoria, Ph.D, *Emotional Trauma in the Womb*, 6/30/2010, http://psychcentral.com/blog/archives/2010/06/29/emotional-trauma-in-the-womb/
Author Unknown, *Sharing Mother's Stress in the Womb Leaves Children Prone to Depression*, 2015, http://www.telegraph.co.uk/news/science/science-news/10177858/Sharing-mothers-stress-in...
Christine Zeindler, *Prenatal Maternal Stress*, 2015, http://www.douglas.qc.ca/info/prenatal-stress
Fiona Macrae, *Stress Such as Bereavement during Pregnancy Can Harm Child's Health for Years*, 7/30/2012, http://www.dailymail.co.uk/health/article-2181368/Stress-bereavement-harm-chi...

48. Anne Marie Helmenstine, Ph.D *Chemistry of Diamond Part 1 Carbon Chemistry and Diamond Crystal Structure* http://chemistry.about.com/cs/geochemistry/a/aa071801a.htm page 1
49. *Ibid.*
50. Unknown Author *The Different Types of Diamonds* October 10, 2014. http://typelist.com/different-types-of-diamonds
51. Hobart King *How Diamonds are Formed* http://geology.com/articles/diamonds-from-coal/
52. http://www.naturalgreendiamond.com/discover/origins.html
53. Abraham Zapata *How Diamonds are Mined* *http://www.whiteflash.com/about-diamonds/diamond-education/how-are-diamonds-mined-1185.htm*
54. Diamond Price Guru- *How Are Colored Diamonds Formed?* http://guide.diamondpriceguru.com/diamond-and-ring-basics/4cs/how-are-colored-diamonds-formed/
   DiamondFacts.Org Sorting https://www.worlddiamondcouncil.org/download/resources/documents/Fact%20Sheet%20(The%20Diamond%20Industry).pdf
55. Unknown Author *The Different Types of Diamonds* October 10, 2014. http://typelist.com/different-types-of-diamonds
56. Cleaving and Cutting diamond process https://en.wikipedia.org/wiki/Diamond_cutting Diamond Blog April 19, 2013 *Red Diamonds: The Rarest of Them All* http://www.capetowndiamondmuseum.org/blog/20113/04/red-diamonds/

Other Books by These Authors

Shattered Hope: Infertility

This 30-day Dust2Diamond Devotional will take you on a journey through the spiritual and practical issues of infertility, while focusing on the presence of God in your life.

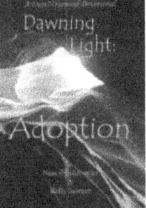

Dawning Light: Adoption-

This 30-day Dust2Diamond Devotional is designed to take you on a walk with God. Not only are the spiritual topics of adoption discussed, but the practical as well.

Diamonds: Tale of Trial

Out of the depths of hardship and pain, diamonds rise.

Have you experienced disappointment, rejection, or pain? Do you wonder if you've been forgotten, like no one cares?

Where is God in the midst of our struggles? What good can come from trials?

In this book, we take a look at Joseph's life through the analogy of a gem quality diamond's journey. Beginning as something ugly and black, it turns, through great hardship, into a wondrous beauty that reflects His light in prisms of color.

Visit us at: www.fromdust2diamonds.com
Our Blog: dust2diamonds.wordpress.com

If you have found this book to be helpful, we would love to hear about it. Please write to us at dust2diamonds1@gmail.com. May God bless you on this journey.

ABOUT THE AUTHORS

From Dust2Diamond Authors
Kelly Sumner and Nancy Faltermeier

Kelly Sumner is a teacher with experience in both public and private schools. Her involvement in the teen pregnancy clinic has inspired her to write about her experience as a teenage birth mother. She has published *Broken Dreams Made Whole* in *Apraxia Now* magazine. A magazine devoted to parents of children unable to speak.

She devotes her time to teaching her own preschool, writing fiction for women, young adults, and suspense lovers. Residing in gorgeous Colorado, Kelly lives with her husband, two children, a dog, and a conversational cat. She loves to travel, camp at the lake, and spend time with friends.

Nancy Meyers Faltermeier writes non-fiction and Young Adult fantasy. In past years she worked full time with a ministry noted for the children's albums *Music Machine* and *Bullfrogs and Butterflies.* There she wrote skits, plays, and songs. Music she wrote, found publication in two songbooks and four recordings by different artists.

She has also taught Bible Studies on many different topics and levels. After homeschooling her children through high school, she is dedicating her time bringing hope to the hurting through the written word. Nancy resides at the base of the Rockies in beautiful Colorado with her husband, two adult children, two parakeets, and a backyard nursery of wild cottontail bunnies. In her spare time, she enjoys hiking, amateur photography, and scrapbooking.

Gone to unearth more truths for hurting hearts.